FILM AND EVERYDAY RESISTANCE

SUPER
IMPOSITIONS

PHILOSOPHY AND THE MOVING IMAGE

Series editor Brian Price

Superimpositions: Philosophy and the Moving Image takes philosophy and visual media as related practices. Books in this series do not simply apply philosophy as a method for reading art or redundantly representing its extant ideas. Following the visual logic of superimposed imagery, we see what philosophy and art share and what remains distinct, and distinctly generative. Superimposition, moreover, resembles thinking itself: an encounter with an object summons the idea of something like it and yet not the same. Twentieth-century philosophers turned increasingly to literature to replace generalized axioms with thick descriptions of the world and our psyches. *Superimpositions* takes the moving image, in all its limitations and possibilities, as central to the task of twenty-first-century philosophy and its refusal to foreclose either thought or difference.

Film and Everyday Resistance

Marguerite La Caze

NORTHWESTERN UNIVERSITY PRESS
EVANSTON, ILLINOIS

Northwestern University Press
www.nupress.northwestern.edu

Printed in the United States of America

10 9 8 7 6 5 4 3 2 1

Library of Congress Cataloging-in-Publication Data

Names: La Caze, Marguerite, author.
Title: Film and everyday resistance / Marguerite La Caze.
Other titles: Superimpositions.
Description: Evanston : Northwestern University Press, 2024. | Series: Superimpositions | Includes bibliographical references and index.
Identifiers: LCCN 2024017153 | ISBN 9780810147454 (paperback) | ISBN 9780810147461 (cloth) | ISBN 9780810147478 (ebook)
Subjects: LCSH: Passive resistance in motion pictures. | Authoritarianism in motion pictures.
Classification: LCC PN1995.9.P345 L32 2024 | DDC 791.436552—dc23/eng/20240417
LC record available at https://lccn.loc.gov/2024017153

Contents

Illustrations

Acknowledgments

Much of the work in this book was carried out in Meanjin (Brisbane), and I would like to acknowledge the country and the traditional custodians of the land. Different versions of the chapters were first given as papers at the Cinematic Thinking Network Workshops at the University of New South Wales; the Film-Philosophy Conference; the Australasian Society for Continental Philosophy Conference; the European Philosophical Society for the Study of Emotions Conference; the International Society for Women Philosophers Conference; the Ethics, Politics, and the Cinema Symposium; the International Association for Genocide Studies Conference; and the workshop titled "Resistance, Violence, and Non-violence" at the University of Jyväskylä organized by Magdalena Zolkos, and I appreciate the support and insightful conversations with colleagues at all these symposia. Roland Bleiker, Ted Nannicelli, the late Tom O'Regan, and others in the "Visual Politics" project at the University of Queensland were enthusiastic about cinema and philosophy, and I really appreciate their collaboration. I would like to thank the anonymous reviewers of the manuscript for their suggestions and their encouragement and offer a special thank-you to Heidy Meriste, who gave me thoughtful comments on chapter 3. I am grateful as always to Damian Cox for his enduring support and encouragement and endless discussions about films and philosophy. Daniel Brennan has given me great feedback on chapter 6, and his work on Václav Havel has been inspiring. My thanks also goes to Brian Price for his interest in and support for this project, and to Faith Wilson Stein for her expert advice.

Chapter 1 is based on my article "Becoming a Victim: *A Dry White Season*," published in *Philosophy Today*'s special issue on victimhood, edited by Jason Alvis and Ludger Hagedorn: 65, no. 4 (2021): 899–916. Earlier versions of chapters 2, 4, and 6 were published as "*The Look of Silence* and the Ethics of Atonement," in *Truth in Visual Media: Aesthetics, Ethics and Politics*, edited by Marguerite La Caze and Ted Nannicelli (Edinburgh: Edinburgh University Press, 2021), 104–23; as "Chile 1988: Trauma and Resistance in Pablo Larraín's *No* (2012)," in *Places of Traumatic Memory: A Global Context*, edited by Amy L. Hubbell, Natsuko Akagawa, Sol Rojas-Lizana, and Annie Pohlman (London: Palgrave Macmillan, 2020), 285–307; and as "Realism as Resistance: The Case of *Wadjda* (2013)," *Angelaki: Journal of the Theoretical Humanities* 25, no. 5 (October 2020): 156–70, https://www.tandfonline.com/journals/cang20, respectively, and I gratefully acknowledge these publications.

FILM AND EVERYDAY RESISTANCE

Introduction

In this book I explore the everyday, nonviolent ways that authoritarian and totalitarian states can be resisted and the affects and situations that foster this resistance through filmic sources. Films provide both a philosophical thinking about an everyday type of resistance and a sense of the experienced texture of the lives of people who engage in this kind of resistance. The forms of resistance, such as amelioration of conditions, exile, legal contestation like plebiscites, and truth-seeking and truth-telling, intertwine with victimhood, atonement and forgiveness, love, trauma and happiness, ethical dilemmas, and desire, and this process reveals that ordinary people have their own ways of creating quiet resistance. I analyze the films through a close interpretation of a single film alongside and interconnected with philosophical theorizing about resistance to oppression and totalitarianism, such as the work of Hannah Arendt, Simone de Beauvoir, Aimé Césaire, W. E. B. Du Bois, and Václav Havel. I focus on the philosophical accounts of resistance that engagement with films can provide, crossing genres between documentary and dramatic film and across time and different countries, including the apartheid regime in South Africa, Indonesia, the German Democratic Republic, the Chilean civic-military dictatorship, and contemporary Iran and Saudi Arabia.

Terms like *authoritarian regime* and *totalitarian regime* are contested and are sometimes associated with either communist or fascist political tendencies, an association that I avoid in that both kinds of regimes are featured here. Authoritarian regimes characteristically restrict personal freedom, expect obedience to their commands, and suppress plurality of thought (Kamenka 1995, 630; Popper 2020). They may be bureaucratic or military or both, and the political system can be close to, or can descend into, totalitarianism. For Arendt (1976, 364–65), what distinguishes an authoritarian government from a totalitarian one is a shift from an expectation that citizens obey orders to the idea that citizens should follow the will of the leader, whatever that may be. Authoritarianism is often defined negatively, encompassing governments that do not respect human rights, or that are not liberal or not democratic, or where there is a general lack of freedom (Repucci and Slipowitz 2021). Each of the chapters here relates to a specific time period in authoritarian societies: some are systems coming toward the end of their authoritarian era, like South Africa, East Germany, and Chile, while others are seemingly quite stable, such as Indonesia, Iran, and Saudi Arabia. That context to an extent dictates the form of resistance and the likelihood that it will be effective.

Much of the discussion of resistance is framed around violence, such that even to speak of "nonviolent resistance" is to frame it as lacking violence, and this does not credit the truly individual ways that resistance has been thought and enacted. Furthermore, it seems that in debates about violence versus nonviolence, language is stretched to conceive the violent as nonviolent. For instance, while nonviolent resistance can often be thought of as involving strikes, protests, and civil disobedience, these contain an element of violence as coercive pressure or force. Judith Butler (2020, 22), in *The Force of Nonviolence*, specifies that in her view "nonviolence does not imply the absence of force or aggression."[1] Her examples are of activists using their bodies as a form of force in creating a barrier, or through embodied performance like the "standing man" Erdem Gündüz, who stood silently with others in Taksim Square in Istanbul in 2013 to protest the authoritarianism of the Erdoğan government. Butler is certainly right in her thinking about the breadth of nonviolence: many of the techniques of nonviolence, such as hunger strikes, involve bringing pressure to bear on the authorities.[2] Yet the everyday resistance shown in the films discussed here does not rely on aggression or force.

The films I examine go beyond the standard idea of nonviolence: their protagonists do not use violence, force, or even dissent or direct protest. Yet while the resistance examined here is without dissent, it can still bring about regime change. The kinds of resistance depicted in the films I consider here involve an assumption of moral responsibility, of considering what actions mean for oneself, for one's loved ones, for the wider society and for the future. Due to these considerations, their path cannot be violent.

THINKING NONVIOLENCE

Recent discussions of violence have proliferated and expanded the concept to take in the use of language, categorization, and concepts of identity, as Ann Murphy argues in her wide-ranging study *Violence and the Philosophical Imaginary* (2012). I understand violence here in a narrower sense than that, but not as just "physical violence," since violence can include force, pressure, and threat. My focus in this book is on individuals who are caught within authoritarian systems and are trying to think of different ways of overcoming or escaping or challenging those systems. One starting point in relating to historical circumstances creatively is suggested by Hans Magnus Enzenberger's (1997, 208–15) use of the phrase "heroes of retreat/demolition" to refer to political leaders who voluntarily relinquish or even enthusiastically throw off their power. His essay was written in 1989 in the wake of the fall of the Berlin Wall. He writes, "The *non plus ultra* in the art of the possible consists of withdrawing from an untenable position. But if the stature of the hero is proportional to the difficulty of the task before him, then it follows that our concept of the heroic needs not only to be revised, but to be stood on its head. Any cretin can throw a bomb. It is 1,000 times more difficult to defuse one" (Enzenberger 1997, 210). His heroes of retreat are ambiguous figures, often hated and often responsible for much wrong: Nikita Khrushchev (Soviet Union), János Kádár (Hungary), Adolfo Suarez (Spain), Wojciech Jaruzelski (Poland), and Mikhail Gorbachev (Soviet Union). Nevertheless, Enzenberger credits them with dismantling, often over a long period of time, the regimes they worked within. The individual characters and real people in the films that I describe are not heroes on a grand scale or leaders like the ones Enzenberger discusses. When multiplied, however, their actions could help bring down a regime, and the actions of all have wide implications. In a sense, they are the citizen counterpart to the heroes of retreat, helping to bring about a change in the climate that the heroes experience.

Although the examples discussed here involve different type of actions, they also have different aims: some do hope to overturn an existing regime, others are focused on living a better life, and some have narrow goals with broader repercussions. For instance, escaping or "exiting" a regime, if it happens on a large scale, can undermine the legitimacy of the regime itself. These forms of challenge to different cases of authoritarian regimes find their best expression in the work of Havel, an influential Czech dissident and playwright who became president of Czechoslovakia (1989–92) and of the Czech Republic (1993–2003) following the collapse of the communist states in Russia and Eastern Europe. He also spent long periods in prison for his political activism prior to 1989. His essay "The Power of the Powerless," originally written in 1978, provides a compelling undercurrent to this book in its thinking of the diverse ways of engaging in resistance. At that time, he was one of the leaders of Charter 77, a group advocating that the Czechoslovak government act consistently by upholding the human rights it had agreed to in the 1975 Helsinki Accords. The banning, trial, and jailing of the underground rock band Plastic People of the Universe in 1976 galvanized public opinion in solidarity with them, and the essay is written in the light of the events surrounding the treatment of the band.

Following a line of thought concerning authentic action and thought from Søren Kierkegaard and Jan Patočka, Havel considers how it is possible to live "within the truth" in an authoritarian political regime.[3] Another way he describes this life is as the possibility of living with dignity ([1978] 1987, 72). More precisely, Havel defines the political system of the Soviet bloc as post-totalitarian, to signify not that totalitarianism is over but that it has taken a different form from how totalitarianism has traditionally been understood. In this essay he uses the example of a greengrocer who puts a sign in his window that says, "Workers of the world, unite!" For him, the sign helps the greengrocer to hide behind the ideology it signifies and acts as an excuse that can "provide people, both as victims and pillars of the post-totalitarian system, with the illusion that the system is in harmony with the human order and the order of the universe" (Havel [1978] 1987, 43). However, the sign's statement is an illusion because the post-totalitarian system does not allow lives to develop in freedom and so are not in harmony in that way.

Within a regime that functions to perpetuate itself and to cover the truth with lies, individuals do not have to believe any of the hypocritical claims; they only have to act as if they do, keep silent, and cooperate with those who do support the system. Thus, in Havel's ([1978] 1987, 45) words, "they must *live within a lie*." That is why resistance for him is living in the truth. Havel provides a brilliant analysis of post-totalitarian regimes, where power becomes anonymous and the system is continued through empty phrases and rituals. Like Arendt, he believes that authoritarian regimes continue only because people are willing to accept the ideology and live within its lies; in other words, "everyone in his or her own way is both a victim and a supporter of the system" ([1978] 1987, 53). Havel's understanding of the regime is that each person is in some way able to come to terms with it. In this system open rebellion is punished with persecution. According to him, this high level of sanction occurs because living within the truth is incompatible with living within the lie, and anyone who tries to live within the truth "denies it [the system] in principle and threatens it in its entirety" ([1978] 1987, 56). Any such action reveals the post-totalitarian situation and has existential, moral, and political dimensions.

The power of open rebellion and even more subtle resistance is that it connects to the hidden realm of life, which Havel calls prepolitical and which has an openness to truth and therefore potential. This power, he explains, can erupt forth in "a real political act or event, a social movement, a sudden explosion of civil unrest, a sharp conflict inside an apparently monolithic power structure, or simply an irrepressible transformation in the social and intellectual climate" ([1978] 1987, 59). Following on from this thought, Havel's idea of what counts as living within the truth varies considerably; it can be "a protest or a letter written by a group of intellectuals. It can be any means by which a person or a group revolt against manipulation: anything from a letter by intellectuals to a worker's strike, from a rock concert to a student demonstration, from refusing to vote in the farcical elections, to making an open speech at some official congress, or even a hunger strike, for instance" ([1978] 1987, 60). This kind of breadth of dissidence makes sense in the systems he is discussing, which are fragile in the manner outlined. Other more open systems could absorb much of this kind of dissidence. In fact, Havel rejects the labels *opposition* and *dissent*, because he maintains that he and others are simply and positively living in the truth and are not trying to set themselves up as opponents or as dissidents as if that were a profession or often even a choice. His way of thinking about it is that the prepolitical living in the truth and creating the independent life of society can be more genuinely political than more obvious dissidence can ([1978] 1987, 86). Nonetheless, their attempts to live in the truth stand out against the background of acceptance of the lies and so become action in an Arendtian sense (Arendt, 1993, 251).

A valuable concept Havel introduces is "small-scale work," an idea elaborated by Czech philosopher and politician Tomáš Masaryk (1850–1937). In the context of the Austro-Hungarian Empire, this concept concerned a sense of independence through "honest and responsible work in widely different areas of life but within the existing social order, work that would stimulate national creativity and national self-confidence" (Havel [1978] 1987, 80–81). This focus on authentic human life is expressed through a dedication to doing one's best in one's occupations, a kind of recognition of their intrinsic worth. On Havel's reading, taking pride in producing good work is itself a way of criticizing the lack of standards of the regime, as in the example of the devoted brewer he provides, and can appear in any walk of life. For Havel, it is the attempts at small-scale work that are significant, not whether they succeed or fail.

The best type of challenge to the post-totalitarianism regimes, according to Havel ([1978] 1987, 92), is an approach that is within the law, open and public, and critical of violence: it "can only accept violence as a necessary evil in extreme situations, when direct violence can only be met by violence and where remaining passive would in effect mean supporting violence." Like other theorists of nonviolent politics, Havel believes respect for human life has to be fundamental. A more developed stage of living in the truth is the creation of what Václav Benda, another member of Charter 77, called "parallel structures," which include what Ivan Jirous, the artistic director of the Plastic People of the Universe, called the "second culture" (Havel [1978] 1987, 100). From these beginnings a parallel political structure may grow. Again the possibilities are very diverse, including publications, small performances, talks, and shows, or parallel trade unions and international connections. Havel ([1978] 1987, 103–4) is quite clear that this approach is not an isolationist retreat and is based around care and taking responsibility for the world and for others.

Finally, Havel describes the regime's typical responses, which involve repression and adaptation. Repression involves actions such as arrest, detention, imprisonment, and persecution that many in the post-totalitarian states and elsewhere endured. Adaptation is a process of attempting to integrate dissent into the structure of the regime. Optimistically, and related to his experience of the Prague Spring of 1968, he contends that ultimately integration will lead to fundamentally different structures that have come from the experiments of living in the truth ([1978] 1987, 108). But Havel does not try to predict the future or set out a blueprint; rather, he suggests a focus on the present life. He envisages a moral transformation, arguing that "the issue is the rehabilitation of values like trust, openness, responsibility, solidarity, love" ([1978] 1987, 118). These values point to the kind of small structures that might be developed in a post-democratic future, as the actions of the parallel structures also point beyond themselves to a better future.

Havel's ideas were an encouraging and powerful account of a sense of true dissidence. They were also remarkably prescient as to how the final blows to the Eastern bloc came, and the Plastic People of the Universe and Charter 77 are often credited with bringing down the Czechoslovak communist government (Kraus 2007). Journalist Mark Kurlansky (2006, 173) views the Czech strategy of resistance as one of the most inspiring, in its "focus on small victories of everyday life" and creation of a life parallel to the state system. Havel's conception of resistance is the greatest influence on my understanding of resistance in this book, and in the film *Barbara* his ideas come most strongly to the fore, as I shall show. Yet each of the contexts that the films portray is one where characters attempt to build their own parallel lives.

Another dissident author who expresses something vital about everyday resistance is Chinese author Wang Xiaobo (1996, 22), who extols the virtue of silence while also describing the silent majority as the "greatest disadvantaged group in history." He thinks people talk too much: "But here's what I think about all the world's suffering people: instead of constantly telling them how we're going to liberate them and punish their oppressors, wouldn't it be better to keep quiet, and then one day liberate them all of a sudden, and give them an unexpected treat?" (1996, 15). His sarcastic comment criticizes those who merely talk about liberating others and contrasts it with the silent resistance of the repressed. Many of the films I discuss here revolve around that kind of silent or quiet resistance, given that speech is so dangerous in some political regimes. Yet the idea is not that a person outwardly and actively conforms to the regime, while having a private disagreement with it. Even Wang Xiaobo began to speak and write in the last years before his death in 1997. Arendt (2003, 48) makes the distinction clear and argues that in totalitarian Germany a refusal to collaborate is a form of resistance, "in fact one of the many variations of nonviolent action and resistance." One can engage in quiet or silent resistance either by leaving or by staying.

As Mónica Brito Vieira (2020, 371) argues, leaving a regime, even without criticizing it, can be disturbing for the regime, especially when it happens on a large scale. Furthermore, silence can mean different things and can come about in different ways, such as through an active decision not to speak, or by remaining silent in a more passive way. A widespread refusal to speak can create what is called the "dictator's dilemma," or what Vieira calls the "paradox of silence," where too much repression leads to a fear of criticizing the regime, and the dictator is thus cut off from the information they need to stay in power. One way out of the dilemma is to have different authorities, so that blame can be shifted for excessive repression. Another factor is "voice," which means allowing citizens to express small grievances and responding to them. The East German government was well-known for this tactic, an experience satirized in *Good Bye Lenin!* (dir. Wolfgang Becker, 2003) Another example is that the GDR sold arms to Ethiopia in order to buy coffee (Apor 2022, 136). Vieira (2020, 377) points out that silence can be "full of menace," as the regime does not know whether events are moving toward a tipping point.

An example of the active use of silence is "the dissident who refuses to speak in court so as to boycott and protest against proceedings she deems illegitimate" (Viera 2020, 379). Still, Viera notes that it is difficult to produce effective collection action through silence, although the Falun Gong protests in China in 1999 are a case of coordinated silent protest. What is really significant about her discussion is bringing silent actions into the realm of nonviolent resistance and seeing that it can take a variety of forms, some of which, like leaving or exit on a wide scale, can change a regime or bring it down altogether.

Another thinker who enables reflection on resistance and its relation to power and violence is Arendt. Her considerations of the power of human beings to act in concert as a contrast to violence, which she sees as the use of instruments to achieve ends, is useful (Arendt 1970, 41–42). For her the collective nature of power makes it the more political phenomenon of the two, and such power can be seen in political promises, alliances, and groups that form to contest governments. However, Arendt's exclusive focus on collective action does not enable consideration of the resistance of individual acts or of common acts that are not necessarily collective, which are my focus in this book. Arendt (1972, 101) takes justifiable civil disobedience to be collective, in views belonging to minority protest groups, such as the protest groups in the United States in the 1960s, in contrast to individual concerns about moral conscience. In these cases, coalitions are formed based on common concerns.

Civil disobedience is an example of power in Arendt's sense when it involves plural actors protesting. Its purpose is to restore legitimacy to a political order when its legality is being undermined, at least in the context of the United States. Any individual acts in the name of a group, and arguably the individuals and characters in the films I interpret here represent a possible group of dissidents. However, they may not be primarily concerned with the public good or concerned to be public and visible.[4] Furthermore, because Arendt (1972, 88) focuses on civil disobedience in the United States, she considers dissent a feature of free or democratic government, while the contexts I discuss in this book are marked by authoritarian governments where dissent is generally not allowed or is only allowed to a very limited extent. Although the forms of nonviolent resistance I investigate are not aimed at the kind of power of minority groups coming together that Arendt had in mind, in some ways their individual actions are inflected and linked with those of others, as I will show in each chapter.

NONVIOLENCE AND FILM

My argument in this book is not a polemic against violence, nor is it an argument that only nonviolence can succeed in creating political change, or that nonviolent political change has better long-term consequences, two views that are sometimes urged, for example by Erica Chenoweth and Maria J. Stephan (2011). Similarly, Daniel Chirot (2020, 6) observes that the most revolutionary changes lead to violent resistance that in turn leads to civil war. Rather, what I seek to explore are the creative forms of nonviolent, everyday resistance that are possible and that are portrayed or imagined through film. Few discussions of resistance consider film, and equally few discussions of film link it to nonviolence.

One exception is the work of Ellen W. Gorsevski, whose *Peaceful Persuasion: The Geopolitics of Nonviolent Rhetoric* (2004) has a chapter that considers *The Spitfire Grill* (1996), directed by Lee David Zlotoff, in relation to nonviolence as social resistance. She notes that films with a clear lack of violence, such as romantic comedies, are often thought of as women's films, even though some nonviolent films are expected to appeal to male viewers as well. For her a concern with nonviolence is a kind of lens through which films can be interpreted as offering nonviolence as a possible way of life. Gorsevski (2004, 50) writes, "Nonviolent theory, properly applied and understood, can be a more hopeful and humane way to theorize how human persuasion operates in film." She suggests that films can help us find and appreciate creative ways of solving the issues that arise in oppressive systems. That idea is close to the concerns of this book, although my approach here involves allowing the films to speak philosophically rather than imposing nonviolent theory on them.

In her analysis, Gorsevski considers how the characters in *The Spitfire Grill* grapple with the problem of structural violence and how the film has been received by critics in order to reveal a nonviolent perspective. She distinguishes between strategic nonviolence, which takes into account and responds to violence occurring on a range of levels, and pacificism, which condemns "*going to war* and *war making*" (2004, 543). Furthermore, those who adopt a nonviolent worldview may qualify that in the sense that they still accept the use of violence as a last resort. To consider the film in more depth, Gorsevski argues that we need to take into account structural violence, which includes class systems, economic injustice, the prison industry, and ignorance and which may be invisible, partly because it is culturally accepted, unlike personal violence. In opposition to this kind of structural violence, a nonviolent approach could encourage a person's growth. Starting from the presumption that human beings have a basic tendency toward love, Gorsevski (2004, 62) sees nonviolence as "overcoming injustice through teamwork, cooperation, creativity, and sacrifice." The film concerns a protagonist, Percy, who has been released from prison and finds work at a café at a small town in Maine called Gilead. For Gorsevski, the nonviolent perspective appears in the film's treatment of the themes of forgiveness and redemption, and its portrayal of acts of cooperation, goodwill, and kindness, and friendship between women. These aspects of the film's narrative were regarded by some critics as "sentimental" or "unbelievable," which she contends reflects their acceptance of violence as inevitable.

Nevertheless, she observes that viewers can be drawn into films that are emotionally affecting and uplifting in a range of ways. Her focus is on the resolution of conflict within a democratic society rather than resistance to specific regimes, but the examples she uses of creative responses to that conflict are relevant. To establish her view about non-violence, Gorsevski focuses on critical responses to the film, and while they are useful in providing context, my interpretations of the movies in this book look more closely at the films to understand their visual and aural texture, their narratives, their characters, individual key scenes, and intertextual references.

To some extent, the attitudes that Gorsevski detects concerning an acceptance of violence and a view that depictions of nonviolent social change are sentimental or "women's films" can be seen in the responses to one of the films I consider below: *Wadjda* (2012), directed by Haifaa Al Mansour. Yet the theme of resistance links films that audiences may perceive differently due to their genre or their having a man or a woman protagonist, for example. All the films I selected for this book were popular and achieved a reasonable degree of critical acclaim. All are very rich sources for philosophical thinking about resistance, and all bear multiple viewings. It is noteworthy that they are a mix of genres, including realism, melodrama, and a documentary, and all set in different times and places: South Africa under apartheid, recent reflections on the 1965–66 genocide in Indonesia, East Germany in 1980, Chile in 1988, and contemporary Iran and Saudi Arabia. With the exception of *A Dry White Season* (dir. Euzhan Palcy, 1989), they were all made around the years 2011–14, possibly reflecting a period of hope for resistance and political change.

Each of my readings approaches the film from its context, the director's view of their project, the film's style and reception, how resistance is portrayed, and the ideas about resistance that emerge. There is no one interpretational method I impose, and the films relate to a diverse group of thinkers: Sara Ahmed, Arendt, Aristotle, Simone de Beauvoir, Aimé Césaire, W. E. B. Du Bois, Václav Havel, Michèle Le Dœuff, Linda Radzik, and Margaret Urban Walker. What I aim to do is connect the films to ideas that are close to their spirit so that they mutually illuminate each other. In *The Cinema of Disorientation*, Dominic Lash (2020, 153) expresses this idea very well: "The best orientational method is the absence of method. By this I do not mean that aesthetic criticism should not be methodical but that it should aim to avoid *general* methods, that the critic should be prepared to attend to the individual film and tailor their method to the demands of the film rather than arriving armed with a predetermined way of forcing the film to give up its secrets."[5] My purpose in this book is not aesthetic criticism but philosophical understanding, yet the point is well taken and will become clear as the chapters unfold. In each chapter I focus on a single film, attempting to elucidate the specificity of the vision and the thought that it exemplifies, although each film is often closely related to other films as part of a diptych or trilogy or through intertextual references.

The first film I discuss, *A Dry White Season*, is set in apartheid South Africa in 1976 and depicts a resistance that is dangerous. This is a good example to begin with to show how much risk is involved in resistance and why different paths might be chosen. Here resistance is aimed at finding out the truth rather than dissenting as such, as Havel explains. However, Benjamin Du Toit (Donald Sutherland), the protagonist, an Afrikaans schoolteacher, is finally murdered by the police. The extremity of what happens is tied to the extremity of the apartheid regime in South Africa, which punishes any questioning of the system. The film portrays Ben as a secondary victim and witness in relation to the Black South African characters, the primary victims. Ben's resistance in pursuit of the truth is nonviolent and everyday, as he is led from one action to the next, but the context is a violent one, so his actions stand out from that background. Ben's way of living in the truth is to search for the truth about the treatment of his Black South African friends under apartheid.

Palcy is Martinican and made the film in difficult and unusual circumstances during the South African apartheid regime. She has made a range of other films, shorts, documentaries, and television series. In chapter 1, I find that looking at the early reception of *A Dry White Season* is central to gaining a deeper insight into the film's portrayal of apartheid and hence the dangers of resistance. In my view, the way early critics of the film missed its significance and the influence of Aimé Césaire's work on Palcy, along with the timing, the difficult filmmaking circumstances, Palcy's activist aims in making the film, the involvement of South African actors, and its relation to the novel of the same name by André Brink, are all factors one must be aware of to appreciate the film and its depiction of this high-risk resistance.

In this chapter I examine key central criticisms of *A Dry White Season*'s depiction of South African apartheid and the way that Black South Africans are victimized, and show how a close examination of the film's narrative structure and style reveals forms of resistance to apartheid. Palcy uses a series of dramatic juxtapositions to convey the experienced texture of life in a militarized state and the brutality of the regime. The interrelation between Césaire's ideas in *Discourse on Colonialism* ([1950] 2000) and the film also enrich recognition of the film's resistance philosophy as anticolonial, cosmopolitan, and future-oriented. I also consider the way literature and film use a privileged protagonist as a victim to underscore the suffering of the less privileged characters who are the primary victims, in this case Jonathan (Bekhithemba Mpofu), Gordon (Winston Ntshona), and Emily Ngubene (Thoko Ntshinga), a Black South

African family. *A Dry White Season* gives a visceral sense of the extreme risks of resistance that is answered by deadly repression. The grave riskiness of truth-seeking also informs the path of truth-telling in the second film I consider here.

In chapter 2, "*The Look of Silence*: Revealing the Truth," I demonstrate how truth-telling is crucial to understanding this documentary. It forms a diptych with Joshua Oppenheimer's previous film, *The Act of Killing* (2012), which focused on killers involved in the genocide of hundreds of thousands of those considered to be communists in Indonesia in 1965–66. Oppenheimer got to know them and filmed them reenacting the killings in a range of film genres. *The Act of Killing* was significant in informing audiences about the genocide and how the perpetrators had not been punished and the victims and survivors had not been apologized to or compensated during the intervening period. Many of the perpetrators stayed in or went on to be in positions of power in Indonesia, so the genocide's consequences are ongoing.

The paired film, *The Look of Silence* (2014), examines the issue of the survivors meeting the genocidaires and their children. On one level, both films are accounts and acts of atonement. On another level, the attempts to get the killers to face the horror of what they have done is a continuous act of resistance in the face of decades of impunity. The film, although a documentary, is partly constructed like a fiction film, as it centers on one main "character," a survivor named Adi Rukun, who is determined to discover the truth of what happened to his brother and to confront those responsible. His search for truth and his revealing of the truth can be understood as resistance in the Havelian sense, and like the fictional resistance of Ben in *A Dry White Season*, it is risky and dangerous for Adi Rukun and all those involved. I examine how the film depicts Adi's search for truth and shows how some forms of atonement, in the context of impunity, are resistance. Again, though, the resistance is life-threatening and only possible under certain conditions. Despite the dramatic nature of some of the scenes with the perpetrators, the film has a quiet, meditative, almost restful quality, with nature as an additional witness to the atrocities. I argue that to understand how the film screens progress in atonement and itself acts as resistance to impunity and the authority of the killers and their supporters, one must take into account the unusual circumstances in the making of the documentary, the perpetrators' and survivors' participation, key scenes, and even the international screenings and subsequent events.

Chapter 3, "*Barbara*: Love and Duty," looks at a fiction film made by Christian Petzold and set in 1980 communist East Germany; the authority here is the government and its network of Stasi secret police agents and informers. In this chapter, I center on a dilemma for the resister, partly because there is an alternative created by East Germany's proximity to West Germany. While the situation is also one where overt resistance could have life-threatening consequences, the film takes a different approach in thinking along Havelian lines and in light of Christa Wolf's argument that one can resist from within the system. This way of resisting creates a hidden world of caring, upholding values, and, to an extent, rejecting the values of the West. As with the previous two films discussed, where caring about friends and family contributes to the resolve of the protagonists, in *Barbara* (2012) the feelings of a genuine or authentic love and a sense of duty toward others enrich the resistance and make it meaningful. *Barbara* highlights a short period of events involving Dr. Barbara Wolff (Nina Hoss), a pediatrician sent to work in a village in the German Democratic Republic. This film, like *Nader and Simin, a Separation* (dir. Asghar Farhadi, 2011), stresses the difficulty of making choices in an authoritarian regime. One choice is whether to resist at all and another is how to resist, as that could be done by leaving.

Barbara is part of Petzold's "love in oppressive systems" trilogy, which also includes *Phoenix* (2014) and *Transit* (2018). He is a founding member of the Berlin School of filmmakers, along with Angela Schanelec and Thomas Arslan, famous for its rediscovery of genre and the beauty of many of the films, described by Marco Abel (2008, 12) thus: "Many of these films . . . thematically focus on the everyday and attempt to capture normality—though they do this so that *in* their visual intensification of normality the extraordinary at the heart of everydayness emerges." This film is very complex, with dense intertextual elements from literature, music, and painting as well as the film language of shots, color, acting, and sound being used to highlight how hard it is to decide. Similarly to *A Separation* and *Wadjda*, the film's title emphasizes the singularity of the main character(s) and, in this case, the specificity of Barbara's choice. The heart of the chapter concerns the way the film enriches viewers' comprehension of her decision and portrays the texture of a life in which everyday resistance means pursuing meaningful goals with others in an authoritarian regime, the motivations of love and duty intertwined and shaping the choice, and I focus on two key turning points in the film.

While Barbara remains in Eastern Germany to try to live out her duties toward others, the next film I reflect on also portrays a resistance from within, using legal means. In the chapter "*No*: Happiness, Resistance, and Trauma," I show how the Chilean film *No* (dir. Pablo Larraín, 2012) depicts a resistant response to trauma based on happiness so that the Augusto Pinochet civic-military dictatorship (1973–90) is defeated by the 1988 plebiscite. This plebiscite involved a "Yes" (*Sí*) vote, in favor of Pinochet remaining as president of Chile for another eight years, versus a "No" vote, in favor of having democratic elections instead. I concentrate on how the film represents the transformation of the trauma of the dictatorship through the concept of happiness. *No* fictionalizes the advertising campaigns for the 1988 plebiscite shown on television. Stylistically, it intercuts the historical drama with long sections of footage from the period, as well as creating new footage using cameras from the period to create a seamless whole. Chilean director Larraín is known for his diverse oeuvre, including biopics of Jackie Kennedy Onassis and Princess Diana of Wales. *No*, like *Barbara*, belongs to a trilogy (with *Post Mortem* [2010] and *Tony Manero* [2008]); each film in the series engages with a different period in the Pinochet dictatorship.

As the film shows, the "No" campaign prepared advertising with footage of military dominance and cruelty to opponents, thus concentrating on negative emotions and trauma, but then René Saavedra (Gael García Bernal), an advertising creative, took over and shifted the focus to galvanize the "No" vote. His pursuit of excellence in the campaign can be likened to the concern for the inherent values of their profession of the protagonists in each film.

In this chapter I deploy two central philosophical ideas alongside Larraín's to draw out the complexity of the process conveyed in the film. The first is Du Bois's ([1903] 1996, 188) writing about the slave or sorrow songs, which express the experience of trauma yet transform that trauma into a new narrative that is more hopeful and positive and can be part of a shared heritage. The parallel in *No* is the new narrative that the advertising campaign creates. The second is Aristotle's (1984, 1097a36–b7) belief, and also seemingly that of the "No" campaigners, that happiness is an intrinsic value. This idea appears in their theme song, "Chile, Joy Is Coming," and throughout the individual sections for the campaign, which I compare with Sara Ahmed's (2010, 160–98) recent discussion of happiness and the future. These two concepts are connected to resistance through providing the emotional and intellectual support for the belief in a better future beyond the regime. Using these ideas, I interpret the film's depiction of a type of resistance that requires an affective and symbolic turn from trauma to happiness, from past to future, and from the individual to the collective.

In the fifth chapter, "*A Separation*: Ethical Ambiguity," I examine how the film represents the conflict between Nader (Peyman Moadi) and Simin (Leila Hatami), a married couple who live in contemporary Iran. *A Separation* returns to the difficulty of making a decision about how to resist, a matter also addressed in *Barbara*. In this film, however, there are two protagonists who see the issue differently and settle on different conclusions about what to do. Nader prefers to stay to look after his father in Iran, while Simin believes that leaving is the best way to resist the circumstances. Their daughter, Termeh (Sarina Farhadi), who is loved deeply by both parents and who also loves them, is torn between the two. In a way similar to that seen in *Barbara*, love for others is the driving force here, but it leads to conflict between two individuals rather than a dilemma for one. Both are ethical people who are concerned with upholding crucial values and confronting the ambiguity of existence in general and in an authoritarian system. Unfortunately, the two ethical approaches to the ambiguity of their situation cannot be reconciled, and their resistance leads to the breakup of their family. Farhadi has made a series of influential and well-regarded films, mostly (although not all) set in Iran, that deal with conflict within families and society. *A Separation* moves between genres, with elements of melodrama, detective, and courtroom drama, and relies strongly on dialogue and ambient sound to convey mood as well as a sense of eavesdropping on the characters.

To explicate the ethical conflict that Nader and Simin are drawn into by their society, I use Simone de Beauvoir's concept of ambiguity in *The Ethics of Ambiguity*. According to Beauvoir (1997, 9, 129), ambiguity entails that life's meaning "is never fixed, that it must be constantly won." It includes human ambiguity as self-conscious and material, between dimensions of time, between individuals and groups, and ambiguous choices in ethical situations (1997, 7). I argue that these ambiguities, which exist in any community, are intensified in authoritarian polities. Beauvoir's experience of the Nazi occupation means that her ethics is informed by the ambiguity of those situations and by an understanding of the ethical loss or remainder after a decision is made. Beauvoir herself was interested in film, and of course her literary works also present the perspectives that arise in different characters with different worldviews. *A Separation* reveals the ambiguity of ethical questions about resistance, as Beauvoir outlines, and how this ambiguity heightened again due to the stresses of life in a theocratic society. Rather than reconciling the ambiguities, the film shows how they lead to different and opposed ways of resisting, even in individuals who fundamentally have shared interests and concerns. It provides not a comforting sense of what the good person does to resist but, rather, an unease concerning the ethical challenges of resistance.

The Saudi Arabian film *Wadjda*—the focus of the final chapter, "*Wadjda*: Realism and Resistance"—is perhaps the most hopeful of the examples here. All of the films I discuss in the book use children or the next generation to represent the possibility of a better future through resistance, but here the child is the absolute center of the film. It focuses on a period in the experience of Wadjda (Waad Mohammed), a rebellious ten-year-old girl growing up in Riyadh, who longs to ride a bicycle of her own. This was Al Mansour's first feature, and since then she has made a number of diverse films connected by their depiction of nonconforming women. It was also the first feature film made entirely in Saudi Arabia. One fact central to understanding the film and its impact is that it was shot on location in Riyadh, even though that choice created more challenges in shooting due to restrictive customs and censorship rules. The film depicts men and women and their lives separately and together in the capital in the light of these restrictions and has a sense of optimism concerning the possibilities of resistance.

In *Wadjda*, there is an evident connection between the realist cinematic approach and the form of resistance. I consider André Bazin's and Rudolf Arnheim's accounts of realism and authenticity in film alongside more recent considerations of realist cinema in the digital age and then show how *Wadjda*'s specific realism and location filming is linked to a philosophy of women's rebellion and resistance. The resistance portrayed in *Wadjda* is detailed by considering Arendt's ([1958] 1998, 8–9) concept of natality, exemplified by Wadjda's single-minded determination to live beyond the rules that are set for her as well as through Beauvoir's account of girls' challenge to their situation (2010, 369) and how new possibilities are won by the child (1997, 141). Furthermore, Michèle Le Dœuff's (2003, 44, 68) idea of "meliorism" in conjunction with the film's realism articulates a sense of thinking differently. *Wadjda* takes a realist approach that describes the constricting situation yet also generates hope about small changes as a kind of resistance. The film is planned and closely structured, not improvised, and depicts a Riyadh that had not yet arrived. In some cases, cinematic realism is linked to support for the current situation and publicity used by authoritarian systems. I consider the opposing potential of realism in film to theorize the resistant measures that women and other oppressed groups can take against the restrictions they face. The vision of the film suggests that gradual change and nonviolent resistance have a crucial place in our ethical and political thought. Moreover, the film shows how realism can work to visualize and encourage these changes, contributing to our resistant imaginations.

The book is bookended by films by two very different films by women directors, *A Dry White Season* and *Wadjda*. One is a representation of the most dangerous resistance, the other a more hopeful tale of resistance's possibilities. Thus, we now turn to *A Dry White Season* to consider resistance in relation to truth-seeking and to understand its dire consequences in the context of a brutally repressive regime.

[CHAPTER ONE]

A Dry White Season

Discovering the Truth

In this chapter I consider how the film *A Dry White Season* portrays a dangerous resistance, a resistance that is not intended to lead to victimhood but in the end does. Although it is a resistance without dissent, it still results in the death of the protagonist, Benjamin Du Toit, an Afrikaans history teacher. This film is essential to my argument because it depicts the horrors of apartheid and shows that within such a system to even ask questions about torture and murder leads to one's own assassination. Each character who is killed or tortured is a victim of the regime, although Ben is a secondary victim and witness. His fate shows how dangerous individual resistance can be in a racist regime. Although Ben is nonviolent, he is surrounded by violence, and that affects everyone, especially Black South Africans. He is not a dissenter but comes to live in the truth in the Havelian sense through his search for the truth concerning the murder of his friend Gordon Ngubene.

The film's director, Euzhan Palcy, is Martinican, and she was the first Black woman to direct a film in Hollywood with a major studio, MGM (Bobo 2016).[1] Palcy has made a number of other films—*Sugar Cane Alley* (*La rue cases-nègres*, 1983),[2] *Siméon* (1992), *Ruby Bridges* (1998), and *The Killing Yard* (2001)—along with shorts, television series, and documentaries, including *Aimé Césaire: A Voice for History* (*Une voix pour l'histoire*) (1994), a television documentary about Martinican author and statesman Aimé Césaire (1913–2008). As I will explain, early scholarly reception of *A Dry White Season* was highly critical of its portrait of apartheid and its victims. Unlike those early critics, June M. Gill (2000, 371) argues that "*A Dry White Season*, with explicit scenes of violence from the Soweto massacre and powerful performances by South African actors, was the strongest anti-apartheid film of the eighties" and recognizes the importance of Aimé Césaire's work to Palcy's cinematic vision.[3] *A Dry White Season* was the last film to be made about apartheid before apartheid was dismantled, so it is notable for that reason alone. Furthermore, the filmmaking circumstances are relevant to articulating how the film contributes to understanding resistance and victimhood. Palcy's accomplishments were finally recognized by the Academy in 2022, when she was given an honorary Oscar for lifetime achievement (Beckett 2022).

Palcy's aim was to create an activist film that would make people realize the harms of apartheid and oppose it (Gill 2000, 374). She cowrote the screenplay with actor and writer Colin Welland, best known for the script for *Chariots of Fire* (dir. Hugh Hudson, 1981); Welland provided the first draft, and Palcy revised it to reflect South African life more precisely. Three well-known US actors—Donald Sutherland (Ben), Susan Sarandon (Melanie Bruwer), and Marlon Brando (Ian McKenzie)—were used to widen the audience for the film, which was well received by audiences if not scholars.[4] Nevertheless, it should be noted at the outset that many elements in filming and the texture of the film in representing daily lived experience under apartheid involved South Africans. South African actors in *A Dry White Season* included Zakes Mokae (Stanley Makhaya), a theater and film actor who left South Africa for the United States in 1960 (S. G. Freedman 1989; McKenna 1989, 35); Winston Ntshona (Gordon), an actor and writer; and Thoko Ntshinga (Emily), who had appeared in a number of films. These actors were not as familiar to international audiences.[5] One should also recall that at that time many South African artists had to live in exile (Maingard 2007a, 512).[6] These actors traveled in secret to film in Zimbabwe and thus risked their lives to appear in the film (Gugler 2003, 85).

Palcy's film is based on the book of the same time title by Afrikaans South African writer André Brink (1935–2015). Interestingly, Brink was inspired to write his anti-apartheid novels from within South Africa rather than living in exile by reading the work of Césaire when visiting France (Hunt 2020). The title refers to a hot, rainless, season. It is from a short poem that provides the epigraph to Brink's book called "For Don M. Banned" by Mongane Wally Serote (1974, 58), a South African poet. It both suggests the destruction of Black African lives by apartheid and presents a strange juxtaposition with the fact of the whiteness of apartheid and of Ben, a white resister. In an interview Palcy explains that "in Soweto it's said apartheid is a season, it's a dry, white season, and seasons don't stay, they are just passing. So apartheid cannot stay forever" (Glicksman 1989, 66). Palcy's hope was that the film would contribute to the passing of apartheid. The narrative of the film follows Ben as he comes to understand how Black South Africans suffer under the system of apartheid, and Ben's growing activism, which finally leads to his murder by the police. While both the film and the book are set in 1976 at the time of the Soweto uprising of school students, which followed the proposal of enforced study in Afrikaans rather than English for half the school curriculum in the townships (Ackerman and DuVall 2000, 341; Lodge 2009, 214), there are differences between the film and the book, which was published ten years earlier (1979). These differences underscore how Palcy heightens the focus on Black South African experience of victimhood and of resistance in the film.[7]

In the first section of the chapter, I consider the central criticisms of *A Dry White Season*'s presentation of victimization. Then I examine the structure of the film and analyze how the film represents a much more complex and inspiring picture of resistance, suffering, and victimization than a number of the critics acknowledged. Palcy's approach to confronting racism cinematically coheres with that of her compatriot Césaire in the passionate and poetic essay *Discourse on Colonialism* ([1950] 2000), and an understanding of those ideas can help to place the film in context. Césaire played a central role in the development of the négritude movement. Négritude, in Césaire's (2000, 92) words, is the view that "our Negro heritage was worthy of respect, and that this heritage was not relegated to the past, that its values were values that could still make an important contribution to the world." However, colonization involves an erasure of the past, and the process of what Césaire (2000, 42) calls "thingification," or the construction of both colonizer and colonized as only a role or instrument. In the essay Césaire (2000, 44) makes a very similar claim to Serote and Palcy concerning the transitory nature of apartheid: "My only consolation is that periods of colonization pass, that nations sleep only for a time, and that peoples remain." Like Havel, Césaire combined a life of writing with that of political leader. The approach Césaire maintains is anticolonial, global, critical of the impact of colonialism on both the colonized and colonizer, and oriented to a future new society. Palcy also follows Césaire in using cultural means to contest colonialism and racism.[8]

In the final section of the chapter, I examine the way the protagonist, Ben, becomes a secondary victim when he is murdered as a result of his concern for the primary victims of apartheid, Jonathan, Gordon, and Emily Ngubene, and how the film uses this narrative to provide a powerful portrait of all those who suffered under apartheid and what is at stake in resisting such a regime. A "victim" is understood here as "a person who is suffering as a direct consequence of the wrongdoing of another" (Cox 2015, 2)—in this case the South African security police, who enforce the excesses of apartheid system—rather than someone who suffers through accident or natural disaster or who merely claims to be a victim.[9] The focus of the film is the structure and the texture of the felt experience of becoming a victim through resistance.

CRITICISM OF THE REPRESENTATION OF VICTIMIZATION IN THE FILM

In this first section, I consider how Ben's resistance was interpreted by early critics of the film. His resistance is a search for truth, which begins when he supports Gordon Ngubene, a gardener who works at the school and Ben's home, and ends in them both becoming victims of the regime.[10] Ben, an Afrikaner, teaches history and lives in Johannesburg. He is reluctantly drawn into resistance after Gordon's son, Jonathan, and then Gordon are killed. While the police claim that Gordon committed suicide, Ben discovers that he was tortured by the Special Branch and that Gordon's son, Jonathan, was also tortured and killed after the Soweto uprising in 1976. Ben hires a lawyer, Ian McKenzie, to act for the Ngubene family, but the judge finds the police innocent. Stanley, a friend of Gordon and his partner Emily as well as a taxi driver, takes Ben in hand and teaches Ben how apartheid affects the lives of all the people in the townships. In the course of gathering evidence about the attacks on Jonathan and Gordon, Ben is harassed and fired; his son is expelled from school; he is left by his partner Susan (Janet Suzman) and betrayed to the police by his daughter Suzette (Susannah Harker); the house is searched and then burgled, and shots are fired through the windows.[11] Finally, Ben is killed by a security agent, Captain Stolz (Jürgen Prochnow), who runs Ben down in the street.

But the information Ben has gathered about the murders of Jonathan and Gordon, including sworn statements from witnesses, is saved, as his son Johan (Rowen Elmes) delivers it to a newspaper, the *Rand Daily Mail* (1902–85).[12] So in that sense his resistance is not wholly in vain. Ben's resistance in trying to discover what really happened to Gordon is ordinary and everyday and shows the reach of apartheid as it violently suppressed any attempt to support Black South Africans. Contemporaneous critical discussions of the film claimed that it centered too closely on the character of Ben. I will consider these criticisms and then argue in the following sections that the film deserves closer analysis and has philosophical insights that remain relevant to understanding resistance and victimization in colonial and postcolonial regimes.

It should be noted that magazine and newspaper reviews of the film when it was first released were mixed. Sheila Benson (1989, 34) criticizes the film as lacking in "insights into life on either side of the color line," finds the portrayal of Stanley "improbable," and compares it unfavorably to *Cry Freedom* (dir. Richard Attenborough, 1987), *A World Apart* (dir. Chris Menges, 1987), and *Mapantsula* (dir. Oliver Schmitz, 1988). Margaret Walters (1990) comments that it lacks "feeling for the townships." Furthermore, reviews tend to praise Marlon Brando's performance (Benson 1989, 34; Maslin 1989, 19; Walters 1990) over that of the other actors in the film. By contrast, Samuel Freedman (1989) remarks on the originality of having an Afrikaner protagonist and the verisimilitude created by Palcy's research into the experiences of both Black and Afrikaner South Africans. Roger Ebert (1989) also claims that *A Dry White Season* "has much more of the South African black experience" than *A World Apart* and *Cry Freedom* do. Thirty years after its first release, some film writers, such as Erin Free (2022), have celebrated Palcy's achievement as the first Black woman to make a major Hollywood feature and have praised Zakes Mokae's performance as well as others'. Jim Hemphill (2019) enthuses that the film, "which was bracing and shattering on its initial release, has only improved with age." Akiva Gottlieb (2019) describes *A Dry White Season* as "an unusually powerful rendering of the costs of principled dissent—as well as a crackerjack thriller." He suggests that the marketing of the film, such as the US film poster showing only Sutherland, Sarandon, and Brando, contributed to the perception of it as a "white savior" film, which could help to explain some of the initial scholarly responses.

Early political critics of the film caricature it as depicting a white savior who dies, while Ben's friend Stanley survives. These critics focus on the broad plot outline of *A Dry White Season* rather than the way the narrative is framed, scripted, set up, shot, and acted. For instance, Rob Nixon (1994, 78) describes *A Dry White Season* in relation to *Cry Freedom* and *A World Apart*, all three of which he sees as ideologically transformed to appeal to US audiences.[13] While Nixon (1994, 275n36) calls *A Dry White Season* "respectable," he argues that Ben is at the emotional center because "the black family remains pretty anonymous" (perhaps revealing his own prejudices), and he asserts that it is implausible that Ben would be hounded more than Stanley. Nixon (1994, 89) acknowledges that the film has a strong and complex character in Stanley and that the plot runs against cliché in making the Black protagonist the survivor while the white friend is killed. However, he believes that there should be more in the film about "the major organizational agents of political change" rather than victimization and individual friendship between white and Black individuals.[14] This criticism implies that the film should be a documentary-like depiction of structural groups rather than a dramatic narrative. I contend, however, that showing the victimization process is central to the film's meaning, not one of its faults.[15]

Similarly, Victoria Carchidi (1994, 54) criticizes the focus on a white protagonist, a choice Palcy explains as helping to finance the film and also as portraying people, both Black and white, in South Africa under apartheid (Gill 2000, 377). When Carchidi (1994, 59) compares *A Dry White Season* with *Cry Freedom*, she discusses Richard Attenborough's role as director of the latter but does not mention Palcy's name, and she claims that "*A Dry White Season* [does] not present the felt texture of South African life."

In a short discussion of *A Dry White Season*, independent filmmaker Peter Davis (1996, 110) contends that "black pain was mediated through middle class whites" and "there was a certain appropriation of that pain: in fiction form, with the murder of Ben Du Toit." He acknowledges that "Palcy rejected the black-as-victim image, and built up one of the African characters, the taxi-driver Stanley, into the embodiment of the resistance" (1996, 111).[16] One major change Palcy makes to the narrative to stress that embodiment is Stanley's shooting of Captain Stolz. Brink (quoted in Davis 1996, 11) was critical of this alteration to the narrative.[17] However, Palcy justifies the change as giving a warning "'that this decent man can be pushed to violence'" (Collins 1989; Herndon 1999, 240). Elsewhere Palcy says that if apartheid is not ended, then Black people "won't have any other alternative but to fight back" (S. G. Freedman 1989; Glicksman 1989, 69). So Stolz's murder can be seen as a protest against the violence of apartheid and as foreshadowing—cinematically speaking, since the film is set in 1976—the violence in South Africa in the 1980s. Palcy (1990, 15) makes the point that the killing of murderous police like Stolz is a significant aspect of the struggle against apartheid and one that was often covered up.[18] Her inclusion of this detail reinforces the idea that some victims will retaliate.[19] Not all will engage only in nonviolent resistance.

Carchidi (1994), Davis (1996), and Nixon (1994) accept that the film portrays apartheid and its cruelties. Nevertheless, Carchidi (1994, 59) says it presents a "schematized representation of the extreme conditions in South Africa." Davis (1996, 11) dismisses the film because it "[places] this power in the hands of righteous white men" and has a "familiar Hollywood ending." Finally, Nixon (1994, 90) writes, "The film's emphasis on victimization appears as a combined product of the more fragile condition of anti-apartheid resistance in the late seventies, Brink's liberal perspective, and studio and mass market pressures on Palcy." One assumption here is that the film is made for international white audiences and thus necessarily cannot properly represent how the racism of apartheid works. Yet if one remembers that Palcy intended to portray people, both Black and white, under apartheid, she must have thought that the film would be seen by mixed audiences. Palcy's approach resonates with that of Césaire (2020, 43), who in an interview with Françoise Vergès explains the irritations of sectarianism, the need for a dialogue of civilizations, and the view that "of utmost importance is humanism, humanity, the respect due to each individual, the respect of human dignity, the right of fulfilment." *A Dry White Season* deliberately appeals to that respect in its depiction of victimization.

Similar kinds of uncharitable readings are made of Brink's novel, where some interpretations ignore the irony and effect of the narrator, a popular writer, describing the events that led to so many deaths, with the narrator's speculations interwoven with Ben's diary and other documents. For instance, Alice Brittan (2005, 59–65) argues that in the novel Brink displaces the descriptions of torture onto the sex scenes between Ben and partner Susan and Ben and lover Melanie, descriptions that Brittan (2005, 76) claims support "the vision of apartheid." However, this conclusion does not draw out the complexities that her own analysis reveals: that the narrator is a popular writer who imposes a distorted vision onto the story and so in that sense is unreliable and should be distrusted.[20] Brink's ([1979]1980, 316) narrator represents a complicity with the apartheid system, but Ben's resistant action and death finally penetrates that complicity, and the narrator becomes a witness so that no one can say "*I knew nothing about it*."

By contrast, Giuliana Iannaccaro (2014, 72–73) stresses the novel's complex, multilayered elements and the way it implicates the system of censorship in South Africa, as does Mélanie Joseph-Vilain (2009), a specialist in postcolonial literature. As Palcy describes, in the film the romance between Ben and Melanie is de-emphasized so that the narrative can stay focused on the political issues of both the violence of the security apparatus and the resistance to it (McKenna 1989, 35). There are flashes of attraction between Ben and Melanie, but that is all. In the next section, I focus on a closer and more sympathetic reading of the film, especially its structure, to highlight the specificity of Palcy's vision of the experience of victimhood.

FRAMING VICTIMIZATION

The structure of the film and the book, intentionally or not, follows a pattern that is used to highlight the egregiousness of victimization for audiences who may not fully recognize its seriousness or its arbitrariness.

One example is *The Boy in the Striped Pajamas* (dir. Mark Herman, 2008), where the inexorable and random nature of the Shoah is depicted through the son of a concentration camp commandant being caught up in the maelstrom through friendship with a Jewish boy of a similar age. Another powerful work deploying this structure is *12 Years a Slave* (dir. Steve McQueen, 2013), where an African American man is snatched from the street in Washington and forced into slavery. Both rely on the contrast between a human life lived in freedom and an abrupt or rapid transition to extreme suffering as a victim in order to deeply affect the reader or audience. The point of this narrative structure is to stress the outrage of the injustices committed against the more typical sufferer by evoking our empathy in the unusual situation. *A Dry White Season* is more complex: this structure runs in parallel with the depiction of the victimization of already oppressed victims, since it concerns two families, one white and one Black. One story shows how questioning the status quo can quickly lead to intimidation and even death, and the other shows how victimization is continuous with a lifetime of deprivation and exclusion.

While the film seems to stay, as the novel does, with Ben as the main character, the film in fact frames Ben's story with the Black South African experience. The film begins with a scene of a Black boy and a white boy (Jonathan and Johan) playing soccer together and ends with photographs of Jonathan and Gordon on the front page of the newspaper, with a photograph of Ben beneath theirs and that of Captain Stolz over to the side.[21] Furthermore, after Johan delivers the documents, he runs to Stanley, who embraces him and says, "Well done, little lanie" (the term *lanie*, in South Africa, means "white person"). Thus Stanley's view and Stanley's action in killing Stolz provide the film's denouement.

After the opening scene of the two boys having fun playing soccer, the viewer is plunged into a scene in a beer hall. This beer hall scene, which does not appear in the novel, depicts another dimension of the economic system of apartheid. A panning shot of a relaxing bar where Black South Africans drink beer and strum guitars is interrupted by an activist accusing them of funding the government bullets used to kill them. In *Discourse*, Césaire (2000, 43, emphasis in original) focuses on the way that through colonization "natural *economies* have been disrupted—harmonious and viable *economies* adapted to the indigenous population." In a compressed way, therefore, Palcy is alluding to the government control of alcohol sales, which superseded a previously independent industry run by Black South Africans, as well as the strategy of suppressing opposition by encouraging inebriation.[22] From there the scene shifts to Jonathan and other children playing and being arrested by the police. It is only after that framing that the scene shifts to the whites at a soccer match and introduces Ben and family.

Although the film was shot in Zimbabwe and Pinewood Studios in England, Palcy adds to the film's authentic representation of apartheid by incorporating dialogue and knowledge of the experiences of Black South Africans. To research the uprising and the torture carried out by the police, Palcy traveled to Soweto, claiming to be recording an album (Gill 2000, 374) or needing technicians to make a comedy in Zimbabwe (S. G. Freedman 1989).[23] She depicts the torture that Jonathan and Gordon endured based on her research and conversations with torture survivors in South Africa, which Brink does not describe directly in the novel (Glicksman 1989, 65; Palcy 1990, 14). Furthermore, Palcy changes Emily's death from suicide to Emily's heart giving way after the family are forcibly thrown out of their house because Black South African widows were not allowed to stay in their homes (S. G. Freedman 1989). Her film represents without flinching the "infinite distance" between colonization and civilization and the brutalization of the colonizer in colonization "to degrade him, to awaken him to buried instincts, to covetousness, violence, race hatred, and moral relativism" that Césaire (2000, 5) describes. This degradation of the colonizer is linked to the victimization of the colonized.

Some interpretations of the film have taken a closer look at what Palcy was aiming for and what is achieved in the film, and those clues will be developed to articulate *A Dry White Season*'s illumination of victimization. For instance, a more sympathetic reading of the film is provided by Marlaine Glicksman (1989, 65), herself a director, who observes that "Palcy alone looks at black South Africans who are neither leaders and intellectuals, like Steven Biko, nor the usual house help. Nor are they silent or symbolic faces." A similar complexity appears in Palcy's depictions of the proponents of apartheid: although Palcy portrays them as evil, the film shows they can also be "charming" and "attractive," like Captain Stolz, who asks Ben for an autograph for Stolz's son, as Ben had been a well-known soccer player (Glicksman 1989, 66).[24]

In contrast to critics such as Nixon, Carchidi, and Davis, who decry the film because it has a white protagonist, Vivian Bickford-Smith (2003, 24) argues that *Cry Freedom* and *A Dry White Season* are important films because they were popular and successful, "the two most influential filmic popularizers of apartheid history," and suggests that "they are particularly worth analysing as filmic histories for this reason alone." As Bickford-Smith (2003, 25–26) notes, early critics disparage the film for portraying Black problems from a white perspective, portraying friendship between Black and white people, making the Black characters less complex than the white characters, not accurately depicting the nature of apartheid and the struggle against it, and not stressing the collective and radical character of resistance. This debate itself shows how scholars can ignore the possibility of solidarity in struggles against victimhood and portrayal of such solidarity.

The depiction of united resistance is arguably a positive feature of the film, because it shows someone who is not suffering under apartheid, and is even benefiting from it, choosing to help those who are oppressed and thereby becoming a victim themselves. Bickford-Smith (2003, 27–28) argues that the views of the Black characters are given greater weight and that their views of apartheid are always the authoritative ones, which he illustrates with dialogue where Stanley points out that Ben's experience of being African was nothing like Stanley's and with an analysis of how *A Dry White Season* uses cross-cutting of scenes to show the obliviousness of the Du Toit family to the reality of Black South African experience. He points out that "a white protagonist does not exclude the possibility that the films also tell black tales, that they can reveal something of black experience as well" and that both Ben *and* Stanley are well-rounded, interesting characters (Bickford-Smith 2003, 30, 32).[25] Samuel G. Freedman (1989) refers to the film's portrayal of a "joint struggle," unlike *A World Apart* and *Cry Freedom*, which focus primarily on white English families. These protagonists can serve to make international audiences aware of the horrors of apartheid, as early critics noted, although they thought the film was distorted by that aim. For her part, Palcy says the film aims "'to appeal to the human side of *everybody*,'" not just white audiences (Glicksman 1989, 66). Further, she makes the point that "'for me, it wasn't really a compromise, because if you want to make a truthful movie about the apartheid regime, you cannot exclude the white people, in the same way you *cannot* leave the Black people in the background'" (Palcy 1990, 13).

Bickford-Smith (2003, 33–34) views the film as an attempt "to describe South African society more broadly to the outside world," including the living conditions for Black urban South Africans, and the relations between white South Africans and their servants, so he considers it a work with "considerable historical merit." He acknowledges that earlier dismissals of the film led to a lack of analysis. That is unfortunate, as the film deals with crucial questions of the role of allies in opposing and witnessing racial oppression in an extreme context, where even what appears to be a nonthreatening approach is met with deadly force. So in the final section of this chapter, I consider the way the film relates the struggles of the Black South Africans to Ben's journey to become a victim and witness.

BECOMING A VICTIM

As described above, most of Ben's formerly central relationships and finally his life is sacrificed to finding out the truth about what the apartheid state has done to Gordon.[26] Ben could have lived as if apartheid had nothing to do with him, but he chose to continue asking questions even if that meant that he would die.[27] It is in fulfilling the intrinsic significance of his profession as a history teacher, as Havel recommends, that Ben loses his position as a teacher and is persecuted. Furthermore, it is quite clear that Ben knew he would be murdered, which is why the documents are entrusted to Johan. The film demonstrates how people who resist oppression risk their well-being and even their lives by doing so and can become victims of the regime. For Césaire (2000, 33), colonialism has "abominable colonialist and racist consequences, whose victims were to be the Indians, the Yellow peoples, and the Negroes." In the film Jonathan, Gordon, Emily, and Ben are all nonviolent but are met with violence. Gordon, his son Jonathan, and his partner Emily are the primary victims, but Ben becomes a secondary victim by caring enough about them to investigate what happened.[28]

Roger Fjellström (2002, 104–7) distinguishes a number of concepts of victimhood. The first is that of the victim as a religious-sacrificial notion, whereby a victim is sacrificed for a god or some other purpose. This type of victimhood does not describe the murders in *A Dry White Season*, which are carried out as a systematic suppression of resistance to and even knowledge of the apartheid regime. However, Ben's role could be understood as a sacrifice for the greater good of exposing and opposing the apartheid regime. Another core meaning of victim is that "a person is subjected to severe injury by another person," a perpetrator (Fjellström 2002, 108). While we do use the term *victim* for those who suffer from accidents and natural disasters, it is this core meaning of subjection to intentional injury that is relevant to understanding what happens to Jonathan, Gordon, Ben, and Emily. Furthermore, the condition of the suffering being due to the wrongdoing of another cited above (Cox 2015, 2) is in strong contrast to someone who is justly injured, as a form of punishment or because of self-defense against an enemy who has attacked (Fjellström 2002, 110). Thomas Brudholm (2008, 185) defines a victim succinctly as "a person to whom a crime has been committed," and that is how the idea of a victim is presented in *A Dry White Season*.

Recent literature has considered the question whether victims have a duty to resist oppression, for reasons such as collective interests, duties to oneself, or as a duty to assist. Ashwini Vasanthakumar (2018, 470–71) argues that victims have both information and experiential knowledge, meaning that they have the standing and authority to both testify and resist oppression, which he conceives as a duty to assist. Of course, a bystander, like Ben when the narrative begins, has more of a responsibility than victims do. Thomas E. Hill places bystanders between primary oppressors and victims. For Hill (2010, 32), a bystander "passively let this [oppression] happen by standing idly by." The kind of responsibilities he argues bystanders have are in moral deliberation, reflecting on one's motivations, and a strong will to act. In *A Dry White Season*, we see how Ben's willful ignorance becomes transformed into an awareness of the suffering of his Black South African friends and thus a recognition of a duty to resist that he follows through in action. He has a kind of moral awakening that is necessary to become resistant and shifts from bystander to ally and finally to victim himself.

Ben is an unusual character because it was more expected that the "English" South Africans would oppose apartheid, as in *Cry Freedom* and *A World Apart*, not the Afrikaners. In different ways, the film and the book enable us to comprehend how Ben experiences a breakdown of trust in the police, the government, family, and the world because of his determination to discover the facts about torture.[29] At first the depiction of Ben is critical of his perspective and lack of understanding, as he teaches the mythology of the Afrikaners to his pupils. In the novel, Ben's increasingly paranoid state is described by the narrator and Ben's diary entries. In the film, that breakdown, which follows his increasing resistance as well as his doom, has to be demonstrated through visuals and dialogue. Once Ben asks the first questions about Gordon, brief shots show police always watching him from a car or on the street or turning up at the house unexpectedly. Ben's psychological state transforms from complacency to disbelief, to shock, horror, anger, disillusionment ("I've been too naive for too long"), and finally a seemingly stoic acceptance of death, a death his son Johan also accepts. However, it takes extreme brutality to shake Ben from a sanguine approach to the South African authorities and to begin to resist. When Ben first sees that Jonathan has been beaten, he says that nothing can be done, and as Gordon points out, Ben says the same thing again when Jonathan has died (fig. 1.1).

There are two key scenes in the film that mark Ben's awakening and victimhood. First, Gordon's death in police custody is a turning point, as Ben did not think anything could or should be done about Jonathan's death, but he saw Gordon's death completely differently. He had already tried to find out how Gordon was by going to the police station and asking about him. Second, Ben's first visit to Soweto with Stanley in order to see Gordon's tortured body is essential to recognition of the cruelty and injustice of the South African regime. It is as if Ben had to actually see it rather than simply hear about it.[30]

FIG. 1.1. Gordon takes Jonathan to see Ben after he was beaten. Still from *A Dry White Season*, directed by Euzhan Palcy (Davros Films and Sundance Productions, 1989).

While the film depicts how Black African anti-apartheid activists are able to draw the Afrikaans teacher into the struggle, the conflict in becoming a resistant witness is apparent. Ben's search for evidence has the consequence of putting the lives of others in danger, as witnesses to Jonathan and Gordon's murders are exiled, kept under house arrest, detained, and even murdered themselves, like Johnson Seroke (Sello Maake Ka-Ncube), who witnesses and testifies about Gordon's torture.[31] In a sense, the film does not promote Ben's version of resistance, since Ben is murdered; in another sense, it does, as the evidence is ultimately published openly. Furthermore, the very making of *A Dry White Season* and its portrayal of resistance promotes activism that can take many forms and be carried out by both Black and white South Africans.

A number of elements in the film articulate an analysis and response to racist regimes that extends Césaire's critique, which primarily focuses on French colonialism. Jacqueline Maingard (2019, 203) argues that if we examine Palcy's oeuvre, we can see a pan-African sensibility where "the local manifestation of black resistance against Apartheid and its brutal repression—at a particular moment in South Africa—in *A Dry White Season* can be seen as an extension of relations between Africa and the Caribbean," and she contends that Palcy's work creates continuities between apartheid and histories of slavery (2019, 211). Such repression is a sign of the brittleness of the regime, which is almost unable to employ the alternative to repression that Havel outlines of integrating resistance. Maingard's interpretation sees a positivity in the global link between

South Africa, Martinique, and the United States, as Césaire outlines, rather than a blurring of significant distinctions and universalizing of the unique South African experience, as has been suggested (Higgins 1992, 109). Similarly, in *Discourse* Césaire (2000, 32) connects colonialism around the world even more broadly: "The colonialists may kill in Indochina, imprison in Black Africa, crack down in the West Indies." He argues, "It is a new society that we must create, with the help of all our brother slaves. A society rich with all the productive power of modern times, warm with all the fraternity of olden days" (2000, 52). For Maingard, the film goes beyond the novel in presenting the perspective of the Black victims/survivors as well as that of Ben. Moreover, the film breaks down apartheid boundaries by "insisting instead on the necessity of collective responsibility and resistance" (Maingard 2019, 205). As Maingard notes, Gordon is the one who shifts the relationship with Ben by asking for help.[32] She observes that the film presents the story of Jonathan's torture not from Jonathan's point of view but in an indirect way, through his friend Wellington's (Precious Phiri) description of how he heard Jonathan screaming in the prison (2019, 207–8). By contrast, the way Gordon is tortured is shown directly in two crucial scenes, as is the view of it by a witness, Johnson Seroke. Palcy places the viewer there to try to create their perspective and their view of the security police who commit these outrages.

The methods of these police resemble that of authoritarian and totalitarian regimes, a parallel Césaire (2000, 32, 34) draws in terms of links between colonialism, fascism, and slavery. The thingification he theorizes as colonization's "relations of domination which turn the colonizing man into a classroom monitor, an army sergeant, a prison guard, a slave driver, and the indigenous man into an instrument of production" (2000, 42) is both graphically and subtly present in the film. *A Dry White Season* aurally and visually represents the militaristic and fascistic nature of the whole South African society. In the massacre scene, dogs are barking and growling, and helicopters are flying overhead. When Ben finds out from Gordon that Jonathan was arrested, a helicopter flies ominously over the yard, as if the government is already aware that Ben and Gordon are discussing the abuses of the regime. At the school, cadets are on parade in the background when Ben tells Gordon that Jonathan is dead, and in another intercut scene the camera crouches to their level as the cadets, including Johan, practice shooting. This militarization shows how maintaining a system of such profound injustice is linked to a warlike approach to governance; indeed, Susan refers to the idea of a war that must be "won."

As well as describing the psychological process of victimization, the film suggests positive paths of resistance to oppression and to victimhood itself, along with Ben's positive move toward acceptance. In opposition to early scholarly critics, bell hooks sees the film as disruptive and providing an ideal of solidarity. She does not draw directly from Césaire; her antiracist thought draws on her knowledge of the oppression of African Americans. Yet her approach shares with Césaire the support for a broader conception of antiracist opposition that includes white allies. Her discussion begins with a reference to writer Lorraine Hansberry's declaration that Blacks "must concern themselves with every single means of struggle: legal, illegal, passive, active, violent and nonviolent" (hooks 2015, 187; Hansberry 1969, 213–14). hooks (2015, 187) asks rhetorically, "How many films show white men acting in solidarity with the oppressed to resist racist white domination? Why is it that so many reviews saw this representation as uninteresting, as though it is a common sight?" Unlike Nixon (2015, 188), who saw the film as portraying liberalism, hooks interprets the film as portraying radicalization and "authentic solidarity with the oppressed" and as having many subversive moments.

FIG. 1.2. Ben hugs Emily after the inquest. Still from *A Dry White Season*, directed by Euzhan Palcy (Davros Films and Sundance Productions, 1989).

One such moment hooks notes is when Ben hugs Emily in public after Gordon's murder and the unsuccessful inquest (fig.1.2). In the novel, Ben's affair with Melanie is considered more shocking than apartheid (Carchidi 1994, 53; Brittan 2005, 64). By contrast, for the film, it is Ben hugging Emily that Susan and daughter Suzette find a step too far: Suzette says, "My God, Pa. How could you let it go this far? You're such a fool." The way hooks (2015, 188) sees it is that "Palcy explores the question of whether a white male who chooses to give up his privilege and work on behalf of the oppressed who struggle against racism does not as a consequence challenge the system of patriarchal male power." From this rejection of patriarchal privilege follows a link between antiracist and feminist struggles, as Ben loses the legacy a man in a patriarchy expects.[33] Another aspect of the film that hooks argues reinforces this reading is the active support for apartheid by privileged white women. Her view is that *A Dry White Season* positions a radical activist perspective as a choice rather than essentializing it as a feature of identity or circumstance "and that the power of that choice will be indicated by the sacrifices and risks taken to fulfil those commitments" (2015, 189). Throughout the film, people choose to risk their lives, sometimes with certainty that they will be killed, to contribute to the ongoing struggle to free South Africa.

Interestingly, hooks (2015, 189) also observes how children in the film engage in political action in demonstrations and testimony, and her diagnosis is that "many viewers allowed their dissatisfaction with the focus on white people to blind them to the powerful representations of black militancy." For Palcy, Jonathan "symbolizes the young generation of blacks who have had enough" (Glicksman 1989, 66), and as hooks (2015, 190) observes, other children play significant roles as both resisters and victims. A specific scene that hooks uses to support this interpretation takes place during the massacre in Soweto: a young girl whose even younger sister has been shot and killed addresses the police (and the camera) saying, "'You have killed my sister. Kill me too. [Shoot me too].'" For hooks, this depiction of a young Black girl should be contrasted with the common passive sexist and racist portrayals of Black girls. It is also much more defiant than Ben's lack of protest against his situation. Another example is the courtroom scene where a Black prisoner, Archibald Mabaso (Ernest Ndlovu), referred to as a "detainee," unexpectedly testifies after signing a false statement under torture, knowing the danger that puts him in. Unlike the many other writers about the film who describe how Marlon Brando steals this scene, hooks *sees* the Black prisoner and the importance of his testimony.[34] Furthermore, hooks (2015, 190) can see the significance of the character of Stanley and his "spirit of militant resistance." Again, she stresses an element of the film overlooked in many analyses, where Stanley is overwhelmed by Emily's death and Ben comforts him. hooks focuses on the risks and sacrifices involved in political commitment—risks taken and sacrifices made by all the central characters of *A Dry White Season* who resist apartheid. Almost all of them become victims through suffering and dying.

Another child is also significant to the film's portrayal of resistance, and acceptance of the victimhood that will result from that resistance. Johan's support for his father, Ben, can be interpreted as one sign of hope for the future of South Africa, along with the other defiant children. He is concerned about Jonathan and Gordon right from the beginning and remains loyal to his father, unlike the other family members. His name implies that he represents the city, Johannesburg. Even though he is questioned by the police and abused by his schoolmates, Johan helps to hide the precious documents from the police and delivers them to the newspaper for publication, which is one of Palcy's interpolations. Johan supports Ben's search for truth at every point in the film. He says, "Don't stop, Pa. Please, I don't want you to give up." Johan also clearly knows that Ben is risking his life through his actions but still encourages him. Ben's suffering and death as a secondary victim of the regime is presented as morally preferable to acquiescence.

CONCLUSION

Although early critics and some reviews found *A Dry White Season* lacking in philosophical insights into racist oppression and the resulting victimization, I argue that a closer reading and discussion of the film, one that takes into account Palcy's goals and the inspiration of Césaire's internationalist and optimistic anticolonial discourse, shows how bystanders can become (secondary) victims and witnesses simply by becoming concerned about the primary victims of an oppressive, racist regime and by trying to live in the truth, as Havel recommends. By depicting this process, the film provides greater comprehension of the workings of such a regime and its creation of victims. *A Dry White Season* also suggests that allies can play a crucial role in gathering information and sharing it more broadly, although in the case of oppressive regimes such as apartheid these apparently nonthreatening and nondissenting actions challenge the regime so much that they entail sacrifice and often death. Furthermore, the film portrays the conflict between the desire to pursue truth and justice and the unintended consequences of harming vulnerable others through that pursuit. Moreover, the film portrays the progressive experience of becoming a victim in a relatively short time in order to throw that experience into sharp relief, as well as depicting the experience of those who are already oppressed and tortured. Palcy's vision portrays a resistance that links these victims in a common struggle, as Césaire recommends. Ben's search for truth can be contrasted with the revelations of truth seen in *The Look of Silence*, which I examine in the next chapter.

[CHAPTER TWO]

The Look of Silence

Revealing the Truth

In this chapter I take the discussion of resistance in a very different direction, both by shifting to documentary film and by considering resistance that comes many years after the worst repression. American filmmaker Joshua Oppenheimer's (1974–) extraordinary film *The Act of Killing* documented perpetrators of the genocide of hundreds of thousands of communists or "suspected" communists in Indonesia in 1965–66, encouraging them to reenact their crimes in the film genre of their choice. These men are largely unrepentant about the killings, although one of them, Anwar Congo, a leader of a death squad that killed thousands of people, appears to show signs of remorse at one point. The film itself can be understood as an attempt at atonement and working toward resistance despite the attitudes of the perpetrators, and may even lead to real steps to atone, since millions of Indonesians have seen the film and responded with concern to the killings. The film raised awareness of the killing, the impunity of the wrongdoers, and the lack of redress after fifty years.

The second documentary released, *The Look of Silence*, actually filmed before the release of *The Act of Killing*, takes this process of atonement and resistance to impunity further by considering how the survivors might confront the killers and build relationships with the next generation, the children of the killers.[1] It focuses on the attempt of one survivor, Adi Rukun, to discover the truth of what happened to his brother who was murdered and to confront those responsible.[2] Adi is an optometrist living in northern Sumatra at the time of the film. His mission has a dual purpose, seeking both admissions and expressions of remorse from the perpetrators, so as a resistant text, *The Look of Silence* is complex. Both Oppenheimer, as filmmaker, and Adi, in pursuing the killers and making use of his skills as an optometrist to interview them, practice what

Havel calls small-scale work, where taking pride in one's profession and its purpose is itself a form of resistance to an authoritarian society. They try to live in the truth by revealing it in different ways. Moreover, the tight connection between their professions and their political commitment to exposing the truth about the genocide makes that resistance more profound.

The question of impunity means that issues around truth are a little different from those explored in *A Dry White Season*. In that film, we see the apartheid government casting a thin veil over its atrocities, so thin that even to point them out is, for its agents, a profoundly threatening act. In Indonesia there is almost an openness about the past killings: boasting, even in public, is quite common. What is not said, however, is that what was done was wrong, and that is what Oppenheimer's films aim at revealing and so resisting a particular way of talking about both the past and present. This focus on truth is linked to the practice of nonviolence in the sense that violence that is not recognized and understood continues into the present and future (Fiala 2018, 245–64). Furthermore, while the situation and the response to the resistance is not as extreme as in *A Dry White Season*, the participants in the documentary are threatened and do have to go into exile either internationally or within Indonesia, as will be explained.

In this chapter, I examine the film's presentation of Adi Rukun's attempt to persuade the perpetrators to tell the truth so the culture of impunity and the resultant fear of the survivors can be overcome. I consider how the process of making the documentary, participating in it, and the screenings in Indonesia and elsewhere contribute to atonement and resistance to the killers' power. First I provide some context for the films, including the historical background and the filmmaking process, and then I explore the multifaceted nature of Adi Rukun's search for atonement and truth as a form of resistance.

THE GENOCIDE AND ITS AFTERMATH

The genocide in Indonesia was set off by the murder of six generals and other high-ranking military on the night of September 30, 1965, by members of Sukarno's presidential guard and air force. These murders provided the pretext for the political takeover and genocide that followed. Sukarno, who became the first president (1945–67) of Indonesia after leading the fight for independence from the Netherlands, was one of the founders of the Non-aligned movement in 1961 for countries that did not want to be part of either the Eastern or Western blocs, including

India, Egypt, Ghana, and Yugoslavia.[3] His successor, General Suharto (president 1967–98), blamed the Indonesian Communist Party (PKI) for the killings, and President Sukarno was overthrown in a military coup and replaced by Suharto, who was backed by the American government, led by Lyndon B. Johnson, and other Western nations, including Australia.[4] Recently declassified documents also show the role of the UK intelligence in fomenting the massacres (Strangio 2021). After Sukarno's ousting, he was put under house arrest in Bogor Palace in West Java and died there in 1970.

In Indonesia in 1965, the victims were taken by the paramilitary (including local gangsters), held in concentration camps, and then murdered. According to one estimate, up to a million or more people were murdered (Buckley 2016; Schenkel 2015, 97), and that is the figure referred to in the films. In an interview, Oppenheimer says the figure is between 0.5 million and 3 million (Goodman 2015). The murders occurred over a period of six months, and the victims included feminists, intellectuals, peasants, and teachers.[5] The genocide can be thought of as a politicide, or targeting of perceived members of a political group, although in some cases ethnicity played a role in who was targeted, as did the allegation that people were "atheists" (McGregor, Melvin, and Pohlman 2018, 5).[6] As Oppenheimer notes, Suharto and his New Order regime (1966–98) also presided over the genocide in East Timor, where a third of the population was killed, and during that period he continued to receive a great deal of financial aid from the United States. One of Oppenheimer's concerns is the US role in the genocide.[7] He portrays how the US government funded and trained the military as an internal force against the population, giving money and weapons to the military for the genocide, and supplied the radios used to coordinate the massacres. Moreover, Oppenheimer claims that US Embassy officials were giving kill lists of thousands of public figures to the military during the genocide, saying, "Kill everybody on these lists and check off the names as you go, and give the lists back to us when you're done" (Goodman 2015). Robert Martens, who worked at the embassy in Jakarta at the time, told Oppenheimer about these lists. Western countries such as the United States praised measures against the Communist Party. He also comments on how Goodyear used people held in the concentration camps as slave labor on the rubber plantations, shown in an NBC report in *The Look of Silence*, and asks whether the anticommunist campaign "was a ruse, a pretext, an excuse, for murderous corporate plunder" (Goodman 2015).[8] These details are presented in the film but not discussed at any length. One of the most surprising things about the two films is that they were made at all: they were made under very difficult circumstances.

Oppenheimer first went to Indonesia to teach plantation workers how to make films about union concerns but was disconcerted by the atmosphere of fear and repressed trauma that he found there, which led him to discover the reasons behind it. As he says, the films are not about 1965 as such, and the historical events are not explained in detail in the films; they are about "the impunity, and fear, and silence, corruption and violence in the present" (Blyth 2016). Oppenheimer was encouraged by the workers to film the perpetrators at first alone and then together. What he noticed is that the killers boasted a great deal individually and even more when together—symptoms or manifestations, he argues, of a collective political impunity (Blyth 2016).[9] Ultimately, he decided to make two films, one to understand the killers' boastfulness, and the other to understand the experience for the survivors living in that atmosphere.

From the beginning of the project the survivors were threatened by the army not to speak, so filming had to be carefully arranged. Because Oppenheimer had made *The Act of Killing* with some of the most powerful perpetrators, such as the vice president, cabinet ministers, and the chief of the Pancasila Youth (an Indonesian paramilitary group), Adi Rukun and Oppenheimer thought that would provide a kind of protection from the regional leaders interviewed in *The Look of Silence* (Schenkel 2015, 99; Goodman 2015). Oppenheimer spent seven years working with the killers; during five of those years, he was making *The Act of Killing*, and then the interviews for *The Look of Silence* were conducted in 2012 before *The Act of Killing* was released.[10] The crew and Adi Rukun and his family had to go into hiding elsewhere in Indonesia after that (Blyth 2016). When he was conducting the interviews with the offenders, they had a getaway car at all times. It should be noted that it was Adi who asked Oppenheimer if he could interview and film the perpetrators himself (Blyth 2016; Goodman 2015). For Adi's confrontations with the killers, Oppenheimer worked with the Danish crew only so that the Indonesian film crew would not be exposed to such risk. Adi's family would be at the airport with packed bags waiting for an okay (Blyth 2016; Goodman 2015). Furthermore, all Indonesians involved in the films are credited as "anonymous" for their own safety. After the end of the filming, Oppenheimer had to move to Denmark, and he received death threats for years (Grierson 2015, 6).[11] In an interview several years after the release of *The Look of Silence*, Adi Rukun said that he feels free and free of fear for the first time in his life, because now he is not surrounded by people threatening him and can speak openly about the past (Buckley 2016).[12] Nevertheless, it takes a twenty-five-person team, including five full-time workers, to protect him and his family, who moved to live in another part of Indonesia

(Goodman 2015). In the next section, I concentrate on the documentary itself to see how it presents the issue of atonement and its complex relation to the truth about the killings.

ATONEMENT AND TRUTH

A notable demonstration of the effects of impunity on perpetrators is depicted in *The Act of Killing*.[13] As Karen Hoffman argues, this film takes an indirect approach to communicating the truth. Hoffman takes as her model of an indirect communicator Søren Kierkegaard in *Concluding Unscientific Postscript* (1992), who in turn models himself on Socrates's process of asking questions to help "others in thinking through the material so that they develop their own sense of what is true and determine what significance that truth has for their lives" (Hoffman 2017, 518). Kierkegaard uses pseudonyms and a variety of literary forms such as journals, letters, and stories to convey truth indirectly. Hoffman (2017, 519) argues that it can sometimes be important to "deceive" someone into truth in these kinds of ways, so that they can come to see the truth for themselves. In the film, the perpetrators are allowed to act out their stories, yet in doing so they may come to recognize the horror of their actions. Similarly, this indirect approach could encourage viewers to take the crimes more seriously and to acknowledge their own complicity. What is significant for thinking about resistance and the link to *The Look of Silence* is that "*The Act of Killing* arguably goes beyond merely using fictional elements and reenactments to document a historical past; it uses them to explore the lingering consequences of that past for the individuals involved and for the larger political and paramilitary forces still in power in Indonesia" (Hoffman 2017, 532). That wider perspective informs the shift to a focus on the victims in *The Look of Silence* and means that the attempt to bring about atonement and reconciliation is a form of resistance in the present.

Other discussions of *The Look of Silence* have focused on testimony (Torchin 2015), ethical witnessing (Sinnerbrink 2017), the question of the monstrosity of the killers (Abbott 2017), and the factors of class and social position (Sutopo 2020), all of which are relevant themes in the film. *The Look of Silence* works on a number of levels to explore truth and its relation to atonement and resistance and has both ethical and political implications. In *The Look of Silence*, Adi's search and interviews with those involved in the killings, including those responsible for the death of his own brother, at least pieces together what happened as well as shows how the perpetrators are guilty and fearful in ways they try to hide. His questioning about the truth of the killings challenges the impunity that has existed for decades. Adi's interviews also show that the next generation may be able to more substantially contribute to atonement. Furthermore, the film itself, in portraying the brazenness of the killers, has pushed Indonesian and international audiences to make some steps to atone and to resist the culture of impunity through a commitment to truth about the genocide.

Atonement involves concepts of apology, compensation, healing, moral transformation, and sometimes punishment or sacrifice as ways to make up for wrongs that have been committed. Several religious rituals and traditions involve atonement—for example, the Jewish celebration of Yom Kippur, or Day of Atonement—and can be broadened to include secular forms of atonement, both individual and collective. In *Moral Repair: Reconstructing Moral Relations after Wrongdoing*, Margaret Urban Walker (2006, 191) characterizes atonement or making amends as "intentionally reparative actions by parties who acknowledge responsibility for wrong, and whose reparative actions are intended to redress that wrong" that make up for the debt to victims. One of the strange features of making amends is that if the wrong is minor, making amends and the recognition of that by victims is relatively easily done. However, Walker (2006, 198) observes that "it is often in the most egregious cases of harm that significant reparative actions are resisted and seem shallow, meagre, and incomplete where attempted." The reasons for this lack of atonement in extreme cases is that acknowledging guilt can be psychologically, politically, and materially painful and that it is difficult, if not impossible, for atonement to really make up for the harms of the wrong, especially in extremes case such as a massacre or genocide, which Oppenheimer's films are dealing with.

Linda Radzik (2009, 175–97) considers collective atonement in *Making Amends: Atonement in Morality, Law, and Politics*. For her, atonement is generally "an action the wrongdoer carries out" (2009, 7), whereas in the case of institutional and group wrongs, nonperpetrating members of the group share the obligation to atone through their membership in and identification with the group, and because in some cases, there is no one else who can do that (2009, 195–96).[14] Furthermore, Kara Barnette (2017, 68–72) regards atonement as "communal, ongoing, and cross-generational" in relation to memory and atrocities from the past.[15] She characterizes atonement this way to distinguish it from atonement as an act or set of acts that can make up for past wrongs once and for all.

Individual atonement may occur through apologies, assistance or community service, confessions or truth-telling in truth and reconciliation commissions, expressions of remorse, or material compensation, and punishment can also be thought of as a form of atonement. Further, community atonement can be carried out through collective apologies, compensation, memorials, monuments, museums, and commemorations. Such atonement is improbable when the offenders do not desire to atone or are even triumphant, as is common in the case of the Indonesian genocide, as Oppenheimer's films make clear. In one sense, they do admit their crimes, but in another, they do not acknowledge the seriousness or wrongness of those crimes, or the continuing wrong of the harm to the survivors and victims.

Thus, in that case atonement often must be undertaken by someone who is not guilty of the original crime but may be a bystander, beneficiary, or descendant. *The Act of Killing* and *The Look of Silence* both won many awards, and both were nominated for an Academy Award for Best Documentary. Nonetheless, Oppenheimer describes *The Act of Killing* as a "flamboyant fever dream" rather than a documentary (O'Falt 2016), with Anwar Congo as "the main character" (Goodman 2015).[16] Furthermore, he explains how he "was interested in the relationship between documentary, collaboration, and performance" (Grierson 2015, 2) and speaks of the importance and power of documentary in giving us "the shock of the familiar," rather than "the shock of the new" (O'Falt 2016).[17]

Jake Wilson (2015, 2) disapproves of *The Look of Silence* for its fictionalizing, and compares it unfavorably to *The Act of Killing*, writing that it is "more lucid but less interesting."[18] He claims that the film is "rather too polished for its own good. Even as he chronicles the search for truth, Oppenheimer turns his subjects into characters in a kind of fiction: it's unlikely any of the confrontations we witness would have occurred without his sponsorship" (Wilson 2015, 2). It is hard to see how this claim is a criticism, however, as Oppenheimer was asked to make the films by the survivors. Oppenheimer was able to create an environment where Adi could confront his brother Ramli's killers and survive, although he is threatened on several occasions, threats that demonstrate how his nondissenting approach nevertheless contests the regime. These interviews would have been much less "coached" than the interviews Oppenheimer conducted with the other killers over five years. Moreover, Wilson finds the image of optometry working as "a heavy-handed metaphor," although optometry is simply Adi's profession, which he puts to a dual use. He hints that the film is really about something else, larger than the story of Adi and Ramli, and even larger than or different from the genocide in Indonesia—such as failures of the rule of law there and in the United States, issues of race, and the genocide of Native Americans (Goodman 2015). Oppenheimer certainly does not deny this point; rather, he reinforces it.

Interestingly, Oppenheimer also rejects the term *storyteller* because it is a flawed metaphor, claiming that he works to "create new realities" (O'Falt 2016). He says, "I try to create these realities that are beyond their [the participants'] comfort zone and make something visible about that space that was previously invisible. I want to immerse the viewer in that space, but with a moral point of view, and I think that can be achieved without distancing" (O'Falt 2016).[19] What he means is that the films create a full experience that draws in the viewer so they can understand that moral viewpoint. They present a reality, a particular interpretation of that reality aimed at the truth, and have a moral and political message. Like *A Dry White Season*, they are activist films that portray and enact resistance.

In contrast to the indirect communication of *The Act of Killing*, *The Look of Silence* is a more conventional film and takes a more direct approach in articulating its truth. In an apparent revision of his comment about storytelling above, Oppenheimer explains what he calls the "sacred role for the storyteller. We can tell stories which invite people to confront painful truths. . . . The other thing that story telling does is open the imagination and the heart to people we normally comfortably overlook" (Nussbaum 2020). This vision encompasses the different approaches taken in the two films. *The Look of Silence* is carefully crafted, using imagery to convey particular effects, and shows parts of the previous film on a television screen. These scenes are primarily of the killers bragging about what they have done, with Adi Rukun watching, as that is how he discovered who murdered his brother. For Oppenheimer, the two films form a diptych, complementing and enriching each other (Grierson 2015, 3, 6). The flamboyance of the first film contrasts with the restful, contemplative mood of the second film. Instead of the killers driving through the streets, or acting out roles in loud costumes, Oppenheimer allows the pace of everyday life, the natural sounds, and the spaces of fields and forest to suggest a gentler rhythm. Bright colors in this film come from nature rather than the elaborate outfits the killers don in *The Act of Killing*. The camera focuses throughout on Adi's face, gazing intently, thinking, and yet usually calm, despite what he is hearing in his interviews and on the television when he watches the earlier footage taken by Joshua. Often we hear cicadas and birds in the background, providing the soundtrack of the tropical forest. Shots of a bridge over a river evoke the violence hidden behind its stillness, a connection with the murders the audience must infer.

Oppenheimer's documentary helps us to listen to silence, and it also helps to make the silence start to speak again. He is trying to "create a world that's always there, but invisible" and film a "poem to all that was lost" (O'Falt 2016). Oppenheimer (2015) writes,

> *The Look of Silence* is, I hope, a poem about a silence born of terror—a poem about the necessity of breaking that silence, but also about the trauma that comes when silence is broken. Maybe the film is a monument to silence—a reminder that although we want to move on, look away and think of other things, nothing will make whole what has been broken. Nothing will wake the dead. We must stop, acknowledge the lives destroyed, strain to listen to the silence that follows.[20]

The film uses images of butterfly cocoons to represent something that we normally do not see or notice but that is having an effect (Stevens 2015; O'Falt 2016). They could also signify new life and hope, as Adi's mother holds them and talks to them, very close to the end of the film. Furthermore, Adi takes eye tests for some of his interviews, and they function as a metaphor for the willful blindness of the perpetrators to the horrifying meaning of what they did (Goodman 2015).[21] It is not as heavy-handed in its use of imagery as Wilson claims, since the dialogue between Adi and the perpetrators is of greater consequence. Both documentaries show how Oppenheimer and Adi Rukun employ their professions to engage the perpetrators—Oppenheimer with his filmmaking talent and Adi with his skills as an optometrist. They both practice the small-scale work Havel talks about as opening the possibility to political change.

One scene just over thirty minutes into the film—a long shot of an open square with children playing on a makeshift stage, jaunty shops, traffic passing, and Western music coming from the shops—appears to have no purpose (fig. 2.1). It can be seen as similar to the shots of the river used throughout the film, as a scene of life going on as if nothing happened, perhaps disturbing because of past events or possibly life-affirming. The river was where many of the bodies of those murdered victims were thrown. The scene could be understood as an establishing shot: this is where people live and work and play locally. Or it could be a moment to meditate. This scene also marks a transition to Adi's more focused interviews, where he questions Inong intently, using his technique of the eye test and the promise of new glasses. Here the shots, like the one used for the film poster, are close-ups of Inong's face in the trial lenses and then side shots of Adi questioning him. Adi tries to help Inong see the inconsistency between his actions and his religious beliefs, a probing that Inong protests against as too deep. These interviews are intercut with scenes of Adi's mother and father; sometimes his mother is talking about his brother Ramli, and at other times she is just relaxing at home. The film can be seen as having two climaxes, which point in different directions concerning the question of atonement and Adi's search for the killers to take responsibility. One is the scene where a killer's daughter asks Adi to forgive her father and think of them as family—a moment of atonement, perhaps? The other concerns the family of the killer Amir Hasan Nasution, whose partner and two sons Adi talks to, who published an illustrated book (*Embun Berdarah*, or *Dew of Blood*) including details of Ramli's murder (Oppenheimer and Uwemedimo 2012, 293). The mother apologizes, adding that "we feel the same way that you do," but this moment is spoiled, as I will explain further on.

FIG. 2.1. A local scene of an open square in *The Look of Silence*. Still from *The Look of Silence*, directed by Joshua Oppenheimer (Anonymous, Final Cut for Real, Making Movies Oy, Piraya Film A/S, and Spring Films, 2014).

Oppenheimer argues that the central problem the films reflect on is impunity, and he wonders whether that is why there are "sweat shop labour and slave labour conditions around the global South" (Blyth 2016). His concern is with the legacy of the killings, "the current regime of fear and thuggery and corruption" (Goodman 2015). He says that the situation in Indonesia was like "wandering into Germany 40 years after the Holocaust, only to find the Nazis still in power" (Oppenheimer, in Behlil 2015, 27). To some extent, the films have led to challenges of that impunity. Oppenheimer's aim was to "show how torn this society is, how urgently truth, reconciliation and justice are needed," whereas he saw Adi as specifically looking for reconciliation with the perpetrators (Goodman 2015). What happens in and because of *The Look of Silence* is closer to Oppenheimer's goal, although there are elements of Adi's. This search for reconciliation could be seen as purely a search for peace, but the penetrating questions Adi asks means that he is resisting the terms in which the past has been described, and thus resisting the legacy of that past.

THE SEARCH FOR TRUTH

The Look of Silence conveys moral resistance by focusing on Adi Rukun throughout, rather than using a didactic voice-over or Oppenheimer as interviewer. The film intercuts scenes of Adi interviewing the men involved in his brother's murder with scenes of his mother, father, children, and partner, and him watching the footage of the men swaggering about their crimes. While his visage expresses "profound sadness," as Torchin (2015, 31) notes, Adi is also quite implacable and persistent in his interviews with these men. *The Look of Silence* presents the process of revealing the truth as one between individuals and centered on one person only at a time. In this film Adi, the survivor, is the "main character," and it is his view of the world that the audience experiences.

Adi and his family had helped Oppenheimer talk to survivors right from the beginning of his project (Goodman 2015). In the film, Adi is trying to find out more about the murder of his brother Ramli, who was killed during the "Snake River Massacre," where over ten thousand people were killed (Schenkel 2015, 99).[22] Ramli was "the village head of a farmer's cooperative" and thus was thought likely to oppose the military dictatorship, so he was murdered by the Kommando Aksi, an Acehan paramilitary group (Goodman 2015). Ramli's murder was one of the few that was witnessed, so his death could be acknowledged, grieved, and his body could be buried. As Oppenheimer says, "So, over the decades, from 1965 until I first arrived in 2003 and started working on this, over the decades Ramli became a kind of synonym for the genocide as a whole" (Goodman 2015). Most other people could not talk in the same way about the death of their loved ones, although they knew they must have been killed.

Rather than referring to every crime, Oppenheimer centers on one person's confrontation with those involved in the killing of his brother. He observes of Adi, "Many younger Indonesians think he's a kind of national hero"—that is, for both the public and the media (Grierson 2015, 6; Blyth 2016). *The Look of Silence* was first shown on National Heroes Day, and a trending topic on Twitter that day was "Today we have a new national hero and his name is Adi" (Goodman 2015). Adi represents his large family and the network of children and other relatives of genocide victims that work together in that area. Oppenheimer focused only on Adi to protect the identities of other family members. During the genocide, Adi's older sister had her head shaved by the local militia, and all the siblings were "routinely intimidated, harassed and extorted" (Buckley 2016).[23] Moreover, they were threatened by the army to prevent them from being involved in the film (*Look of Silence*, DVD notes).

There are also a number of reasons why Adi in particular was so determined to participate. Adi is the youngest in the family, and born after the killings, so could see them differently from those directly involved. He is seen by his mother, Rohani, as a kind of replacement for Ramli, and he grew up hearing his mother endlessly talking to him and others about the murder. Now he wants his children to grow up without fear of their neighbors (Goodman 2015) and not be taught that people like his brother deserved to die. In *The Look of Silence*, schoolteachers are shown teaching Adi's son that the communists deserved to be murdered and that their grandchildren are under suspicion by association. Communism and Marxist-Leninism are still banned in Indonesia (Santoso and Klinken 2017, 595).[24] That is why his interviews can be seen as acts of resistance. As Tim Grierson (2015, 5) points out in *Rolling Stone*, "The director has . . . given what's hopefully a growing movement towards truth and reconciliation a now-recognizable everyman face." While the idea of reconciliation is hopeful, there is also reason to think that the truth-telling of the film, because it threatens the perpetrator's narrative, may make some aspects of reconciliation challenging.

In the documentary Adi confronts a number of his brother's killers, giving some of them free eye tests, as mentioned, and an offer of free glasses if they are needed as he does so, and tries to get them to confess responsibility and acknowledge the wrong.[25] However, the killers do not take responsibility. For example, Amir Siahaan, the commander of the Snake River death squads, says, "We had commanders above us. And we were protected by the government. So you can't say I'm responsible." He asks Adi where he lives, and Adi refuses to answer (Goodman 2015). While a number of the perpetrators menace Adi in this way from a position of power, Benedict Anderson (2012, 282) questions the extent to which they were rewarded for what they did during the genocide; rather, he sees Ramli's killers as "actually nobodies," and any benefits were gained from decades of criminality.[26]

Anderson's use of the term *nobody* recalls Hannah Arendt's characterization of Adolf Eichmann and other desk murderers in *Eichmann in Jerusalem: A Report on the Banality of Evil* as nobodies—bureaucrats who were more concerned with their own careers than with the lives of others or the events of history. This is part of what makes them exemplars of the banality of evil (Arendt 1992, 252). She reported on Eichmann for the *New Yorker* when he was tried for "crimes against the Jewish people, crimes against humanity, and war crimes" (1992, 21). Eichmann was responsible for the deaths of millions as he organized mass deportations to concentration and extermination camps. He was found guilty of the majority of the crimes and executed. For Arendt, the banality of the evil of such murderers is *not* that their *acts* are banal—they are extreme and shocking. Nor does she mean that such crimes are everyday or "commonplace" (1992, 288). Rather, "banality" describes the apparent lack of monstrous motives, or the lack of a desire to "prove a villain," which is how Arendt (1992, 287) sees Shakespeare's Richard III; the term signals that they would commit these horrible crimes and simply think of it as part of their "job." Her interpretation of Eichmann's character is that he spoke in clichés, and these are a sign: "The longer one listened to him, the more obvious it became that his inability to speak was closely connected with an inability to *think*, namely, to think from the standpoint of somebody else" (1992, 49). According to Arendt, the so-called inability to consider others is linked to his focus on his own career. In her view, although bragging is a common vice, and Eichmann boasted continually of his responsibility for the deaths of 5 million Jewish people prior to his trial, his key character flaw is his failure to consider the viewpoint of others (1992, 46–48).

These genocidal killers in *The Look of Silence*, like Eichmann, speak in clichés, even if the clichés are at first startling and unfamiliar, such as the claim that drinking their victims' blood will prevent them from being harmed by their spirits. They also concentrate on their own advancement in recounting their life stories and avoid reflecting on their victims' perspectives, with the brief exception of Anwar Congo, mentioned above. That is a rare moment of lucidity evoked by Oppenheimer's encouragement to reenact his crimes in the role of one of the victims. There are key differences in that unlike Eichmann and others involved in the crime of "administrative massacre" (Arendt 1992, 294), most of the perpetrators interviewed by Oppenheimer and Adi did the killing themselves. Furthermore, they were never brought to trial and so were not challenged by prosecution and judges.

A different view from Anderson's is provided by Oki Rahadianto Sutopo (2020, 292), an Indonesian sociologist, who argues that "the reenactment of killings in both films rejustify the perpetrators' actions as investments to deal with social forces in the field, not only in the past but also in the present." He lived through Suharto's authoritarian regime and the Reform Era and discusses both *The Act of Killing* and *The Look of Silence*. For him, the killers' detailed accounts of the murders are not confessions but part of a strategy to keep their dominant class position, especially in relation to the victims and survivors. In his analysis, the more successful they are in social terms, the more likely they are to be proud of their past. Furthermore, maintaining their position of dominance ensures that their victims remain silent (2020, 294). This stress on the present is key to understanding their unwillingness to properly acknowledge the past, as Adi tries to bring his interviewees to, and is deeply connected to their continuing impunity for the murders.

The Look of Silence also portrays how Adi's own family is implicated—his uncle (his mother's brother) worked as a guard in the prison where Ramli was held, which he admits on camera. However, he claims that he was under orders, that he would have been accused himself if he did not obey, and that he did not know that Ramli would be killed, which Adi's mother says is a lie. Ultimately, Ramli's uncle refuses to accept any responsibility or express regret. Nevertheless, there is an emotional moment following their discussion where both Adi and his uncle are teary and silent, a silence that is more telling than the uncle's words. In Adi's view, he should have at least admitted an indirect responsibility. A troubling aspect regarding Ramli's mother, Rohani, is that she gave him up under duress after the first attack and became in her own mind a collaborator, although that is far too harsh a judgment on herself. Ramli had been attacked and managed to crawl home, but the death squad returned for him and threatened the whole family if he was not given up. The death squad tried to hide their true intentions by saying they were taking Ramli to the hospital (Goodman 2015). It is her acceptance of that pretense that she blames herself for.

Some critics and audiences objected to the film sequence showing Adi's father, Rukun, crawling through the house, not realizing he is at home, and saying that he needs help (Stevens 2015). However, Oppenheimer explains that it is the only scene filmed by Adi, and shows that his father has forgotten his son, Ramli, but has not forgotten the fear that he might be beaten up in a stranger's house (Stevens 2015; Goodman 2015; Blyth 2016). This scene is a telling presentation of the continuing legacy of the genocide, and Adi's singular confrontations with the local perpetrators also link to wider possibilities of atonement and resistance, the idea that his and Oppenheimer's work could flow from small-scale work to deeper parallel structures in the ways that Havel outlined.

COMMUNAL ATONEMENT AND RESISTANCE

The problem of institutions, groups, or individuals not feeling remorse for their actions can mean that wrong is not atoned for and also that the victims are still in a precarious or dangerous position due to continuing repression, as depicted in *The Look of Silence*. The torturers and killers of the communists and alleged communists are largely unrepentant and are hailed as heroes in Indonesia. *The Act of Killing* shows Anwar Congo (now dead), one of these petty gangsters, coming to a sense of what he has done through indirect means, as Hoffman describes, and having some experience of remorse when he asks, "Have I sinned?" and says, "I know I have done wrong," but he immediately adds that he "had to do it." This lack of repentance or remorse makes atonement especially difficult, and as another perpetrator says in that film, "There is no reconciliation, there can be no reconciliation": in other words, he seems to mean, the survivors are not in a position to expect or demand reconciliation.

In that situation, communities and those who are not directly responsible for the original crimes can, and arguably should, take on the responsibility to try to atone and to change thinking about the past, and that could lead to the original offenders recognizing what they have done. Film, both documentary and fictionalized works, has played a vital role in raising awareness and understanding of genocide and other atrocities, even if that does not necessarily lead to acts of atonement. For example, the film *Katyn* (dir. Andrzej Wajda, 2007) dramatizes the full horror of the massacre of more than twenty thousand Polish officers and civilians in World War II in 1940, known as the Katyn massacre.[27] Other massacres and genocides, such as those during the Yugoslav wars and "ethnic cleansing" of the 1990s and the genocide in Rwanda, have been witnessed in a range of films (Torchin 2012, 99–135). In relation to *the Act of Killing*, Grierson (2015, 2) observes that it was criticized for the "stylized dramatizations overshadow[ing] any examinations of past barbarous deeds." It was also criticized for neglecting US complicity in the genocide and not interviewing survivors, criticisms Oppenheimer contends are answered in *The Look of Silence* (Behlil 2015, 30), and it takes the projects of finding the truth and atonement much further.

The Look of Silence links the search for atonement with resistance. While the film focuses on Adi Rukun, the effect of the documentary itself, in empowering victims, survivors, and their descendants, is exemplary as a form of collective atonement and resistance. The making of the documentary, participating in it, and the screenings in Indonesia and around the world supports communal atonement despite the killers' lack of repentance and the lack of state compensation or care. Oppenheimer's view is that the killers' reenactments and discussions of what they did provide a document: "Above all, they transformed rumour into evidentiary account. Rendering the spectral explicit allows it to be critically reframed, and this process opens on to the potentially redemptive and retributive possibilities of this project" (Oppenheimer and Uwemedimo 2012, 307). Here Oppenheimer hints that the survivors can use the films in a number of ways that could contribute to resistance and atonement. It should be noted that much of the work toward reconciliation in Indonesia has been carried out by grassroots local organizations—the powerless trying to morally transform their nation—rather than national bodies (Pohlman 2016; Santoso and Klinken 2017, 595). International attention has been drawn to the genocide through *The Act of Killing*: the film was launched in The Hague in 2013, and an International People's Tribunal (IPT65) was held there in 2015 after the screening of the films and talks with Oppenheimer (Santoso and Klinken 2017, 595).[28] The tribunal concluded that Indonesia was guilty of a series of crimes against humanity, that of genocide against a national group according to the 1948 Genocide Convention: "severe deprivation of physical liberty, enslavement, torture, enforced disappearance, sexual violence, and exile" (Santoso and Klinken 2017, 598–603).

Both films have also been widely seen in Indonesia and are free to watch online, as they have been distributed by the National Human Rights Commission and the Jakarta Arts Council (Blyth 2016). That means that many people can come to know the truth about what happened and to reflect on the need for a just response to the killings.[29] Furthermore, there were a number of serious steps forward toward justice after the film was released. The Indonesian president's office admitted that 1965 was a crime against humanity and that truth and reconciliation are needed (Blyth 2016). Moreover, a Truth and Reconciliation bill was introduced by the government (Goodman 2015), but unfortunately it has not been implemented. This was the first step in what will be a long process. In April 2016 the Indonesian government held a two-day symposium on the genocide, with Islamic groups, military, and survivors (Kwok 2016, 1). There were discussions between victims and the military, although no apology was given. The current president of Indonesia, Joko Widodo, established a reconciliation committee but did not apologize to the PKI (the Communist Party of Indonesia) in his state address on August 16, 2016, although he had committed to addressing human rights violations (Buckley 2016). Muhammad Rizieq Shihab, the leader of the FPI (Islamic Defenders Front), threatened to impeach him if he apologized, so it is not that surprising. Additionally, media silence ended when testimony of perpetrators was published in *Tempo*, Indonesia's most influential news magazine, as Oppenheimer notes (Blyth 2016; Oppenheimer 2014). In 2023, Widodo acknowledged that "gross human rights violations" have been perpetrated in Indonesia in the past, including the 1956–66 politicide; he said, "'I strongly regret that those violations occurred'" and that the "government would seek to restore the rights of victims," although he did not say how (ABC News 2023).

In relation to the US role in the genocide, documents released earlier showed that the United States helped and encouraged the anticommunist groups, as Oppenheimer relates (Buckley 2016). Indonesia's National Commission on Human Rights asked President Barack Obama to release documents as well (Kwok 2016), and almost thirty thousand pages of records from the US Embassy in Indonesia 1964–68 were released in 2017 by the National Declassification Center, created by Obama in 2009 (Varagur 2017). Journalist Krithika Varagur (2017) contends, "It is hard to overstate the impact of the documentaries *The Act of Killing* and *The Look of Silence*, which are respectively about the perpetrators and victims of the 1965–66 killings, on the renewed conversation over Indonesia's mid-century anti-Communist purge." She is referring to the conversation in both Indonesia and in the United States, so the films have played a substantial activist role in resistance by revealing truths about the genocide.

By contrast, there has been a backlash against this recognition of the genocide, with screenings shut down, supposedly to prevent violence (Schenkel 2015, 101; Kwok 2016, 2); however, this attempt at censorship has undermined by the film's availability online at no cost. An anticommunist symposium was held in June 2016, and symposiasts demanded that the Communist Party "apologize to the people and the nation of Indonesia" (Kwok 2016, 3). There also still remains the need for monuments for the victims. The only existing material acknowledgments are markers for a very few of the mass graves that Indonesia is peppered with (Associated Press 2016). In 2016, the government said it would excavate mass graves, and such graves have been excavated in Bali and Central Java (Santoso and Klinken 2017, 595). There is a small grave for Ramli in the palm plantation where he was killed (Goodman 2015).

Atonement is also linked to forgiveness as a possible response to atonement. This was clearly what Adi Rukun had in mind from the beginning. For instance, he said, "We can forgive them if they can just admit what they've done was wrong" (Blyth 2016; Goodman 2015). That is the principle that Adi holds on to in his resistance to the narrative and reality the perpetrators have created, and that is also precisely what they will not admit. Oppenheimer notes that Adi initially hoped that one or more of the perpetrators would be glad to find forgiveness from one of the victims (Goodman 2015). The filmmaker warned Adi that he would not get an apology from the killers (Blyth 2016); he thought it was much more likely that they would "get defensive and angry" and threatening, after experiencing shame and guilt (Goodman 2015). Indeed, the local perpetrators seem even less perturbed by talking about their crimes than Anwar Congo did.

Some hope of a changed relationship is raised in the film through the relationships Adi begins to build with the children of the killers.[30] When the daughter of one of them asks him to forgive her father and think of them as family, as mentioned, Adi hugs her father and shakes his hand, in one of the more touching moments filmed. But in fact she does not apologize; she just repeatedly asks Adi to forgive her father. The partner of the killer who authored the illustrated book, Amir Hasan Nasution, does say, "Adi, we apologize. We feel the same way you do." And Adi nods. These developments, albeit small, suggest, as Barnette (2017, 70) writes, that atonement can only come with a new generation, from those who were not involved in the genocide. However, the moment is ruined by Nasution's sons' noisy claims that they know nothing and that Joshua is making trouble. His sons demand that they stop screening footage of their father showing off his book. They deny knowing anything and complain that Adi is opening up a wound, that he is seeking revenge, and that they should forget the past. The scene ends with a close-up shot of Adi's pained face, similar to many shots that recur throughout the film (fig. 2.2). The limited nature of these glimmers of atonement, or recognition of the truth, supports the need for a broader acknowledgment of the past crimes. Unfortunately, the very last scene of the film, showing the lights of a truck driving through the night, does not augur well for justice in the future.

FIG. 2.2. Adi Rukun's expression after Amir Hasan Nasution's sons say they know nothing about the killings. Still from *The Look of Silence*, directed by Joshua Oppenheimer (Anonymous, Final Cut for Real, Making Movies Oy, Piraya Film A/S, and Spring Films, 2014).

CONCLUSION

The Look of Silence demonstrates the power of documentary to perform and portray resistance against the impunity of the killers. It makes vivid Adi's search for his brother Ramli's killers to tell the truth and take responsibility for the actions, and although he does not really find the remorse or apology he seeks, Oppenheimer does expose the guilt and fear that he tries to reveal. Oppenheimer practices the small-scale work of resistance that Havel's powerless can claim in so single-mindedly pursuing an understanding of the killers and the victims and survivors, while Adi does the same in using his profession as an optometrist to disarm his interlocutors so that they reveal the truth about their deeds. Their work may lead to wider structural changes. Furthermore, the film suggests that some of the next generation, the children of the killers, will contribute to atonement in a way that makes Adi's resistant efforts worthwhile. However, other perpetrators and bystanders continue to deny the genocide or even claim that a communist threat still exists, and the anticommunism law is still in place. The film succeeds on many levels in contributing to communal atonement and so to resistance to the culture of impunity about the past and continuing repression even if as a work of art it does not, in the main, portray the individual atonement that was Adi's aim. In the next chapter we shift again to a different time period and another part of the world—1980 in East Germany—to consider a different kind of filmmaking and a very different form of everyday resistance.

[CHAPTER THREE]

Barbara

Love and Duty

In some cases, resistance consists of working within an oppressive system to try to improve the circumstances for others and make it as good as it can be, perhaps with a hope that one day that goodness will overcome its worst elements. One might choose this form of resistance when it is perceived as better than the alternative, which, in *Barbara* (dir. Christian Petzold, 2012), is fleeing to life in West Germany. This approach to resistance is that advocated by writer Christa Wolf and Václav Havel: to stay and be a critical voice and "defend moral values" (Wolf 1997, 10), or create "parallel structures" (Havel [1978] 1987, 100). Havel's elaboration of "living in the truth" as a form of dissidence is exemplified by the main character Barbara (Nina Hoss) in the practice of her vocation as a doctor. The idea of flight is supported by exiles and expatriate dissidents everywhere.

Here in *Barbara*, love plays a role, in that authentic love for a particular person and dutiful caring more generally can make it more sense to stay and to give meaning to that choice. The film follows a sequence of experiences and events in the life of a pediatric doctor, Barbara Wolff.[1] Barbara is sent from East Berlin to a small town in the German Democratic Republic (East Germany) in 1980 as punishment for trying to leave the country, or "exit."[2] She is still in contact with her West German lover, Jörg (Mark Waschke), who is going to try to help her flee the GDR, but she starts to be drawn into the life of the town, becoming attracted to one of the other doctors, André, and caring for the patients, especially a young girl, Stella, who herself is desperate to escape the work camp, Torgau.[3] *Barbara* is an intense drama that conveys Barbara's inner life as she contends with a difficult moral choice, whether to leave for West Germany or not, as well as the texture of life in that period and place.[4] It is a richly atmospheric and emotional film, tracking the protagonist

Barbara closely, without being invasive, and using all the elements of film language to dramatize the difficulty of her decision. The film is densely layered with allusions that are unlikely to be observed directly on a first viewing, especially by a non-German-speaking audience, but become more obvious through closer attention.

Barbara is played by Nina Hoss, who also appeared in *Phoenix* (2014), another film in Christian Petzold's "love in oppressive regimes" trilogy, along with *Transit* (2018), which stars Paula Beer. He is known as perhaps the most successful member, or even the "godfather," of the Berlin School group of filmmakers, who began to direct films in the early to mid-1990s while studying at the Berlin Film and Television Academy (DFFB) (Abel 2008). Petzold (quoted in Fisher, 2013, 154) describes his approach and that of the Berlin School as the rediscovery or reconstruction of genre, saying, "It is a kind of archaeology. And therefore we, with the Berlin school and such, wanted to build it back up again." Daniela Berghahn (2016, 328) explains the aesthetic approach of the Berlin School as creating an art object "in which ordinary life becomes suffused with a sensuous intensity, even beauty." Marco Abel (2010, 261) describes the Berlin School style in more detail as an "aesthetics of reduction" characterized "by long takes, long shots, clinically precise framing, a certain deliberateness of pacing, sparse usage of extradiegetic music, poetic use of diegetic sound, and frequently, the reliance on unknown or even nonprofessional actors who appear to be chosen for who they are rather than for who they could become." Many of these features apply to *Barbara*, although one could hardly call Nina Hoss an unknown actor.

I read *Barbara* in this chapter as a film where little appears by accident or just to create a beautiful scene or appealing mood, although that occurs as well. Rather, most of what the audience sees and hears is symbolic of the choice Barbara has to make. Even the film's title is resonant in a number of ways. The name "Barbara" derives from the Greek *barbaros*, meaning "foreign" or "strange," and the film's title can indicate that the choice is Barbara's alone; it is not meant to be generalized for everyone living in authoritarian societies. Barbara's name is also used a great deal by the different characters, much more than theirs are—André (Ronald Zehrfeld),[5] Jörg, and Stella (Jasna Fritzi Bauer), for example. In one of the last scenes in the film, as Stella floats away on a dinghy to a new life in the West, she calls "Barbara," as if in recognition of the gift of freedom Barbara has given her and as an expression of love. Barbara's surname, "Wolff," is also symbolic: it suggests that she is a forest creature, so perhaps her decision to stay in East Germany was also shaped by a horror of the sea journey. The name "Wolff" also references Christa Wolf's novel *Divided Heaven* (1963), about a woman torn between East and West

Germany who chooses the East, while her lover chooses the West, and Konrad Wolf, who directed the film based on that novel (1964).[6] Some of these elements, like the use of Barbara's name, can have an effect on any audience; others, such as the allusions, may require extra knowledge or research. All can contribute to a richly embellished sense of Barbara's turmoil and the difficulty of her choice.

To examine how the film contributes to our understanding of such a choice, I consider the idea of an everyday nonviolent resistance as working within an authoritarian society, as Havel explicates; then the moral choice that Barbara is faced with, and the two main factors influencing her decision, love and duty; and the crucial scenes that determine her final decision.

RESISTANCE

In relation to *Barbara*, I understand resistance as an engaged resistance rather than a refusal: making the system as good as one can by living according to what you value. Barbara's stance can be seen as accommodation or coping with an oppressive situation, but we can also delineate more complex motivations. The film shows rather than tells here, so it is only by looking closely at the individual scenes that we can interpret or speculate about what is going on in Barbara's mind. Barbara must choose whether to escape to West Germany or stay and help those living in East Germany. She has two love interests, Jörg and André, who represent the different life possibilities for her, as I discuss in the following section. Also, Barbara has to consider, under great pressure, whether she should help Stella, a young woman who needs to leave East Germany more than she does, and stay and help other patients in the hospital.[7] Stella had escaped from Torgau and been taken to the hospital where Barbara begins working, and Barbara finds that she has meningitis. Torgau was a Wehrmacht (German army) prison and Soviet special camp called Fort Zinna; then, from 1950 to 1990, it was a GDR prison. The conditions were bad in terms of surveillance and control, with poor hygiene and overcrowding, and inmates had to engage in hard labor. Some inmates were criminals, some were political prisoners, and juvenile offenders were imprisoned there from 1964 to 1989. It is not clear why Stella is being held in Torgau, only that she wants to escape the labor, which we see her carrying out when she runs away a second time.[8] Perhaps it is because she also wanted to leave East Germany. Duty also suggests that Barbara should stay—she can help people here, whereas in Western Germany she would be idle, as I describe further below.

A model for Barbara's dilemma and her decision can be found in the work of novelist Christa Wolf's idea of the choice involved in resistance. It is portrayed differently in the film *Divided Heaven* (dir. Konrad Wolf, 1964), based on her novel of the same title, where the protagonist, Rita, visits her lover Manfred in West Berlin but returns to Halle because she finds the noise and commercialism of the West unbearable. This story is set just before the building of the wall between East and West Germany in 1961, so its atmosphere is not as claustrophobic as *Barbara*'s. In later years Wolf characterized her approach and those of likeminded people thus:

> For years we had been addressing certain tasks in what we intended to be our opposition literature: to name the conflicts which for a long time were expressed nowhere else, and thus to generate or strengthen a critical attitude in readers; to encourage them to resist lies, hypocrisy, and surrender of self; to keep alive our language and the other traditions of German literature and history from which attempts were made to cut us off; and, last but not least, to defend moral values that in the dominant ideology were cynically earmarked for sacrifice. (1997, 10)

While Wolf's profession of writer distinguishes her from Barbara's as doctor, the concerns with taking a critical attitude and maintaining artistic traditions and moral values all resonate in the film.

Havel advocated a similar stance of "living within the truth" in his essay "The Power of the Powerless," as I explained in the introduction ([1978] 1987). Recall that he labels the system of the Soviet Union and the Soviet bloc "post-totalitarian" to distinguish it from earlier conceptions of dictatorships ([1978] 1987, 40–41). While Havel ([1978] 1987, 60) advocates forms of protest and rebellion, he also notes that a way of living in the truth could involve "ordinary citizens who were able to maintain their human dignity." His argument is that any attempt to live within the truth becomes political in a society driven by ideology: "Every free human act or expression, every attempt to live within the truth, must necessarily appear as a threat to the system and, thus, as something which is political *par excellence*" ([1978] 1987, 65). One of the features he identifies in these post-totalitarian systems is that politics has to be practiced in new ways and thus that people from many traditionally apolitical or nonpolitical professions, including doctors, may become involved. What distinguishes what may be called "dissidents," according to Havel ([1978] 1987, 79), is their "interests in others, in what ails society as a whole, in other words, on an interest in all those who do not speak up." They practice "small-scale work" that is "honest and responsible" and creates a kind of independence ([1978] 1987, 81). To see whether Barbara is such a dissident, I examine the film's attention to her experience, which must be conveyed through cinematic means. The film also asks questions about Barbara's thought process and the sources of moral values: Can they be understood in terms of love and duty? What kind of factors go into making a moral choice of this kind?

MORAL CHOICE

Barbara's moral choice between staying and working in East Germany and going to live in the West is underlined and represented by the film's events; its colors and scenes; the dialogue, sound, and music; and even the names of the characters, as I mentioned in regard to her name.[9] Petzold says that he is influenced by the opening line of a short poem called "Wünschelrute" ("Wishing-wand," 1838) by Joseph Freiherr von Eichendorff (1788–1857), "A song sleeps in all things around" (Fisher 2013, 167), which is followed by "Which dream on and on unheard, / And the world begins to resound, / If you hit the magic word." That idea can be a guide to interpreting his film in the sense that everything symbolizes the choice or crossroads for Barbara. She even rides to a cross that stands on the corner leading to the path to the beach, André's favorite place and the place for her planned escape; she conceals the money for her escape under some rocks near that cross.[10] The unnamed town in East Germany is near the Baltic Sea, and André suggests an excursion to the beach, but she says, "I hate the sea." It is not clear from the film whether Barbara really hates the sea or is just saying that to put him off. Either way, the road to the sea implies a choice between the interior and the exterior, symbolized by the sea, a choice to stay or to go. For many in East Germany, leaving was almost the only way to effectively protest against the regime while escaping it at the same time, so the choice for Barbara is stark.[11]

Throughout the film Barbara responds to nature. The forest is a kind of liminal space between East and West, as is "air," which Barbara seeks outside the hospital. It is always windy, and that is what she wants: air. The wind in the trees, whenever Barbara is riding alone on her bike, signifies freedom, which she might find by leaving. But the forest is ambiguous. When she meets her lover Jörg, the birds are singing in the forest, and they run to each other to embrace, dropping their belongings like a fantasy of reunion. Afterward he gives her blue cigarettes, and tights. When André sees the cigarettes later, under the bed at the hospital, he looks hurt, as if they are a sign of betrayal. They also signify the privilege of her contact with the West, and the exchange aspect of the relationship with Jörg, as I explain below. Highlighting the natural beauty of the place again underscores its appeal, whereas West Germany is represented by objects like Jörg's friend Gerhard's (Peter Benedict) car, a Mercedes. The encounter sets up a conflict between the material benefits of the West and the frugality of life in the East, as well as between Barbara's relationship with Jörg and with André.

Music is absolutely central to the film and often acts as a connection to and commentary on the action. Rather than a musical score, the music, apart from that over the end credits, arises from the film's action. A series of telling scenes concern the piano left in Barbara's flat, initially unplayable, as it is out of tune. She becomes irritated when André sends someone to tune the piano and give her some sheet music, perhaps because she feels he is interfering in her life. Nevertheless, Barbara derives great pleasure and release from playing it, and it is one of the signs that she is beginning to feel at home in the village.[12]

Music highlights Barbara's moral choice between staying and going—between her work as a doctor and the life she might lead in West Germany. Roger Cook (2017) argues that music and literature do not become "subordinated to the hegemony of the narrative." They are not didactic references, yet they play the role of engaging viewers with Barbara's dilemma and suggesting her inner life. Early in the film, following Barbara's first day at her new job and her discovery of a bicycle in the cellar of her flats, she listens to a radio program about Wilhelm Furtwängler (1886–1954). Debbie Pinfold refers to the discussion as a "snippet of radio commentary preceding the opening bars of Carl Maria Weber's *Der Freischütz*" (*The Freeshooter*, 1821), and focuses on the significance of the opera, as a love story with an equivocal ending, to approaching the film. For her, the radio presenter's comment about hearing the opera as if for the first time suggests that we should read the film "with an openness to the new and a reflective, questioning attentiveness" (2014, 298). However, I argue that the program can also be seen as particularly resonant for Barbara as a character due to the details of Furtwängler's life. Furtwängler famously stayed and continued to conduct orchestras during the Nazi era while other conductors fled. Like Christa Wolf, he felt a duty to contribute to culture in spite of the barbarity surrounding him. Controversy still surrounds his decision today: some see him as a collaborator, while others believe he courageously represented hope and the cultural life of Germany during a crisis (Gutmann 1999).[13] Furtwängler represents the idea of working within a system in order to defy it and keep the best ideals alive, and the program can be inferred to influence Barbara's reflections, as it will affect audience members who know Furtwängler's biography. The music follows Barbara as she walks into the hospital for her next shift, thus suggesting it is playing on her mind in some way.

Similarly, one night after Barbara reads to Stella from Mark Twain's *The Adventures of Huckleberry Finn* (1884), Stella sings Barbara a lullaby, "Abendlied" ("Evening Song"). The song refers to neat solutions being a delusion that take us off our path:

> We, with our proud endeavor,
> Are poor vain sinners ever.
> There's little that we know.
> Frail cobwebs we are spinning,
> Our goal we are not winning,
> But straying further as we go. (Claudius 1916)[14]

At the end of the film, over the credits, the band Chic performs "At Last I Am Free" (1978).[15] The song could be interpreted either as ironic or as sincere, implying that Barbara is free from Jörg or free from wanting to leave.[16]

The references to literature in the movie further indicate Barbara's inner moral struggle, and it is notable that Petzold did a master's in literature before studying film, since there are a number of significant literary references in *Barbara*. For instance, from a selection of books at the hospital, Barbara chooses *Huckleberry Finn* to read to Stella. The idea that a doctor would have time to read a novel to a patient could be surprising for a contemporary Western audience, and shows her dedication. At times the reading of the story seems to parallel Barbara's life. After meeting her lover Jörg in the forest, she reads a scene where Huck talks about his adventures in the forest.[17] Also, the book is a novel by a Western writer about the search for freedom, and an escape by raft like Barbara's proposed escape by dinghy. Huckleberry Finn experiences a moral dilemma between the mores of the slave society he lives in and his own feelings, which he resolves in favor of his friendship with Jim, who is escaping slavery: Huck decides to help him evade capture.[18] Stella can be seen as the parallel to Jim in this tale, and Barbara's aiding her escape as a disobedience to the rules of the system. Reading the story would also be operating on her like the Furtwängler program.[19]

We also hear a radio broadcast from the 1980 Summer Olympics in Moscow after Stella is taken back to the work camp. The event described is the women's 1,500-meter race, which had the following results: gold, Tatjana Kazankina (USSR); silver, Christiane Wartenberg (GDR); bronze, Nadezhda Olisarenko (USSR); and, in fifth place, Ulrike Bruns (GDR).

That Olympics also represents a moral choice, as the United States, West Germany, and sixty-three other countries boycotted the games due to the Soviet invasion of Afghanistan. Barbara seems uninterested in the news, but each of these presentations of a dilemma and indeed of the answer of staying within the authoritarian system despite its privations must be working on her mind, influencing her final decision.

In contrast to the music underscoring the ethical quandaries of the film, the sounds in the environment are often quite threatening: a doorbell ringing, a dog barking, or a wolf whistle. Most of these sounds in the film are diegetic: that is, the actor is hearing them on set (Kasman and Phelps 2012). The shrill ring of the doorbell is like that in *The Lives of Others* (dir. Florian Henckel von Donnersmarck, 2006), although it is not manipulated like that bell.[20] In Barbara, the doorbell announces the arrival of the woman who will strip-search Barbara as her punishment for being absent or unable to be found.[21] The Stasi are looking for contraband, but it is also an act of humiliation. These sounds could portend the need to leave and could thus oppose some of the other elements.[22]

Even colors are symbolic in the film. Color was crucial to Petzold's stylistic choices for *Barbara*, where he wanted to portray the colorful place he remembered from childhood visits and avoid demonizing East Germany, in contrast to the drab grays of *The Lives of Others*, for example (Fisher 2013, 140, 161; Pinfold 2014, 282).[23] Jaimey Fisher (2013, 141) mentions the colors of "lovely summer landscapes and of the remarkable beauty of decaying buildings," yet there are also many colors in Barbara's wardrobe of brilliant blues, her blue eyeshadow, and her red vanity case.[24] The warm colors underline the warmth of the life Barbara becomes accustomed to over the course of the narrative. All these elements stressing the difficulty of her choice are further underlined by conflicts of love.

TWO KINDS OF LOVE

Two different kinds of love are presented in the film, or perhaps two aspects of romantic love. Havel ([1978] 1987, 118) calls for human factors to create a "new spirit" in post-totalitarian societies, contending that "the issue is the rehabilitation of values like trust, openness, responsibility, solidarity, love." So what role does love play in resistance? These types of love track the moral choice Barbara has to make. Barbara's love for Jörg is passionate, sensual, and full of longing, like the erotic love of Plato's *Symposium*, expressed in the Aristophanic myth of the beings cut into halves and so fated to search for each other. The myth represents the idea that "this love is always trying to reintegrate our former nature, to make two into one, and to bridge the gulf between one human being and another" (Plato 2006, 191d). However, this love also suffers from the dangers of what Simone de Beauvoir (2010, 683–708), in her discussion of "the woman in love" in *The Second Sex*, calls "idolatrous" love: the love between men and women in a patriarchal society.[25] This can be thought of as erotic or romantic love that is asymmetrical, lacking in equality and reciprocity. Beauvoir is making the point that love in contexts where women are treated as inferior and where women do not have their own projects will involve women expecting men to give them their reason for living.[26] Barbara at first lives for her meetings with Jörg, distancing herself from her new life, plotting to join him in his world. That love is unequal, and the inequality is shown by the way Jörg does not take her work as a doctor seriously; rather, he wants her to worship him. By contrast, her love for André Reiser develops slowly, through their common interest in medicine, medical research, painting, music, and literature. He also gardens and cooks, activities that she does not engage in but is perhaps interested to learn more about. It will be equal, mutual, and reciprocal, combining respect and desire, like the authentic love that Beauvoir (2010, 694, 706) champions, where both experience each other's "lacks, limitations, and originary gratuitousness." Ultimately, a love relationship with André seems like it will have more depth and enrich her life, whereas a relationship with Jörg starts to look shallow and alienated.[27]

André is another doctor at the hospital Barbara starts to fall in love with. His given name, "André," means "brave," while "Reiser" traces back to "branch" or "twig" and thus represents the forest as well as solidity. At first Barbara sees him merely as a stooge, an informer for the Stasi, spying on her and reporting back to them, which indeed he is doing.[28] But soon she is attracted by his work in the medical lab he has set up; his appreciation of art, literature, and music; and the simple country life. Furthermore, André's concern for his patients, his excellence in his profession, and his warmth are all attractive to her. He explains to her that people in the town are sensitive, so she should not upset them by being too separate from them, as they could feel she thinks she is above them. That is André's first attempt to touch her feelings, and of course when he says "People here are sensitive," that includes himself. His attitude and that of his colleagues hint that they think her desire to leave East Germany is a form of snobbery, rather than a need or political action. Coming from the exclusive Charité hospital in East Berlin and wanting to leave for the West makes her seem like she thinks she is better than others. However, from reading her file, Klaus Schütz (Rainer Bock), the Stasi agent, remarks that her circle of friends disintegrated after she was discovered applying to leave, so her cool manner is more a sign of desolation and isolation.

Art provides another point of contact and interest. While Barbara thinks that his sole object is to talk her into withdrawing her application to leave (*Ausreisentrag*), André says he would like to go to The Hague to see the Rembrandt painting *The Anatomy Lesson of Dr. Nicolaes Tulp* (1632). After she points out errors in the painting of the hand, his reading is that Rembrandt deliberately painted the hand too large and in reverse to demonstrate how the doctors are looking at the textbook, not the body itself, so they are seeing what they expect to see rather than what is there.[29] André's didacticism here could be taken as an attempt to show that as a doctor he properly sees the patients and that as a person he sees Barbara herself, not as she is seen by the state. He is embarrassed about showing off with the lab and the analysis of the painting, but it serves to point out to Barbara that she should look beyond the surface of her experiences of people in the town, especially him.[30] Also, the question whether the doctors are paying attention to their work is relevant to Barbara's sense of concentration and absorption in her own profession.

André continually attempts to befriend Barbara in a range of ways. For instance, André adapts to Barbara's routine by getting a bicycle as well, and describes himself as also being punished by being sent to that town. He tells a story about his past experiences to draw those connections and to underline the need for a focus on work, but Barbara is not sure whether to believe it or not. André relates that he was working at a hospital in Eberswalde, his hometown. They had a new incubator from New Zealand for premature babies, and were caring for twin babies, Maik and Jennifer. However, the instructions were lengthy and in English. A medical assistant affected to know more English than she did to impress him, and because she confused Fahrenheit and Celsius, they set the incubator's heat too high, which blinded the two children.[31] As a result, André had to take responsibility for her actions and was sent to the provinces. Thus, the affair was hushed up, but he has to report on colleagues like Barbara. She doubts the story, saying, somewhat sarcastically, "Is the story true? Maik and Jennifer." Still, their camaraderie grows, as they drink coffee together and eat the monotonous hospital cafeteria lunches.[32]

Their growing love is noticed by others before they realize it themselves. For example, junior doctor Schulze (Christina Hecke) (a name very similar to that of the Stasi agent Klaus Schütz seems to think Barbara is in love with André from the beginning, as she indicates through her expression of derision as Barbara seeks out André in the cafeteria to ask for time off. Furthermore, Mario, a young man who had tried to commit suicide, raises the question of the romantic emotions of love and jealousy.[33] Barbara sees a young woman, Angie, crying at his bedside and follows her to find out why. Apparently, she danced with some Cuban men, and in a fit of jealousy Mario tried to kill himself. Angie notices that he seems normal but does not feel emotions, as he only talked about the food in the hospital and does not remember the note he wrote to Angie. That is a sign for Angie that he is not himself and a clue for Barbara that he has a clot in his brain and urgently needs an operation. Thus, Barbara discusses Mario's coldness with André, and he implies that she is cold in the same way. Her embarrassment then is a sign that she would prefer to be seen as warm, at least by him.[34] The action of the film moves to a climax as the operation on Mario is planned for when Barbara needs to escape, and Barbara agrees to be there as anesthetist, forcing a choice. However, she does not show up for the operation, and the Stasi officer Schütz assumes that she has gone and tells André. But she has not, as several other motivations that revolve around the concept of duty are working to keep her there.

DUTY

As well as finding love, Barbara can do so much good in the village, where people are suffering from the abuses of the regime. The Hippocratic oath tells her to heal, not to run away and become a kept woman. Her duty is tied up with relationships that develop—to the young patients in the hospital, Stella, and André. In that sense, her duty is mixed with care and love. Working in a children's hospital means that Barbara thinks of the future, but not in the sense of a far-off utopia. Rather, she considers the near future, for those children and young people. Her duty here is a kind of practical benevolence, or beneficence, as Immanuel Kant would have it in the "The Doctrine of Virtue" in *The Metaphysics of Morals* (1996, 6:452–55). He distinguished between respect and love and argued that both should have practical forms in the sense of issuing in acts that help others to achieve their goals. In that sense, love can be a moral emotion because it is an important way of valuing others.[35] For Kant (1996, 6:452), the duties of love were beneficence, gratitude, and sympathy. Barbara's practice as a doctor is one of beneficence, "to promote according to one's means the happiness of others in need" (Kant 1996, 6:453).[36] The representation of Barbara's transition from being desperate to leave to staying works through uniting duty and love, and through her finding the sort of authentic love that Beauvoir articulates, one that is equal and reciprocal because she has her own profession and projects.

Barbara enjoys the lab, where she can do research, and has a great deal of empathy and insight, despite André's claim that she is cold. For example, André misses the information about the tick bites relevant to diagnosing Stella's meningitis as he does not read her file, and Barbara reminds him to call Stella by her name. Stella, who is recovering from her meningitis, is pregnant and wants her child to grow up away from the GDR. Barbara signals early that Stella's child would be taken away from her if she returns to Torgau.[37] Barbara also takes her duty of care seriously by sacrificing her own hopes for Stella and her unborn child, as well as defying a law that would require her to report Stella.

That sense of duty is highlighted again when we see how André helps the Stasi agent Schütz, who interrogates Barbara, as his wife is dying of cancer. The other woman helping Schütz and his partner gives vegetables to André and Barbara in gratitude. They both assume that André and Barbara are a couple and are surprised that Barbara speaks formally to him. The vegetables—eggplant, tomatoes, and zucchini—are perfect for making ratatouille, and in the scene where André cooks it for Barbara we get a sense of the "niche society" or cozy socialism that West German journalist and politician Günter Gaus pointed to, whereby citizens in the GDR created a closely protected space of intimacy and small pleasures (Mueller 2013, 198).[38] When Barbara says, "Why do you help assholes?" André responds by saying that he helps assholes who are sick. The needs of others go beyond their official patients in the hospital.[39] Jaimey Fisher (2017) notes that the film is interested in "the satisfaction and solidarity one can derive from" work, and a sense of hope alongside the brutality of the regime. The film underscores how there are intrinsic values that persist despite the insidiousness of surveillance and indoctrination and that in their own ways André and Barbara pursue those values to try to create parallel structures.

As the film progresses, love and duty start to point in the same direction for Barbara, unlike for Simin, in *A Separation*, where love and duty are torn apart, as I discuss in chapter 5. There is also an implicit, if obvious, critique of capitalist commodification of relationships that is another factor in her decision, as we see in the next section.

THE DECISION

The film shows two crucial turning points that reveal to Barbara and to the audience what really matters to her. In the first of these scenes, Barbara is at the Interhotel, a chain of GDR luxury hotels, another in-between space where she meets her West German lover, Jörg, and talks to his friend Gerhard's lover, Steffi (Susanne Bormann) (fig. 3.1). It prepares the audience for a shift in Barbara's thoughts and feelings about escape to the West. In the second, Stella appears at Barbara's flat, and Barbara actually makes up her mind to stay.

FIG. 3.1. Barbara and Steffi in the Interhotel. Still from *Barbara*, directed by Christian Petzold (Schramm Film Koerner & Weber, ZDF, and ARTE, 2012).

The first turning point begins with Barbara arriving in a small town at night.[40] We hear a dog barking, and a wolf whistle as she walks toward the hotel suggests how she is perceived by the townspeople—perhaps as an escort. She has to get into the hotel room through the window. It also implies the inequality in Barbara's relationship with Jörg, like Beauvoir's characterization of idolatrous love. Earlier Gerhard is sarcastic about Barbara and Jörg's tryst as they drive back to the West, and he asks Jörg, "Was it at least worth it?" His attitude expresses disdain toward the Easterner and toward Barbara, who is equated with Gerhard's Eastern girlfriend, Steffi. Notably, in the hotel scenes Barbara, Jörg, and Steffi all speak in whispers, underscoring the clandestine nature of the relationships. When Jörg tells Barbara that she can sleep late, she will not have to work in the West because he earns enough for them both, that is a bad sign. It shows that he does not understand how much she loves her work and how central it is to her life. In Jörg's patriarchal view, a woman in a relationship does not need to work, and the man will provide the connections with the world, an asymmetrical situation Beauvoir articulates as typical for women under oppression. Then Barbara would be completely dependent on Jörg—"condemned to dependence," in Beauvoir's words (2010, 684)—so that what appeared to be freedom can be seen as a trap. As Beauvoir (2010, 691) writes, "The paradox of idolatrous love is that in order to save herself, she ends up totally *disavowing* herself." Furthermore, Jörg's escape plan conflicts with Barbara's duty to be at the hospital, both in the specific context of Mario's operation and in the life-altering idea that she would give up her profession.[41]

What is even more strongly indicative of a problem in their relationship is Barbara's dismissal of her lover's idea that he could come and live with her and be happy: "You're nuts," she says. "You can't be happy here." Her furious rejection of that possibility at the same time as she is starting to acclimatize to life in the village implies that she may not even want him to join her there. Barbara is fiercely independent: for instance, she fixes a bicycle so that she does not have to accept lifts from André, and she is annoyed by André arranging for someone to come tune her piano. It is difficult to imagine how Jörg could live in East Germany if the roles were reversed and Barbara had her own life separate from his. The implication is that their relationship exists only on the condition of *her* dependence and could not be transformed into an authentic love in Beauvoir's sense.

The conversation with Steffi, who slips into her room through the adjoining hotel room door, is also crucial in illuminating how Barbara makes the decision to stay. Steffi's assumption that Barbara is an escort who should be given presents in return for sex is disconcerting and reinforces the suggestion that Barbara's lover Jörg is primarily interested in her for sex.[42] Such a relationship is a form of capitalist exchange rather than an authentic and equal companionship. Barbara does not correct Steff's assumption but looks a bit shocked at the idea of being given something in exchange and says he gave me "nothing." Her words here are ambiguous: not that she wants a necklace, but that she thinks he gives her nothing.[43] Equally, Barbara could have champagne and a ring from her lover, but she does not care about these things. They are only material and do not matter, unlike looking after patients and doing medical research. The scene makes a stark contrast with the solidarity between Barbara and André and the way they help each other become better doctors and better people. While there is no dramatic change after this scene, it can be imagined that the experience is working on Barbara's thoughts as she prepares for her departure.

The second turning point is when Stella arrives at Barbara's flat wounded, with a deep gash in her leg, having escaped from Torgau (fig. 3.2). Barbara must make up her mind then that rather than leaving, she will help Stella escape. The plan involves crossing to Denmark on a motorized rubber dinghy with a skin diver, an escape that could not work for two people. After Barbara binds Stella's leg, they travel together to the beach and she helps Stella into the dinghy, giving her a note for Jörg and the money she has hidden so carefully. Her decision to stay is final and irrevocable. That decision can be seen as multiply motivated by her duty of care to her patients, her love for André, and her concern for Stella and her unborn child's future.

FIG, 3.2. Barbara embraces Stella. Still from *Barbara*, directed by Christian Petzold (Schramm Film Koerner & Weber, ZDF, and ARTE, 2012).

An alternative reading of the film is that Barbara is so beaten down by the system that she loses the energy to run away. However, that would fly in the face of the symbolism, action, and dialogue of the film, as I have argued throughout the chapter. In the final scene we see Barbara arrive at the hospital, where a saddened André, sitting over Mario, suddenly stirs and brightens at her entrance. Barbara's expression in this shot appears to be slightly embarrassed and yet also nonchalant, as if to say, "What did you expect?"[44] It seems that Barbara, unlike Jörg, can be happy there. The difference is that she is not alienated from her work; she is "living in the truth," engaged in her work in a way that is consistent with her values. We can see Barbara as someone who is "defending humanity" as Havel recommends ([1978] 1987, 89). Furthermore, Barbara's and André's treatment of their patients, their research, and even the love between them begin to create a "a parallel structure" (Havel [1978] 1987, 100) that could be the beginning of something more organized.

CONCLUSION

Should we conclude that Barbara made the right decision? In its focus on Barbara as an individual, the film appears to imply that she had a number of compelling reasons for her decision, both to stay, and not to leave, without suggesting that it was wrong for others to choose to "exit." Barbara's love for André and her duty as a doctor and a citizen come together to determine the form of her resistance, as a decision to stay and improve the lives of those who require care. That is her way of "living in the truth" and practicing "small-scale work" as a form of resistance. Barbara is also openly resistant to the regime in helping Stella to escape to freedom. Instead of exiting herself, she enables Stella's exit. The film's aesthetic and narrative elements stress that this is Barbara's choice, not necessarily the right choice for everyone, and there could be good reasons to leave as well. All the elements in the film—the colors, the music, the references to literature and painting, even the seemingly incidental ones such as snatches overheard on the radio—combine to emphasize the difficulty of the decision and, to some extent, ambivalence about it. However, the stress on its difficulty also demonstrates its seriousness as an act of resistance. In the next chapter I examine a resistance that emerges from within the existing governing structures in a fictionalized Chile in 1988.

[CHAPTER FOUR]

No

Happiness, Resistance, and Trauma

The Chilean film *No* (dir. Pablo Larraín, 2012) portrays how the concept of happiness can inform resistance, in this case to the Pinochet civic-military dictatorship (1973–90).[1] The film's narrative concerns the 1988 plebiscite on whether Pinochet should stay as the president for eight more years—the "Yes" or "*Sí*" vote—or hold democratic elections—the "No" vote. In this chapter I analyze how the film represents the transformation of the experience of the trauma of the Pinochet dictatorship into the idea of happiness. As Havel suggested, happiness is such an essential experience and value of the "independent life of society" that to maintain a focus on it is to challenge the regime ([1978] 1987, 86). *No* is a fictionalized account of the television campaigns for the 1988 plebiscite that plays with the historical drama genre by incorporating large portions of archival footage—around 30 percent of the film's two-hour running time—and by using film and cameras that would have been used at the time (Lyttelton 2013). According to the film, the initial idea of the "No" campaign was to condemn the abuses of the dictatorship by showing images of torture and brutality and the resulting trauma and negative emotions. However, as the film shows, this approach was altered and combined with more positive material because of a determination to win the campaign. Instead of repeating the trauma in a gesture acknowledged as futile, the supporters of the "No" vote in the film take up the challenge to "retemporalize and detranslate" the trauma, to create the possibility of a new narrative that Kristin McCartney finds in W. E. B. Du Bois's (1868–1963) articulation of the importance of slave or sorrow songs; this possibility of a new narrative is one that must be recognized, taken up, and recounted to be effective (McCartney 2009, 85–86). *No* depicts how a new collective narrative with a different temporal structure is created in the context of the Chilean plebiscite.

In the film, the "No" campaign, headed by René Saavedra (played by Gael García Bernal), a creative director in advertising, uses the chorus of a catchy theme song, "Chile, Joy Is Coming" ("Chile, la alegria ya viene"), to illustrate Aristotle's idea that happiness is an intrinsic value and thus the best concept to galvanize a traumatized nation in favor of change. While the campaigners were not directly inspired by Aristotle, the focus on joy (*alegría*) was used in the "No" campaign as the first step to happiness (*felicidad*) on the understanding that happiness is an intrinsic value. The resistant "No" campaign shown in *No* portrays a possible future happiness if the regime were to end through the portrayal of joyful happiness, and I connect Aristotle's idea of happiness with Sara Ahmed's suggestion that the concept of happiness promises a better future. The narrative of *No* follows René from his initial reluctance to direct the "No" television campaign to his enthusiastic and determined pursuit of its success and ends with his ambivalent return to his advertising agency to work with his boss, Lucho Guzmán (Alfredo Castro), who directed the "Yes" campaign. Compared to Barbara, who works as a pediatrician, René, the advertising director, is a more surprising exemplar of Havel's notion that following one's profession with integrity is way of living in the truth and a practice of resistance in itself. The conflict with the regime "has not come about through any conscious intention on their part, but simply through the inner logic of their thinking, behavior or work" (Havel [1978] 1987, 78). While the film has been criticized for oversimplifying events and omitting the grassroots campaign to register and mobilize voters (Rohter 2013; Khazan 2013; Peirano 2018), I center on the narrative of the film's representation of the shift of attention from painful trauma to happiness as a form of resistance.

Rather than seeing the film as a flawed how-to manual for ending dictatorships, I explore the importance of the symbolic transformation in the film of emotion from a negative past orientation to a positive future one, and from individual suffering to collective happiness in the specific context of the Chilean 1988 plebiscite. *No* uses original footage from the period and filmic techniques with old film stock in the Academy ratio and cameras that often blur the new footage with the old, so the film feels like a work from that time and place. In order to provide another link with the period, the director also chose to cast as actors some individuals who were involved in the campaign. The film's focus on the television campaign refers us to television as a locus for resistance to trauma here, by showing how television was able to influence and change public opinion and responses to past trauma through its use of a positive narrative. I first explain how Du Bois's work provides an understanding of the way traumatic experience can be transformed into a more hopeful orientation, an understanding relevant to the 1988 Chilean referendum represented in *No*, then how the concept of happiness is presented as essential to resistance in the film, and finally I show how the character of René, the advertising man behind the campaign, exemplifies the connection between individual and collective transformation toward happiness and the future.

RETEMPORALIZING TRAUMA

I begin from the idea of how past trauma can be retemporalized and detranslated, terms McCartney takes from psychoanalyst Jean Laplanche (Laplanche and Pontalis 1973, 465–73) and trauma theorist Cathy Caruth (1996) by linking the past with the present and future, and developing a resistant culture. These psychoanalytic sources suggest an understanding of how experiences of oppression can be transmitted through the generations and how they can be transformed, and I link this thought to Du Bois's articulation of African American experiences of the legacy of slavery. McCartney (2009, 81) follows Caruth and Laplanche in thinking of retemporalization and detranslation as a "struggle to make sense of the remainder of the enigmatic" or the fragments of past experiences of trauma, such as the sorrow songs. Retemporalization is creating a connection to the future as well as transforming the emotional valence from memory of suffering to tempered hope concerning the future. For McCartney (2009, 81), detranslation of what is "untranslatable" in trauma begins "the unending hermeneutic process of temporalizing and narrating the self." Du Bois's *The Souls of Black Folk* ([1903] 1996) arguably foreshadows the pan-African work of Aimé Césaire I discussed in the first chapter (Rabaka 2016, 16). McCartney's interpretation of Du Bois's work provides a precedent for the way I read the narrative of hope recounted in *No*. She shows how Du Bois articulates forms of identification resistant to the dominant white symbolic. McCartney (2009, 79) argues that Du Bois is able to retemporalize trauma "through the unburial of racial history and race ideals" in his account of the sorrow songs. Thus, the problem of trauma Du Bois sets out is one of kinship bonds being broken, rather than unconscious fantasies being passed on, and sorrow songs can be a force for resistance and connection of the disrupted generations. Sorrow songs, including the well-known example "Swing Low, Sweet Chariot," are the songs of enslaved people in the southern United States, popularized by the Fisk Jubilee singers from Nashville from 1871, beginning a tradition that continues today. Du Bois ([1903] 1996, 189) writes, "They tell us in these eager days that life was joyous to the black slave, careless and happy." While many of the songs speak of trouble and toil, he holds that "through all the sorrow of the Sorrow Songs there breathes a hope—a faith in the ultimate justice of things" ([1903] 1996, 196).

In *The Souls of Black Folk* Du Bois broadens the analysis of individual trauma to theorize the oppression of African Americans and resistance to it. For him, black Americans have a double consciousness, or a "sense of always looking at oneself through the eyes of others," which engenders a longing to combine this "double self into a better and truer self" and "to be a co-worker in the kingdom of culture" (Du Bois [1903] 1996, 7). On McCartney's (2009, 80) reading of Du Bois, double consciousness involves the disturbance of the capacity to narrate one's own experiences. Part of the history of dispossession and oppression that creates that double consciousness is the temporal disruption of intergenerational order (Du Bois [1903] 1996, 147). Thus, resistance has to take the form of reestablishing the broken ties to form an identity through continuity over time and generations, and community between Black and white Americans. While Du Bois describes a different situation from the Chilean dictatorship, the torture, disappearances, and murders in Chile marked breaks in temporal continuity and in community solidarity, and the film *No* dramatizes a specific detranslation of those breaks.

The detranslation McCartney focuses on is renarration of intergenerational trauma. The "enigmatic" refers to a fragmented narrative of original loss and is here, for McCartney (2009, 80), the sorrow songs, which are partial links to a lost past that become "vehicles for identification and catharsis [whereby] Du Bois imagines a counter-force of intergenerational strength and Black cultural resistance." Du Bois ([1903] 1996, 188) contends that the songs are "the most beautiful expression of human experience" in America. The sorrow songs express trauma and loss and provide a connection to history, which Du Bois "tries to translate into a message of hope" (McCartney 2009, 85). Fundamentally, he contends that the songs must be recognized as a heritage of the whole nation.

Similarly, Paul E. Kirkland (2015, 415) argues that "Du Bois concludes *Souls* by showing the way that the 'Sorrow Songs' exhibit a capacity for joy when suffering is transfigured as art and self-knowledge when aesthetic experience helps to reveal the character of human longing." This suffering transfigured into joy is contrasted with *blind* optimism, despair and resignation, and grounded in an experience of the tragedy, disappointment, and suffering of African American history (Kirkland 2015, 432–36). McCartney's and Kirkland's focus on Du Bois's transformation of trauma into hope and connection is one that is followed in different forms by other trauma theorists, and theorizing that transformation is essential to my interpretation of the representation of the "No" campaign in *No*. Furthermore, Du Bois provides an account that puts individual suffering in relation to a broader sense of community.

How individual and collective trauma are related should be clarified here. Trauma theory developed in the twentieth century from Sigmund Freud's work on individual trauma and following World Wars I and II. Much research on trauma concerns how people respond to traumatic occurrences, especially how it affects memory; for example, Susan Rubin Suleiman (2008, 277) shows how psychiatrist Judith Herman and others connect trauma with repressed memory of repeated traumatic events. These events involve a life-threatening force that makes the person feel helpless (Herman 1992, 33; Brison 2003, 39). Others, such as psychologists Elizabeth Loftus and Richard McNally, argue that "memories of trauma . . . cannot be dissociated or repressed—on the contrary, the more violent the trauma, the more subjects are likely to remember it, indeed to never forget it even if they want to" (Suleiman 2008, 279). Suleiman concludes that trauma is "primarily a drama of survival" with themes stressed by psychiatrist Robert Jay Lifton, such as "the inability to move beyond images of death, guilt about having survived while others died, psychic numbing, lack of trust in the world, and struggle for meaning" (Suleiman 2008, 280). Like the intergenerational suffering that Du Bois describes, trauma can also be communicated intergenerationally, as E. Ann Kaplan (2005, 37) observes. She takes a syncretic approach that includes both conscious and unconscious processes. Trauma can mean both a response to personal traumatic incidents and to the trauma caused by political events.[2]

I examine trauma here as a response to the atrocities committed by the military in Chile, but in the specific situation depicted in *No*, the dictatorship is still in power and the trauma is ongoing, rather than a response to events from the past and their legacy, as in *The Look of Silence*. The Pinochet regime in Chile committed atrocities, murdering or "disappearing" thousands of people (at least 2,000), torturing many thousands more (27,000), and sending many more (200,000) into exile.[3] Such experiences create trauma, affecting the emotions and self-identity of victims and survivors in ways that reverberate throughout society. Jeffrey Blustein (2018, 234) describes how the suffering of atrocity "is registered in the emotions, memories, and psychological deficits of victims." He follows Herman in seeing the typical response of victims of atrocity as traumatization. His work is significant because he describes how the emotions that traumatized victims experience are diverse, ranging from anger and desires for revenge, to fantasies of forgiveness, to "detached calm" (Blustein 2018, 236), along with "fear, alienation, distrust, hopelessness, guilt, and shame" and grief (2018, 240, 242). Nevertheless, Blustein (2018, 236) observes that an emotion like anger as a traumatized response to atrocity differs from everyday anger in being helpless and uncontrollable, and "it lacks a definite target and a corrective aim. Moreover, instead of asserting autonomy and empowering the agent, traumatic anger of this sort subverts the victim's autonomy because it lashes out at the wrongdoer in a usually futile attempt by the victim to regain some measure of control over his or her life." For these reasons, Blustein argues that such futile anger must be transformed to be experienced as righteous anger or moral indignation. Presumably, this transformation would involve finding an appropriate target and aim, being controlled, and having a point.

After atrocities, Blustein's main example being genocide, people need to recover agency, especially moral agency. The atrocities in Chile under the Pinochet regime can be understood as a political genocide, a policide or politicide (Harff 2003), comparable to the politicide in Indonesia discussed in chapter 2. Steve J. Stern (2004, 31–32) argues that the political project of Pinochet's government was "policide, an effort to destroy root and branch—permanently—the ways of doing and thinking politics that had come to characterize Chile by the 1960s." One of the greatest moral harms to victims of atrocities, Blustein (2018, 238, 249–50) contends, is to self-respect, self-esteem, and other related capacities, as victims of atrocities feel degraded. Furthermore, personal autonomy, or capacities to self-define and self-legislate, which relies on moral autonomy on Blustein's account, are undermined by the inability to trust others or oneself. He adds that a genocide (such as politicide) harms self-respect in specific ways because it attacks the group *and* individual and aspects of the self that are linked to the practices of the group (2018, 250).[4] In the Chilean dictatorship and the acts of murder, torture, and disappearances, political ideals and values associated with communism and socialism were under attack. Blustein observes that the traumatic experience of being attacked as a collective can bring people together, creating a sense of community; on the other hand, it can also divide them.

To recover from the trauma, in Blustein's (2018, 239) view, victims must be able to "mourn their losses, including loss of livelihoods, friends and loved ones, homes, and prestige, and also, fundamentally, a sense of security in the world and trust in themselves and others." In her account of her own recovery from sexual assault, Susan Brison distinguishes between traumatic memory and narrative memory and explains that the latter transforms the former (Brison 2003, 31; Blustein 2018, 240). Traumatic memories are fragmented and not integrated with other memories, whereas narrative memories are coherent in themselves and in relation to other memories, according to Blustein (2018, 255). However, Brison

(2003, 31) also identifies similarities between the two kinds of memory: "Traumatic memory, like narrative memory, is articulated, selective, even malleable, in spite of the fact that the framing of such memory may not be under the survivor's conscious control." She argues that our traumatic experiences are always influenced by cultural meanings and categories. The transformation of memory is a process that must be effected to recover from trauma, which Blustein (2018, 253–54) sees as recovering cognitive and emotional equilibrium. For Brison (2003, 57), relating our narrative "to caring others who are able to listen" enables that transformation. Another process required is overcoming the feeling of "acute helplessness" and loss of personal autonomy (Ashwin Budden, cited in Blustein 2018, 243–44).

Blustein also examines *collective* processes of recovery from trauma. He accepts that communities may dwell on and obsess over the past in ways that undermine agency, so tempering that approach and adopting an appropriate mourning will be necessary (2018, 257). On a collective level, that can be done through memorialization and commemoration, practices shared with atonement.[5] Both individual and collective processes are aimed at developing effective agency. In the next section, I consider how the film *No* shows that a focus on positive affect in the form of happiness can construct effective agency and resistance, instead of a traumatic focus on remembering suffering.

NO AND HAPPINESS

As I mentioned above, *No* has been criticized for depicting the "No" television campaign unrealistically and not presenting the preceding years of activism (Khazan 2013; Rohter 2013; Peirano 2018). However, I concentrate on the philosophical articulation of resistance that drives the campaign, as depicted in the movie. Director Larraín describes the film as a "strange balance between documentary and fiction," and Bernal, who plays the protagonist, René Saavedra, calls it a "fable" (Rohter 2013) and suggests that it provides "a thorough political analysis of the subject" (Lyttelton 2013). It forms a loose trilogy with Larraín's earlier films *Tony Manero* (2008), and *Post Mortem* (2010), which portray life under Pinochet and the military coup itself respectively, each with different characters. It contrasts strongly with more recent works such as *Jackie* and *Neruda* (both released in 2016), *Ema* (2019), and *Spencer* (2021), which have political elements but are not historically and politically focused.[6]

Robert Wells (2017, 504) analyzes the trilogy along with Larraín's first feature film, *Fuga* (2006), as posttraumatic cinema, focusing on "visualization of trauma, male fantasies, and cultural capital."[7] He allows that the films both act out and contribute to a working through of trauma, partly through implicating the viewers in the trauma (Wells 2017, 516–17). His characterization of posttraumatic film draws on that of Joshua Hirsch, and he notes that *No* both directly and indirectly references the trauma of the Chilean dictatorship through historical footage and through the way the videocamera filming blurs the images (Wells 2017, 514–15). In *Afterimage: Film, Trauma, and the Holocaust*, Hirsch (2004, xi) defines "posttraumatic cinema" as "a cinema that not only represents traumatic historical events, but also attempts to embody and reproduce trauma for the spectator through its form of narration." The trauma is that of experiencing extreme events and being unable to either assimilate them into memory or forget them (2004, 15–16). Thus, posttraumatic films "formally repeat the traumatic structure of the experience of witnessing the events themselves" (2004, 3). They are defined by the attempt to "formally reproduce for the spectator an experience of suddenly seeing the unthinkable" (2004, 19). They use stylistic devices such as unexplained flashbacks (2004, 98) to represent the disruptions to time and memory that traumatic events engender. For Hirsch (2004, 7, 162), Holocaust documentaries and fiction films such as *Night and Fog* (dir. Alain Resnais, 1955), *Shoah* (dir. Claude Lanzmann, 1985), and *Schindler's List* (dir. Steven Spielberg, 1993) play the role of getting the audience to admit the existential significance of the Holocaust by representing its trauma, and they possibly even assist in the process of mourning and healing.[8]

No occupies an unusual position within the films in this book in narrating a period of transition. Larraín originally made a much longer film—four and a half hours—which had much of the history of resistance in it. However, he cut it down to focus on the marketing side, which interested him (Rohter 2013).[9] Here, as is typical in films, a complex history is compressed into a short scene or single character. For example, instead of showing some of the focus groups that led to the positive approach of the "No" campaign, the creatives ask René's housekeeper, Carmen (Elsa Poblete), what she thinks, since she represents the people whom they must convince. She is concerned about preserving her children's employment aspirations and is afraid of change, so she is likely to be a "Yes" voter.

The film concentrates on the month of the political advertising campaign for the plebiscite that follows growing resistance against, and international pressure on, the dictatorship. Its portrayal follows closely the way that the "No" and "Yes" campaigns had only fifteen minutes of screen time each daily to persuade people to vote their way in the referendum, although of course the government-sponsored "Yes" campaign had the rest of the airtime as well, due to its control of television content (Hirmas 1993; Simón 2018, 42–48). The programs, *Franja de Propaganda Electoral* (*Official Space for Electoral Propaganda*), were shown late on weeknights (10:45 p.m.) and at lunchtime (11:45 a.m.) on the weekends. They are made within these restrictions and in that sense follow the "stress on legality" Havel ([1978] 1987, 91) sees as characteristic of the dissidents of post-totalitarianism.

What happens, as the audience sees in the film, is that instead of repeating the trauma in images, as is initially proposed, the creatives turn away from them. René insists that the campaign and programs must focus on positive experiences and on what life would be like without the dictatorship. This change, René argues, is a pragmatic break in the remembrance of atrocities to make way for a future where they can be remembered properly. The Chilean referendum was complicated: there was no distance in time from the traumatic events, so it is understandable that people would want to register their suffering. Like the breaks in continuity of life for African Americans through early death, separation of families, and lack of support for well-being into the future that Du Bois describes, the disappearances and murders in Chile broke kinship bonds that must be reconnected. While Du Bois ([1903] 1996, 12) is concerned with the holistic progress of Americans in "work, culture, liberty," the thread of a cultural narrative of hope is fundamental to understanding the events depicted in *No*. A new narrative must be created to overcome trauma and transform affect from fear and powerlessness to joy and to focus on the future rather than the past, and that narrative must be one that can influence more than half of the Chilean population. The idea is that people might not necessarily feel happiness, but they should focus on a happy future through images of joyful experiences, like dancing, picnics, and a mime artist, all used in the campaign and shown in *No*. These depictions of experiences might not be culturally authentic, as critics in the film observe, but they are like fragments of a possible future happy life.

To explain the context of the referendum shown in *No*, by 1988, Pinochet had been in power since 1973, Chile had not had an election since Salvador Allende's 1970 election, and the opposition campaign had to register people to vote and convince them to vote no. This background is given in a series of titles at the start of the film. Once voters had registered, voting was compulsory; these aspects are not detailed in the film, as it centers on the television programs.[10] While *No* can be seen as promoting the values of the advertising industry or as criticizing modern society, I argue that the film shows how the campaign finds success by concentrating on the philosophical concept of happiness. When the advertising creatives brainstorm ideas for the campaign at a retreat, they arrive at the concept of happiness by thinking of what could not be surpassed, asking, "What's happier than happiness?" The slogan and catchy jingle used in the campaign after that discussion is "Chile, Joy Is Coming," as I mentioned above. The concept involves joy, delight, spring, calm after the storm, a party—anything associated with happiness. For example, René leaves baguettes in a picnic scene the campaign is filming despite protests from his colleagues that baguettes are not typically Chilean, claiming that using the baguettes "works." His idea of happiness is that it is a universal political concept that cannot be argued against, and he presents it in advertising language. The "No" programs also discuss abuse and misery, but they do not make them the focus of the fifteen minutes. They further include interviews with "No" voters and, following interviews with focus groups about the campaign, comedy sketches, as shown in *No*. Wells (2017, 513) implies that the spectacle of the film, with its blending of original and new footage, makes it impossible to conceive of resistance, but I argue that the discourse of happiness *is* a discourse of resistance in this case. To explain how the concept of happiness can function in this way, I consider Aristotle and Sara Ahmed's reflections on happiness.

Aristotle's conception of happiness is distinct from the contemporary idea of happiness. In the *Nicomachean Ethics*, he contends that anything worth pursuing in itself is more complete and more unqualified than anything pursued for the sake of something else. Aristotle concludes,

> Now such a thing is happiness . . . for this we choose always for itself and never for the sake of something else, but honor, pleasure, reason, and every excellence we choose indeed for themselves (for if nothing resulted from them we would still choose each of them), but we choose them also for the sake of happiness, judging that through them we will be happy. Happiness, on the other hand, no one chooses for the sake of these, nor, in general for anything other than itself. (1984, 1097a36–b7)

Aristotle also maintains that happiness is self-sufficient and is thus the end of action.

The advertising campaigners' brainstorming session follows a similar train of thought, although it is not directly based on Aristotle's ideas. In the "No" campaign, happiness is a form of active resistance to the negative emotions of fear and anxiety, and the pressure to support the status quo (fig. 4.1).[11] The happiness of the shows, as recounted in the film, must connect to a future of happiness without referring to an earlier time before the dictatorship, as that could remind people of a period of uncertainty or hardship. Of course, Aristotle (1984, 1098b22–23) is not thinking of the emotion of happiness as such, but flourishing, the well-lived or virtuous life—*eudaimonia*—"as a sort of living and faring well." However, feelings always play a role in our responses to our actions and life experiences. The "No" campaign must use images depicting joy (*alegría*), such as dancing, horseback riding, or countryside picnics—all shown in the film—to evoke that kind of flourishing.[12] The positive programs could be seen as a repression of the traumatic memories, in their turn from a real past to the desire for an imagined future, but that interpretation is not borne out because there is reference to that past.

FIG. 4.1. The "No" campaign considers happiness as their concept. Still from *No*, directed by Pablo Larraín (Participants, Funny Balloons, La Fábula, and Canana, 2012).

Sara Ahmed (2010, 2), in *The Promise of Happiness*, considers what happiness does, why we wish to be associated with happiness, and what happiness is associated with. She contrasts contemporary conceptions of happiness with Aristotle's, as they tend to treat happiness as a means to other ends, like becoming optimistic or altruistic, what she calls the "instrumentalization of happiness" rather than happiness as an end in itself (2010, 10). For Ahmed (2010, 13), happiness involves good feeling, although she believes it is more than that, and "the promise of happiness is what makes certain objects proximate, affecting how the world gathers around us." In other words, happiness brings us into contact with things because we experience a positive affect in relation to them, like the images that the "No" campaign presents. Ahmed (2010, 26) notes that Aristotle's (2010, 29) conception of happiness means that other goods become means toward happiness and suggests that "the very expectation of happiness gives us a specific image of the future." For her, a conception of having the right feelings in relation to the right actions means that the happy and good life "regulates desire" (2010, 37). The programs in *No* are portrayed as providing an image and an idea that is linked to the expectation of happiness. They show a variety of different experiences rather than promoting one single ideal, and they are not closely focused on the virtuous life.

In *No,* the programs are met with skepticism at first, but the film shows that in time more voters are swept up into the enthusiasm. Ahmed (2010, 44) suggests that feelings of happiness or joy are not simply passed around, yet what is passed is a promise of the feeling because "you *share an orientation towards those objects as being good*" (emphasis in the original). The ads appeal to a shared notion of the joy that could be taken in the depicted activities and so encourages them to resist the past regime. The view of happiness Ahmed presents is useful, as she focuses on the futurity of happiness, its promise of something better emerging from the present. She also points to the importance of collectives forming to conceive the possibility of change: "Communities take shape in such moments of suspension, where a 'we' is assembled by being thrown together, acquiring a sense of purpose in throwing the meanings of *this* into question" (2010, 192). *No* shows how a group can be formed to resist, to question the dictatorship, and to become a "we" in challenging the despair of oppression. There is a sense of happiness as contentment or comfort that the idea of saying no also rejects, just as Ahmed suggests that people can revolt against certain demands for happiness. Her view of happiness is of moments: "Moments of happiness create texture, shared impressions: a sense of lightness *in* possibility" (2010, 219). This point is where her view intersects with the ideas in the programs of *No*, as they provide a sense of possibility, of moments, of experiences, and the sense of possibility is enough to evoke resistance.

In contrast to the focus on happiness in the "No" programs, the film has a number of scenes characterizing how the "Yes" campaign struggles with how to present Pinochet: Should he be in uniform or civilian clothes? Eventually they decide on civilian clothes as a sign of democracy and progress, which proves to be a mistake: for the first time, people see him as able to be defeated (International Commission of the Latin American Studies Association 1989, 6). They begin by combining an emphasis on economic success (using the slogan "Chile—a winning country") with a scare campaign against "No" votes and end up parodying the "No" programs with scenes such as horseback riders carrying Soviet flags and dancers wearing balaclavas. The "Yes" campaign also focuses strongly on the past: instead of arguing that it would be good to extend Pinochet's government, they warn that economic gains would be lost and chaos would ensue with a return to the "Popular Unity" coalition.[13] In that way, they associate voting "Yes" with the traumatic images René rejects for the "No" campaign. The optimistic note of the "No" programs' shots of happy groups can also be seen as creating a narrative whereby the past can be connected to the future, and the individual linked to their community, so in that respect they involve the remaking of the self that Brison recommends.

NO AND THE TRANSFORMATION OF THE SELF

The complexity of the protagonist René and how he becomes drawn into the campaign needs to be explored to comprehend the link between trauma and resistance in *No*. I argue that the film's narrative should be interpreted as a transformative one where René's character and actions both prompt and track the main elements of happiness as a form of resistance. By contrast, reviews of the film have referred to René as a sellout (Felperin 2012), apolitical (Toledo 2013; Howe 2015), cynical and unscrupulous (Matheou 2013), neoliberal (Qandt 2016), showing "political apathy" (Dzero 2015, 123), being "self-regarding" (Dargis 2013) or indifferent to democratic ideals (Dzero 2015, 130), and so on. Wells (2017, 514) claims that the approach of the campaign "is not meant to be celebrated, however, but rather exposed as another male fantasy that taps into and dominates the collective fantasies of others." He further argues that "*No* visualizes how traumas were made invisible, and how this was done in order to 'win' and thereby construct a pacifying, neutralizing, amnesiac 'consensus' for the future" (2017, 515). Other critics decry the focus on a "single heroic individual" as simplifying and distorting the campaign (cited in Jung 2015, 119).[14] Irina Dzero (2015, 124), for example, thinks of René as passive and unconcerned with democracy, noting that he does not try to defend himself when one of the opposition coalition members accuses him of silencing what really happened. Likewise, she sees him as equally enthused about all his projects, as I discuss below.

However, could René's seeming apoliticism itself, as portrayed by Bernal, be a feature of traumatization, like the "detached calm" Blustein (2018, 236) describes as a consequence of subjection to atrocities? In fact, as the audience is made aware of, René is no stranger to trauma, since his father was sent into exile when Pinochet took over Chile. Nevertheless, his character is an outsider precisely because of that exile, and his advertising profession is seen as collusive with the regime by the other characters, and that may help explain his willingness to focus on a positive message rather than on showing representations of the trauma.[15] Unlike the protagonists of *Tony Manero* and *Post Mortem*, but like Adi Rukun and Barbara, he is extremely good at his occupation and lives in the truth in relation to it in his own way, by treating it with seriousness. René is approached by socialist leader José Tomás Urrutia (Luis Gnecco) for the campaign, and he is initially skeptical, like many Chileans were, arguing that the referendum will be "completely fixed." They want René to give an external opinion, since he does not want to direct the campaign, but he begins to get involved and then agrees to run it. René conflicts with his boss, Lucho Guzmán (Alfredo Castro), when he tells him that the Americans are with the "No," while Lucho claims the Americans will remain with Pinochet and works for the "Yes" campaign.

One aspect of trauma can be a reduced affect, first as a self-protection from a violent regime, and second as a self-protection from exposure to emotional pain. Barbara's quiet watchfulness is a related example. Blunted affect, or emotional numbing and lack of expression of emotion, especially positive emotions, is one symptom of posttraumatic stress disorder (Herman 1992, 42; Kashdan, Elhai, and Frueh 2007). This aspect of trauma is subtly represented in the film through Bernal's performance. In his review of the film, Omer M. Mozaffar (2013) observes that René "speaks in whispers. He rarely smiles." He clearly wants to get back together with his former partner Verónica (Antonia Zegers), but when he sees her with another man, he says and does nothing. Only by noticing his eyes, thanks to Bernal's superb acting, can a viewer see how much he is suffering. Demetrios Matheou (2013, 101) acknowledges that René may have "chosen apathy as an escape from a painful past" but suggests that his character is ambiguous and his motivations not clear—perhaps he just loved the challenge of the campaign (Dargis 2013). Larraín (2012) himself claims that René "is in a deep existential conflict, in doubt about his job and his partner."[16] There is a mystery about his motivations that leads to reflection on the questions about the nature of resistance that arise.

Images of trauma are initially filmed for the "No" campaign, and that is what René rejects. The leftist strategists argue that they want to open people's eyes, raise awareness. He says to them, "Do you want to win?" and "Do you think you can win?" and they say no to the second question, but they believe the traumatic images should be shown. Their memory of that trauma is clear and detailed, and quickly shown in a short film through images of tanks, soldiers with guns, and statistics about torture, exile, executions, and the disappeared. However, the affect behind those ads could be seen as the pointless rage that Blustein outlines. The socialist coalition members who despise René could have been lost in endless squabbles, as the "Yes" campaign predicts in *No*, if he had not taken over the campaign. Their reluctance to take the vote seriously and belief that a "No" result will not be honored, shown in a crucial scene, links back to a feeling of helplessness as well as a distrust of the authorities (Blustein 2018, 243, 245). All the members of the Chilean opposition felt this way, at least initially, due to the success of the previous referendum on a new constitution in 1980, and the film represents the coming together of all the parties, including socialists and ultimately the communists as well.

However, the very idea of a "No," like that in the campaign, can be empowering. As part of her recovery from the trauma of being attacked, Brison (2003, 14) took part in self-defense classes where the women in the class had to yell "No!," something that was difficult for them to do. She connects this "no" with resistance, maintaining that "The 'no' of resistance is not the 'no' of denial. It is the 'no' of acknowledgment of what happened and refusal to let it happen again" (2003, 64). Of course, the referendum vote could have been framed the other way, but it was framed as "Yes" for a continuation of the regime, presumably on the assumption that was likely to be the more triumphant approach. Likewise, Maurice Blanchot finds refusal to be a powerful political action. He writes, "Those who refuse and who are bound by the force of refusal know that they are not yet together. The time of common affirmation is precisely what has been taken away from them. What they are left with is the irreducible refusal, the friendship of this sure, unshakable, rigorous No that unites them and determines their solidarity" (2010, 7). It is the coming together of those who refuse.

Thus, it is at this level of solidarity with "No"—a fundamental refusal of the dictatorship and Pinochet—that René does his work. Despite intimidation *and* an inducement to withdraw (an offer of partnership) from his boss Lucho who is working for the "Yes" campaign, René continues with the "No" campaign. As noted, Dzero (2015, 122) argues that René does not believe in democracy or that his motives are at best unclear. She contrasts the film unfavorably to Antonio Skármeta's play *El plebiscito*, which she contends shows a genuine commitment to democracy, unlike *No*. Dzero also argues that working on the campaign had no transformative impact on René and that his approach to the campaign is interchangeable with his work on an ad for a soft drink called Free and a soap opera, *Bellas y audaces* (*Beautiful and Bold*), both of which are real. She contends that René uses the same pitch—"What you are going to see now is in line with the current social context. . . . Today, Chile thinks about its future"—for the soda branded Free, for the "No" campaign, and for the serial, thus showing that he is completely cynical about the campaign (Dzero 2015, 127).[17] This reading seems simplistic, as René's character is more complex and motivated in complex ways. The hero's journey narrative of departure, initiation into an adventure, and return, is closer in its broad outlines to the structure of the film (Vogler 2007). Furthermore, the film shows René to be concerned with the principles at stake, since he discusses the importance of the concept of happiness to the political future. Moreover, while René uses the same introduction about the social context and the future in Chile, each time it has a different meaning—the introduction to the Free cola in Pinochet's regime is ironic, in the campaign for change it is earnest, and then for the soap opera it is a kind of celebration of success, tempered with some ambivalence, as René is awkward and hesitant in the final presentation.[18] These differences can be understood because the audience sees René change over the course of the film.

Early in the campaign, René's estranged partner, Verónica, says that the ads are "a copy of a copy of a copy of a copy of a copy," an obvious and hyperbolic reference to Plato's well-known argument in *The Republic* that art is a copy of an object that itself is a copy of its form or idea (Plato 1989, 596e-602c). She cannot see why René would work to validate Pinochet's referendum, but for him it is there to be won. But later Verónica changes her mind, saying, "You are hitting the old man hard," and her new boyfriend is wearing the campaign's signature rainbow T-shirt. Similarly, René clearly changes as the campaign progresses, in contrast to Dzero's (2015, 122, 127) claim that "Larraín and Peirano [Pedro, scriptwriter] insist that the campaign has no impact on him" and has "no transformative or educational impact on the adman." Caetlin Benson-Allott (2013, 61) also sees in René a "growing disillusionment with his vacuous profession" rather than a political change, a view repeated by Fabrizio Cilento (2015). However, while early on René does not intervene to help Verónica when she is beaten at the police station, later he is drawn in to help her at the demonstration and he is kicked in the stomach and thrown to the ground.[19] Furthermore, he accepts the abuse painted in red on his window ("Homeland-peddling Marxist"), being followed, and threatened as a result of his work for the campaign (fig. 4.2).[20]

FIG. 4.2. Graffiti on René's house. Still from *No*, directed by Pablo Larraín (Participants, Funny Balloons, La Fábula, and Canana, 2012).

René's transformation is linked to a collective transformation that is expressed in the film's style. Dzero analyzes the film as a simulacrum, where there is no concern about the distinction between the media images and reality, expressed by René's setup of a group enjoying a picnic, including baguettes, and saying, "It works" (2015, 129–30). However, this interpretation seems not to take seriously enough the way the film draws attention to its artifice at certain points, as Larraín casts real figures from the campaign, with their younger versions in the documentary footage, such as Patricio Aylwin, Chilean president after Pinochet, playing an elderly politician (Dzero 2015, 129; Larraín 2012). For Larraín (2012), the actor's body "returns to where it once was. It returns, returns, and that's the work of memory. It's beautiful." He sees these roles as doing some of the work of recovery from trauma, and as helping others to avoid making the same mistakes. The presence of the individuals both evokes their place in the past and reminds viewers of how things have changed.

Moreover, Larraín immerses the audience in the narrative and reflects the period by filming on old videotape on an Ikegama camera so that the archival film footage used and the new film blend together, and uses the squarer Academy ratio (1.40:1) to evoke the past (Lyttelton 2013). This ratio, in contrast to the narrower ones used for the grimmer films, can signify an opening up of the society through collective resistance. *No* never loses sight of the distinction between fact and fiction, even if the old footage is not immediately distinguishable by color and image quality. Writers find the bleeding and blurred colors and images to signify trauma or moral and political ambiguity (Wells 2017, 515; Benson-Allott 2013, 62–63).[21] Wells notes that these references could be taken as a homage to video resistance in Chile and to Aylwin's Concertación de Partidos por la Democracia (Coalition of Parties for Democracy), a coalition of center-left political parties that governed Chile from 1990 to 2010.[22] The coalition is represented by the rainbow symbol that appears throughout the film in the show, posters, and T-shirts for the campaign, predating the global use of that flag to represent LGBTIQ struggles. However, Wells (2017, 514) concludes that "these tributes are oblique, or better said, bleak." Yet these tributes to collective resistance in the form of original and new video footage and their significance would be obvious to a Chilean audience, much like some of the intertextual references in *Barbara*.

It is significant to the film (and history) that the campaign was a success, with 54.7 percent of Chileans voting "No." At the beginning, most people were afraid to vote and afraid of a return to socialism. People were skeptical about whether the vote would be accepted, yet they had to support the vote in the hope that it would be accepted. What is crucial to the success of the "No" campaign are not just the shifts to positivity and to the future, but also the shift from individual suffering to collective defiance, which the ads contribute to as depicted in the film. Instead of looking at the trauma and the negative effects as those of an individual, the campaign focuses on the *shared* capacity for happiness, presented in the shots of groups enjoying the imagined future after "No" wins.[23]

Nevertheless, the film's conclusion is ambiguous, since René leaves the celebration for the plebiscite win with his son, and commentators have remarked on his "muted response," taken as a sign of apathy or quietism (Wells 2017, 515; Benson-Allott 2013, 61). However, an alternative interpretation is that rather than depicting cynicism about democracy, the film's ending depicts the ambiguity and ambivalence of political change.[24] The theme of ambiguity is central to the following chapter, where I consider Simone de Beauvoir's (1997) concept of ambiguity in relation to the moral decision-making of the couple in *Nader and Simin, a Separation*. Here her reflections on our relation to the future are relevant, as she notes that we have a limited hold on the future (1997, 119) and while we aim at concrete goals with longer-term ends in mind, others "will have to live its joys and sorrows" (1997, 128). Larraín dramatizes the ambiguity that carries into the future through René's muted response.

Any transition from a dictatorship to a democracy is bound to be multifaceted and have both positive and negative aspects, so the events of the transition are unlikely to support a one-sided reading. The Chilean transition is variously described as "a beautiful, almost mystic moment of national euphoria, a unique time of people collaborating" (Cronovich

2016, 173–74) or the beginning of the mediatization of Chilean politics (Simón 2018, 67–71). Mediatization often refers to the media becoming autonomous from politics and yet dominating it, whereas Harry L. Simón Salazar (2018) contends that politics and media/marketing became fused in the Chilean case. One of the negative aspects of post-Pinochet Chile was the impunity of the Chilean killers, in the main, which Larraín sees as an open wound (Larraín, in Lyttelton 2013), although there have been trials of perpetrators in recent years and recovery of some of the bodies of the disappeared in more recent years (Wadi 2022). He notes that the ending is "the wonderful thing, but there's a bitter taste at the same time" because "we kept some of the 'Yes' in our system, in our logic" (Lyttelton 2013; Larraín 2012). By this "Yes" Larraín means the economic logic of capitalism and neoliberalism, which includes the use of advertising to influence people's feelings and behavior. Seeing René skateboarding through a city street toward the end of the film gives an impression of joy, although Mozaffar (2013) suggests it is a scene of loneliness. In the final scene, he is back at the advertising agency working on the soap opera, an ambivalent presentation on how some things will stay the same even after the switch to democracy. Furthermore, in Chile, democracy did not begin overnight after the plebiscite, as the civic-military rule continued for another eighteen months.

By contrast, there are also signs of hope beyond the winning of the plebiscite in the film. Verónica and René are united in their care and concern for their son, Simón (Pascal Montero), and to some extent became united in their desire for the "No" case to win. Unlike the generations of Black Americans who suffered under slavery and successive forms of oppression, Chileans in the film are the first generation, although a new generation was starting to grow up under the dictatorship. René's son in the film is the future, representing those to whom the promise of happiness is held out. He is only eight and would have known nothing but the regime, as even a fifteen-year-old would. Will his generation suffer less trauma? The film *No* frames the relation between the generations differently from the other two films in the trilogy. *Tony Manero*, set during the civic-military dictatorship, concerns an aging Raúl, a dancer who kills with impunity under the cover of the murderous regime and is also trying to win a *Saturday Night Fever* (dir. John Badham, 1977) Tony Manero look-alike context. He stymies the ambitions of the much younger Goyo, also interested in the same contest, by spoiling his Tony Manero suit. Similarly, in *Post Mortem*, concerning the military takeover, the older Mario, a pathologist's assistant, is rapidly corrupted by his exposure to the bodies of those murdered in the coup at the hospital where he works. Rejected by his young neighbor Nancy, whom he had been obsessed with, he murders her and her boyfriend. But in *No*, René's youth and even childlikeness is stressed, as he goes skateboarding, playing with train sets, and looking after and engaging with his son. Wells (2017, 514) suggests that he is petulant because of these activities and Mozaffar (2013) that he is "a soft-spoken kid" with "an empty life of toys and opulence." However, while these presentations could be seen as mocking, in the context of the trilogy, it also implies that in postdictatorship Chile, youth and the next generations will have a chance.

CONCLUSION

The possibility of transforming trauma by altering its relation to time and by creating a new narrative that links the past and future—retemporalizing and detranslating—is affirmed by writers on trauma such as McCartney, Du Bois, Blustein, and Brison. *No* explores this possibility of a retemporalizing and detranslating shift to a conception of collective happiness in the future rather than simply focusing on discussions of the atrocities and trauma of the past and present in the 1988 Chilean plebiscite campaign. Larraín's mix of archival and new footage made on old film and cameras, and the use of individuals from the earlier period playing roles in the film, provide an enactment and embodiment of place and time that enable a connection to be drawn between the past and present. The film's depiction of the campaign and the scholarly responses to it reflect the debates that continue in Chile concerning the Pinochet regime and the postdictatorship period. In this chapter I have focused on the positive philosophical elements of *No* and how they contribute to our understanding of everyday resistance, yet the film, the memories of the campaign, and subsequent developments are all highly contested in Chile and beyond. In addition, the role of television in the "No" campaign as a site of resistance is itself challenged by those who stress the prior grassroots activism. However, the highlighting of happiness in the film and the campaign is itself a form of resistance to oppression in an authoritarian regime and the perpetrators of atrocities as it shifts our affects away from fear, from desire for material things, and even from comfort bought at the cost of democracy and the suffering of others. In the face of the regime, this focus stands out in the way that Havel argued the pursuit of the essential values of life must. *No* also shows how happiness brings together a variety of different political actors in a refusal of dictatorship, a refusal to let the trauma continue. The transformation of René's character in the film as he becomes more engrossed in the campaign shows the importance of sharing in collective resistance. While the "No" campaign in the film and its success cannot be imitated, as it depends on a specific location (Chile) at a specific time (around the plebiscite), the temporal, affective, and pluralistic approach to resistance is one that can inspire. In the next chapter I consider resistance that in a sense accepts that regime change is not an alternative, in contemporary Iran.

[CHAPTER FIVE]

A Separation

Ethical Ambiguity

Nader and Simin, a Separation (dir. Asghar Farhadi, 2011) in some ways returns to the subject matter of *Barbara*: the decision of whether to stay and make the best of things in an authoritarian regime, or to leave. But there are two notable differences. The first is that there is some sense in which the East German regime was finite and would come to an end and both leaving and staying put pressure on the regime. The second is that in *Barbara* a single protagonist struggles with a decision that to a great extent is represented symbolically, whereas in *A Separation*, two central characters explicitly have the philosophical debate with each other.

A Separation addresses the problem of how to live ethically in a society that puts pressure on that possibility.[1] Using the genre or mode of melodrama, the film portrays how the two protagonists, a married couple, take different approaches and come to different ethical conclusions in facing that difficulty. Their resistance is not a conscious resistance to try to change society but a resistance through following their principles, creating in different ways a parallel to their political context. One, Nader (Peyman Moadi), spouse, father, and son, struggles to maintain his personal standards despite the consequences, although he also makes compromises to adjust to the society's restrictions. The other, Simin (Leila Hatami), spouse, mother, and daughter-in-law, proposes to act pragmatically, to compromise from the beginning, and ultimately to withdraw or "exit" to escape the regime. Both are good, caring people who confront the ambiguity of existence in general and in an authoritarian system. They face a specific kind of ethical loss from their decisions: in this case, for Nader and Simin it is the loss of each other and, for one of them (the audience is not told which one), their eleven-year-old daughter, Termeh (Sarina Farhadi, the director's daughter). Their decision is further complicated when Nader is accused of causing the miscarriage of the woman who comes to care for his father, and then his ensuing attempts to clear his name, while the woman's husband becomes increasingly threatening to the family.

A Separation also evokes the emotions felt in response to these predicaments. In the film, ethics, religion, and social and political context collide to entangle the characters in a web of both perceived and felt guilt and shame that makes any resistance difficult. Shame is invoked as pressure to capitulate to the external norms and rejected by many of the characters, yet guilt is felt for small breaches of internal ethical standards by some of them. The different ethical paths taken by Nader and Simin lead to an even further separation, implying that the two ethical approaches to the ambiguity of their situation and the kind of resistance engaged in cannot be reconciled.

In the chapter, I explicate the distinctive way that *A Separation* exposes the ambiguity of ethical questions, as Simone de Beauvoir outlines in *The Ethics of Ambiguity*, an ambiguity that is heightened by the strains of life in an authoritarian state such as contemporary theocratic Iran.[2] Her sense of ambiguity encompasses our ambiguity as self-conscious and physical beings, between past, present, and future, as individuals and part of collectives, and as referring to ethical situations where choices themselves are ambiguous (1997, 7). Her approach to living in the truth in Havel's sense is to accept ambiguity. Of this ambiguity, Beauvoir (1997, 9) writes, "Since we do not succeed in fleeing it, let us therefore try to look the truth in the face. Let us try to assume our fundamental ambiguity. It is in the knowledge of the genuine conditions of our life that we must draw our strength to live and our reason for acting." For her, ambiguity implies that the meaning of existence "is never fixed, that it must be constantly won" (1997, 9, 129). Beauvoir outlines an ethics that follows from the assumption of ambiguity, a series of attitudes we might take to our situation, and a series of antinomies in action. Her text, written after the ethical complexities of the Nazi occupation of France, and the French resistance to that occupation, has insight into the difficulty of making ethical decisions when constrained by life under an authoritarian regime. Given the ambiguity of these situations, even when trying to make the right choice—say, by choosing the lesser evil, sacrificing oneself, or focusing on opposing one form of oppression over another—we will feel the ethical loss or remainder, often experienced in the form of regret or even despair or anguish (Beauvoir 1997, 89, 108–9, 150).[3] Beauvoir's account of ethics can contribute to an understanding of resistance, and interpreting *A Separation* can extend and challenge her insights.

Furthermore, Beauvoir's approach to philosophical and literary writing are relevant for thinking about how to interpret and question a film.

Christine Daigle and Louise Renée (2015, 77) argue that Beauvoir's own writing is a kind of performance, like a novel or film, and that *The Ethics of Ambiguity* performs ethical ambiguity in a way that makes us feel it. In their view, ambiguity is performed through articulating the paradoxes of the human condition, and the series of character types or attitudes and the way they shade into each other (2015, 78). Thus, Beauvoir's writing of ethics is open to the kind of testing of ideas concerning resistance that a film like *A Separation* can undertake through presenting the different perspectives of the characters.

The film does not try to resolve the ethical ambiguities depicted, but shows how they can lead to what appear to be fundamentally opposed positions and different forms of resistance for protagonists reflecting with care on the situation. First, I discuss the relationship between the genres and modes of the film and ethical ambiguity about resistance, then show how that ambiguity emerges in the ethical conflicts of the film, and consider the relation between ambiguity and guilt to explore how the film portrays the exaggeration of ethical ambiguity and the resultant conflicting decisions about how to resist in an authoritarian society.

BEAUVOIR'S AMBIGUOUS AMBIGUITY

Beauvoir (1997, 7) sees our ambiguous condition as tragic because we experience the fundamental ambivalence between being a consciousness and an object, between existing in time and being aware of a sense of existence that is beyond time, and between the life of an individual and a member of a collective. Other ways she describes these ambiguities are as that "of my solitude and my bond with the world, of my freedom and my servitude, of the insignificance and the sovereign importance" of each and every person (1997, 9). Yet another sense of ambiguity appears in our wanting to be an absolute being, a project that cannot be fulfilled (1997, 13). All these features of ambiguity affect our capacity to make choices and contribute to a sense of tragedy in those choices. While Beauvoir (1997, 9) supports the view that human beings are supreme ends, the demands of action mean that we are often compelled to treat each other as means.

Her account is that philosophical tradition, prior to existentialism, tried to evade or reduce the ambiguity of human existence, whereas we should "assume" it or take it up, by accepting the tensions and failures of ambiguity. In doing so, we have to know whether we want "to live and under what conditions" (Beauvoir 1997, 15). Taking these ambiguities seriously is the beginning of ethics, of trying to formulate what values to support through our actions. More crucial than defining ourselves in absolute terms or even succeeding in our goals is disclosing being through "a perpetual tension to keep being at a certain distance, to tear oneself from the world, and to assert oneself as a freedom" (1997, 24). Beauvoir's thinking of ambiguity can be linked to Havel's concept of living in the truth; indeed, their views have a common source in the work of Søren Kierkegaard. For her, we can live in the truth only insofar as we recognize and assume our own ambiguity and acknowledge that ethical and political decisions reflect that ambiguity. The ethical wish and the wish for freedom are one for Beauvoir, and freedom itself is a feature of our ambiguous existence and can be realized only in action. Unlike many of our other attitudes toward ambiguity, as I discuss further below, Beauvoir (1997, 68) finds the attitude of critical thought one that assumes that ambiguity. For her, "critical thought attempts to militate everywhere against all aspects of the serious but without foundering in the anguish of pure negation" (1997, 68). Such a person has independence of mind, and searches for truth in the ambiguity of their situation, although there is a danger of falling into the trap of the "serious," or taking their judgment as absolute and not realizing its subjectivity.

In *The Ethics of Ambiguity*, Beauvoir (1997, 129) carefully distinguishes absurdity from other concepts it might be confused with, such as Albert Camus's idea of absurdity (although she does not use his name), which she sees as denying that existence "can ever be given a meaning" rather than the search for meaning that is involved in the recognition of ambiguity. In spite of failure and what she calls "le scandale," the antinomies of action that ambiguity entails, we still have to act. Freedom itself is ambiguous and always implies violence that could be invoked to affirm freedom, but because we do not have pregiven justifications for our actions, we have to invent an "original solution" to ethical problems (1997, 142). The method Beauvoir (1997, 152) proposes for choosing one's actions in the light of the ambiguity of existence is to confront "the values realized with the values aimed at, and the meaning of the act with its content." Her treatment of specific ethical problems in relation to the problems raised by *A Separation* and its cinematic examination of ethical ambiguity sheds light on the different paths of resistance.

AMBIGUITY AND GENRES

One of the directors of what is known as the new Iranian cinema, which dates from the late 1980s and focuses on art cinema, Farhadi has established a distinctive oeuvre over years, beginning with his first feature, *Dancing in the Dust* (2003).[4] *A Separation* is the most complex of his films in its plotting, its themes, and its mix of genres, including his later films *The Past* (2013), *The Salesman* (2016), *Everybody Knows* (2018), and *A Hero* (2021).[5] His work evolves from his earlier films, which focused on working-class Iranians, to the different milieu of the urban middle class, who feel doubt about the justification for their actions. This doubt reaches a high point in *A Separation* as the protagonists doubt both themselves and each other as they try to deal with a number of complex problems that pit the different individuals and classes against each other, and lead to opposing conclusions. Simin is seeking a divorce from Nader so she can go abroad. Her reasons for this aim are kept vague, but one clear reason is to provide a better life for her daughter. Thus, we can see her resistance as "exit" or escape from the system. Many thousands of Iranians, especially educated Iranians, leave Iran each year in what can be called a "brain drain" for the country (Mahmoudi 2021) that ultimately has political effects. By contrast, Nader insists on staying to care for his elderly father (Ali-Asghar Shahbaz), representing the values of care and duty, which provide a reason to work within the system, as in *Barbara*. His resistance is very subtle, but if amplified, such care could be powerful too.

The film, like Farhadi's other films, such as *Fireworks Wednesday* (2006), *About Elly* (2010), *The Past*, *The Salesman*, and *Everybody Knows*, is structured like a gripping detective film with a central mystery that is intriguing and partly drives the narrative.[6] In this case, the film is not so much a whodunit as a "Did he do it?" Farhadi wants the audience to play the detective role rather than inserting a detective character into the narrative. The various investigators in the film itself seem quite bored and unconcerned about the outcome. In an interview, Farhadi comments that he creates a film where the audience has to imagine what they cannot see, leaving a free space between the lines in the film for this aspect of the imagination.[7] *A Separation* uses this technique extensively through its puzzle-like structure. The audience also has to think back to and remember earlier scenes to make sense of what is going on and to solve some of the film's mysteries, as they are not all explicitly elucidated. Reflecting Farhadi's background in theater, the film is strongly concentrated in dialogue, character development, action, and intricate plot twists that are all philosophically significant.

Due to these elements, the third genre that the film straddles is that of melodrama, as the conflicts within and between the families carry a weighty emotional effect. Melodrama has often been seen in film studies as a genre of mass entertainment (Gledhill 1987, 5). However, in Linda

Williams's (1998, 42) reconsideration of melodrama, she shifts from the concept of melodrama as genre to thinking of the melodramatic *mode* of films "that move us to pathos for protagonists beset by forces more powerful than they and who are perceived as victims." Her focus is on American films such as *Way Down East* (dir. D. W. Griffith, 1920), *Stella Dallas* (dir. King Vidor, 1937), and *Schindler's List* (dir. Steven Spielberg, 1993), and it is worthwhile to consider the transformation of melodrama in an Iranian context, as well as to reflect that while Nader and Simin are victims in many ways, they are always acting, always choosing, making their own ethical judgments even if the choices available to them are limited in certain respects. The argument Williams makes is that although the spectator is emotionally moved in melodrama, they retain the capacity to think, and to think critically about the situation of the protagonists. Writing about the role of emotions in long-form melodramatic narratives, E. Deirdre Pribram (2018, 251) concludes that "melodramatic modes of storytelling, grounded in emotions and felt recognition—involving us in perceptions of how we do, might, or ought to feel things—enable us to connect with and understand the narrative and social worlds we occupy." Farhadi's use of free space for the spectator's imagination as well as the need for the viewer's knowledge and memory of the elements required to piece together what has gone on heightens this critical capacity to reflect on our emotions and the emotions portrayed. The film's use of the different views of Nader and Simin also enables a critical perspective, one that ultimately does not have to involve taking sides with either of them.

Following Christine Gledhill (1987, 38), Williams contends that melodrama is always based on realistic contemporary social problems. The most obvious of these in *A Separation* are conflict in marriage, how to care for an elderly parent without state support, and whether to continue to live within an authoritarian regime. Yet it is not an "issues" film about individuals in that the drama takes place within a specific cultural and political structure that creates many of the problems and limits the possible solutions to them.[8] One of the noteworthy features of this film is that the family drama is so engrossing one could almost forget or not realize that fundamental issues about resistance are being thematized.

A further aspect of the melodramatic mode Williams (1998, 55) emphasizes is the search for "moral legibility," "the achievement of a felt good, the merger—perhaps even the compromise—of morality and feeling." This search for the good in *A Separation* is one that appears most strongly in Nader and Simin's struggle to do what they believe is right, even though social forces seem to be arrayed against them. This aspect is clear once we realize that the conflict between them is not one between moral rightness and wrongness, but an ambiguous ethical situation. *A Separation* is more complex and subtler than many of the melodramas that Williams describes: for instance, Farhadi avoids presenting a Manichean view of good and evil (1998, 77), and it is not clear who is the victim, at least in contrast to a villain. As David Edelstein (2012) observes in his review of the film, "What makes it so good is that no one is bad." It is this moral intricacy that gives the film its philosophical richness and power. Taraneh Dadar (2014, 224), discussing *About Elly*, also notes this feature of Farhadi's work, arguing that his nuanced approach "undermines the moral legibility typically associated with the melodramatic mode" and that he perfected it in *A Separation*. She follows Gledhill and Williams in treating melodrama as a "mode of expression . . . rather than a distinctive genre" (2014, 226). While the melodramatic mode is thought to contain direct moral judgments, Dadar notes that ultimately *About Elly* remains quite ineffable and evasive. Niklaus Reichle (2014, 68) observes that Farhadi's practice of omitting key events from the screen is typically melodramatic and serves to make "the spectator dependent on the narrations of the different characters," and such omissions are relevant to the other genres of *A Separation*. He also contends that the variety of moral perspectives that Farhadi presents in his films as a result is one reason his films have not been banned in Iran. The mixing of genres and the mode of melodrama contributes to the film's ethical complexity.

Moreover, the film's direction underscores the ethical ambiguity that Nader and Simin are contending with, as well as different forms of separation.[9] Many scenes in the film are shot through glass doors and windows, often frosted or otherwise obscured, in their flat, at the school, the bank, the law offices, courtrooms, and even car windows, so the viewer experiences the characters as trying to understand their world, but always finding a barrier between them and the world and others. The separation of the characters makes their claims ambiguous as well: Can they see through the glass? Can they hear through it? It seems that they sense only ambiguously, and this possibility of overhearing is central to the film's puzzle. Also crucial to the mood Farhadi creates is the very limited use of music combined with ambient sounds that are used to evoke atmosphere instead, for example the sound of the photocopier used to copy travel documents over the opening titles.[10] This use of ambient sound, which recalls its similar use in *Barbara*, contributes to the audience's sense of being there, while the film's narrative ellipses of some of the crucial incidents adds to a feeling of the events occurring elsewhere as well as creating suspense.

The characters, Nader and Simin, are driven to act against strongly held principles to protect each other and their father and daughter. But do they still "exact a perpetual contestation of the means by the end and the end by the means," as Beauvoir (1997, 155) argues we should?[11] As I show in more detail below, she sees means and ends as inseparably linked, ethically speaking: "One may say that in cases where the content of the action falsifies its meaning, one must modify not the meaning, which is here willed absolutely, but the content itself; however, it is impossible to determine this relationship between meaning and content abstractly and universally: there must be a trial and decision in each case" (1997, 134). Farhadi creates a very tightly structured and complex narrative to challenge a conventional understanding of Nader and Simin as in conflict because they are hostile to each other, and to question identification or side-taking with the man's or woman's point of view, although it is tempting to. This complexity also means that neither form of resistance is necessarily endorsed against the other. In the next section the narrative of the ethical conflict of the film is reconstructed, as that is necessary to articulate the ethical ambiguities concerning resistance that are exposed.

AMBIGUITY AND ETHICAL CONFLICT

In the first scene of the film, shot from the point of view of a judge, Simin and, to some extent, Nader are trying to persuade him to allow them to have a divorce. As Farhadi points out, this opening scene of the film is influenced by Ingmar Bergman's *Scenes from a Marriage* (1973), since the shot only shows Nader and Simin and not the judge they are talking to, just as in Bergman's film the couple is shot in strong close-ups. His intention is to create a documentary-style effect in that scene and throughout the film, by attempting to efface the very tightly composed script and his imprint as director (Special Features: *A Separation*, 2011). Simin seeks a divorce because she wishes to leave Iran, while Nader is set on staying, as he has to look after his aged father, who is elderly and unwell with Alzheimer's.[12] They have the visa to leave, and it will expire in forty days, a situation dramatized by the shots of passports and other documents being photocopied. However, the judge does not conclude that they have grounds for a divorce, so they agree to separate instead, and Simin moves out of their flat to live with her parents, perhaps only as a temporary measure. Termeh, their daughter, stays with her father and grandfather. The conflict between the couple here partly concerns the nature of ethical obligations. Simin believes they should leave Iran because of "the conditions," which she does not specify. For her, leaving together as a family would better fulfill their duties to each other and their daughter.

However, Nader believes his obligations to his father are more fundamental or at least as important, so his ethical judgment is that he should stay in Tehran. When Simin says to Nader, "He doesn't remember who you are," Nader replies, "But I remember that he is my father." This relationship of obligation to his father continues regardless of whether his father is aware of it. Furthermore, to some extent Nader's father is aware of his situation, as the film shows by the way he clings to Simin and his distress after she leaves. A further complication is that Nader will not give Simin the permission that she needs to take Termeh abroad with her, so she would have to exit alone.

This is the context in which the film's central conflict concerning how to resist the strictures and challenges of their society unfolds. Nader works in a bank, so he cannot stay home with his father, and because Simin, an English teacher, is now living with her parents (supposedly only for two weeks), Nader needs someone to help him look after the flat and his father. He engages a woman, Razieh (Sareh Bayat), introduced by a family friend, Azam (Sohibanoo Zolqadr), to look after his father while he is at work. She comes with her small daughter, Somayeh (first-time actor Kimia Hosseini). Somayeh is a witness to what goes on, and a co-conspirator at times with both her mother and Nader. She makes a pair with Termeh, Nader and Simin's daughter, and their child's perspective contrasts with and provides a silent critical commentary on that of the adults.[13]

In addition to the conflict between Nader and Simin over their duty are the class and religious conflicts set up between them and Razieh and her husband Hojjat (Saahab Hosseini). Razieh is a devout person, and a religious question arises on the first day she is employed at the flat and needs to change the father's soaked clothes.[14] After unsuccessfully asking Simin for help, Razieh rings a religious hotline on a number she keeps in a notebook to find out whether she is permitted to change him, and she receives an affirmative answer. Somayeh says, "I won't tell Dad," revealing the conflicts that can emerge from different interpretations of religious obligations. Razieh's job working in a home where a man lives without his wife is itself a secret from Hojjat. After the first day, she decides the job is too difficult and clashes with her religious beliefs and her duty to him.

A further layer of conflict, highlighting the ethical pressure on the protagonists, is introduced through this connection with Hojjat, an out-of-work and indebted shoemaker. Razieh asks Nader to employ Hojjat instead, and he agrees, but she has to return when Hojjat is held in jail by his creditors. On the third day of her employment, Nader and Termeh come home early to find Nader's father on the floor, as Razieh tied him to the bed while she left on an errand. He is seriously harmed by this abandonment: earlier in the film he was able to speak, but after this incident he says nothing.[15] So Razieh is sacked for deserting her responsibilities by an angry Nader, who also accuses her of stealing some money. The film's viewers know—if they notice and recall it—that Simin took that money to pay the movers who were carrying away her piano, which she is selling. Razieh takes great exception to being suspected of theft and keeps returning to deny it although she is asked to leave several times. She also wants to be paid even though she has abused Nader's father. Nader is so incensed that he pushes her out the door of the flat.

The scene is then set for the accusation of a crime that drives the film's narrative toward its desolate conclusion, where a family is split over the best way to resist "the conditions." Later that evening, after a call from Azam, Nader and Simin discover that Razieh is in the hospital, and when they go to see how she is, they discover she has had a miscarriage.[16] The tensions are further enflamed when Nader and Hojjat focus on the question of shame, Nader telling Simin that Razieh is "shameless" for what she did to his father, while Hojjat loses his temper when he finds out Razieh was working at the flat in Simin's absence.[17] In a surprising development, Razieh and Hojjat accuse Nader of pushing Razieh down the stairs and causing the miscarriage. Hojjat has Nader charged with what is called "murder" in the film, but is in fact the crime of "criminal abortion" in Iran, or intentionally causing a woman to have an abortion, the penalty for which is one to three years in prison.[18] This accusation sets up a puzzle about what happened and an ethical question concerning how to resolve the problem.

The battle between the two families plays out against the backdrop of the class and religious differences between them, thus providing a window onto the tension within Iranian society. On the one hand, Hojjat is humiliated by the judgments of middle-class Iranians like Nader and Simin, which makes him angry and frustrated. On the other hand, because Iran is a theocratic society, Hojjat can wield a certain level of power over Nader by accusing him of murder. The courtroom drama aspect of the film comes to the fore when the families have the "murder" claim investigated.[19] Hojjat says to Nader in front of the investigator, "Aren't you ashamed? You call yourself a man." After some questioning, the examining magistrate stipulates that "blood money" (*diyat*) of 40 million rial should be given to the couple as compensation for the miscarriage.[20] Given that Hojjat is unemployed, getting this money appears to be a strong motivation for the accusation. Of the character types that Beauvoir outlines in *The Ethics of Ambiguity*, Hojjat most strongly presents the "serious man" who clings to his beliefs, unconcerned about his effects on others. He "gets rid of his freedom by claiming to subordinate it to values which would be unconditioned" (1997, 46). By contrast, Nader and Simin struggle to make authentic choices, a task that "appeal[s] to the existence of others" (1997, 67). Such authentic choices are in contrast to the bad faith of acting as if we are provided with ready-made values, as the "serious" person does (1997, 47). They struggle to live in the truth in spite of the forces that are ranged against them.

Nader is kept in jail overnight after the meeting with the magistrate, and Simin pays bail to get Nader released, although Simin appears to believe that he is guilty. The next day, Hojjat insults the magistrate and is about to be arrested. However, Nader gets *him* released by asking the investigator to forgive him.[21] Under questioning from the magistrate, Nader states that he did not overhear an earlier conversation about Razieh's pregnancy, which he in fact did, as is revealed later.[22] The little girl Somayeh also divulges to Nader that Razieh left Nader's father alone because she was going to see the doctor. Again, viewers might remember that the poor grandfather had walked outside into the street on the previous day—wanting to buy the newspaper from a nearby newsstand—and Razieh had followed him, but what transpires is not portrayed so that the two events can be connected. The question becomes whether Nader both pushed Razieh down the stairs and knew that she was pregnant. The possibility that he did complicates the ethical conflict between Nader and Simin concerning staying and going. The puzzle about Nader's actions and intentions raises the question of guilt, its importance to ethics, and the way it is defined differently in law and personal ethics. It also raises the question of ethical principles and their relation to the need for ethical compromise in certain circumstances, which both Nader and Simin show they are willing to do when other deeply held values are at stake, an aspect of the ambiguity of ethics Beauvoir examines in terms of antinomies. The reasoning that Nader and Simin follow is what leads them to opposite judgments about resistance.

ANTINOMIES OF RESISTANCE

Beauvoir (1997, 96–115) sees ethics as constituted by "antinomies of action," whereby chains of reasoning lead ethical agents to opposing conclusions. These antinomies are related to the ambiguities between the individual and the community, means and ends, one person's freedom and that of others, and the present and the future. According to her, ethical decision-makers always have to bear in mind the possibility of failure, for example, in the sense that an action carried out for one person will be against the ends of others (1997, 99). Much of Beauvoir's discussion involves political causes and violence, partly because for her these are the questions that are the most pressing. Nevertheless, according to Beauvoir (1997, 131), the same considerations of ambiguity will guide our ethical and political judgments or ought to, as some political perspectives that she identifies as "political realism" tend to focus on the state or collective at the expense of the individual, on the ends without considering the means, or on the future without concern for the present.

Beauvoir also discusses more personal ethical antinomies, and her view is relevant to the character of the decisions Nader and Simin make, in that by leaving Simin deserts her beloved father-in-law, and by staying Nader knows he will lose Simin, and they both risk losing their beloved daughter Termeh. Throughout the film, there is no question that they love each other, even though at times it seems as if they do not fully trust each other. All of their ethical decisions are shaped by the legal and political context in which they live, and these decisions have political ramifications.

In *The Ethics of Ambiguity*, Beauvoir tends to describe a difficult dilemma and then suggest a single solution that takes seriously the importance of respect for ends while also accepting that the means will sometimes be in conflict or tension with them. As Maša Mrovlje (2019, 80) argues, Beauvoir's account of judgments stands out for its acknowledgment of "the unavoidable specter of tragedy and sacrifice." Nevertheless, Beauvoir appears confident and certain about what judgment should be made in the situations she describes. For example, she condemns the action of a French magistrate who gave up a communist to save ten hostages, as that act destroys the very meaning of resistance to the Nazi occupation (1997, 131–32). The antinomy of action should have been dissolved in the moment of pure rejection of the occupation, she argues. Yet in another case that cannot be understood as that kind of rejection, in deciding whether to refuse an addict drugs or provide those drugs, Beauvoir (1997, 136) suggests that we should help a drug addict take drugs if that will prevent their suicide. Furthermore, she concludes that once children are involved in an oppressive situation, "freedom and the future" are on their side, so "these are the ones who must first be taken into account" (1997, 144). In other words, we should choose the children's freedom to live in a safe place over the parent's freedom to live in a slum, for instance.

Additionally, one has to consider the likelihood of success of helping concrete individuals (1997, 150–52). These considerations again lead to definite conclusions in Beauvoir's eyes, where a costly strike can be justified by the raising of consciousness concerning exploitation, whereas the sacrifice of miners for publicity for the Communist Party cannot. These examples are from John Steinbeck's *In Dubious Battle* (1963) and John Dos Passos's *Adventures of a Young Man* (1939), respectively, and Beauvoir does not hesitate to support the heroes' decisions. However, *A Separation* shows that ambiguity and its "methods," considering our freedom and the freedom of others, and the meaning and content of our action (1997, 134), can go further and lead to two opposing solutions: proper antinomies, in other words. Nader and Simin are using these methods, and are confident of their choices being effective in aiding their loved ones, yet they are opposed.

The series of conflicts in the film come together in the question whether Nader and Simin should pay the blood money, and what it would mean to do so: Would it be an admission that Nader is guilty? As Simin says to the judge at the beginning of the film, Nader is "a good, decent person." If that is so, why does Simin want to leave him? And since she is also a good, decent person, why do they disagree about what is good and right to do? Guilt is raised in the film in connection to the telling of lies, which Nader and Simin find abhorrent and yet have to face the significance of doing so, either by telling a lie or refusing to. For instance, a scene portrays how concerned Nader is with accuracy, as he corrects one of the answers Termeh's teacher has given her, even though she dreads bringing that up in class. Nader says, "What's wrong is wrong, no matter who says what."[23] Yet the situation of conflict will lead him to violate this principle.

Following her realization that her father knew about Razieh getting the phone number for the gynecologist from Ms. Ghahraii (Merila Zare'i), Termeh asks Nader if he lied about knowing of Razieh's pregnancy. He admits that he heard everything, but his explanation is that if he had not lied, he would go into prison and he was worried about what would then happen to Termeh. So Termeh asks Nader why he pushed Razieh if he knew she was pregnant, and he replies, "I knew but didn't know in that moment. The law doesn't care about this. Either I knew or I didn't." He had forgotten or was not paying attention at the time. Thus, the law does not recognize the ambiguity of ethical action, only what seems to be the case given his knowledge. Nader's assertion of the ambiguity of his knowledge is a way of resisting the rigidity of the legal system.

Yet Nader repeats to the judge that he did not hear their conversation about the doctor, and while he does not ask Termeh to lie for him to the magistrate, he clearly hopes she will do so.[24] After her own encounter with the magistrate, where she lies very convincingly that she had told her father only later about the doctor's number, Termeh cries all the way home. Nevertheless, the film demonstrates that she does realize this ambiguity, after Nader explains how he could have acted as he did. In a very powerful scene, Nader says to his daughter, "Termeh, if you think I'm guilty, go get your mum and we'll go see them and pay the money." The following shot shows Termeh getting in the car with her mother and they drive away, making her view evident. So both Nader and Termeh lie to the magistrate because they care so much about each other. Nader's principled stance against lying is pushed to the limit by the risk and danger to Termeh.

By contrast, Simin is unsure about Nader's innocence and is focused on solving the problem in a practical way by paying the blood money. However, her pragmatic approach clashes with Nader's refusal to admit a guilt he does not feel. Simin argues that they should just pay the blood money, and they have a bitter argument, filmed in the kitchen of their apartment and alternating between close-ups of both of them (fig. 5.1). Nader responds to her concern about Termeh's safety by saying, "Shame on you for putting pressure on me." "Put yourself in their [Razieh and Hojjat's] place," says Simin to Nader. She accuses him of "fighting and obstinacy," while Nader accuses Simin of cowardice. From his perspective, Simin's decisions to go abroad and to pay the blood money look like running away from what really happened and from the circumstances of caring for his father rather than a rejection of an authoritarian and dangerous situation. The two cannot reconcile their ethical concerns for Termeh and for Nader's father, which have different outcomes: leaving Iran or staying.

FIG. 5.1. Simin and Nader argue about paying the blood money. Still from *A Separation*, directed by Asghar Farhadi (Asghar Farhadi Productions, Dreamlab Films, MPS APSA Academy Film Fund, and Memento Films, 2011).

The ethical stakes of their argument rise as the situation becomes more dangerous, highlighting and supporting Simin's primary focus on Termeh's safety. While the film does not underline how Simin is in a more difficult situation than Nader and her daughter is more vulnerable too, reflection on Beauvoir's discussion of the oppression of women in a patriarchal society can shed further light on this aspect of the film. In *The Second Sex* (2010, 6), she argues that women in all cultures are oppressed and regarded as the other to men, to varying extents. The Other is opposed to the subject, the essential, the absolute, and in this case the differentiation is not perceived reciprocally, so that women are also the Other to themselves. This oppression cannot be justified by appealing to biological, psychological, or historical explanations, Beauvoir (2010, 21–156) contends in a long and complex argument examining the justifications that have been put forward. Women's capacity to assume ambiguity and to overcome myths and limiting conceptions of femininity are constrained in cultural, material, and social ways.[25]

This constraint can be seen in the film in the unspoken expectation that Simin should stay to care for Nader's father rather than seek a different life abroad. However, one reason it is difficult to overcome oppression is that women do not form a group in solidarity, as other oppressed classes and ethnic groups do, Beauvoir (2010, 8) argues. This point can be seen in the two couples in *A Separation*—for all their internal conflicts, they form a kind of unit against the other couple, although the two women have some solidarity in trying to forge a compromise.[26] Again, the film does not stress Simin's specific difficulties, such as needing the permission of her husband to travel abroad, or that a woman's testimony counts as only half of a man's in some criminal matters, that their murder is considered to be worth less, or that fathers have preference for custody of children after divorce (Maranlou 2015, 128–30). Nevertheless, the judge's dismissal of Simin's reason for wanting a divorce in the first scene exemplifies the conditions she is trying to escape from.

However, as Farzaneh Milani (2015, 211) notes, both Simin and Razieh in different ways challenge the authority and dominance of their husbands. As a woman and a mother, Simin is willing to sacrifice her marriage for her daughter, as Termeh is what Beauvoir (1997, 102) calls "the living affirmation of human transcendence." Simin is trying to live by Beauvoir's (1997, 73) dictum "To will oneself free is to will others free." While restricted in many ways, she is able to see that there are other possibilities, other ways of living, so she transcends and is not completely limited by psychological oppression. In relation to the antinomy between past and future, Simin chooses the future for Termeh. This is a future that is bound to the present, not a concept like "Glory, Happiness, or

Justice" that the present is sacrificed for, as Beauvoir (1997, 116) sees it. In a sense, by choosing to stay and look after his father, Nader chooses the past. However, both think of others, and act in a concrete way, considering specific individuals rather than abstract causes, as Beauvoir (1997, 113) maintains we should, because that is the only way to take the value of freedom seriously.

Against the background of their differential situations and Nader's and Simin's ethical deliberations, the dangerousness of the situation increases. Hojjat goes to the school to harass Termeh's tutor, Ms. Ghahraii, making her swear on the Koran that Nader did not know Razieh was pregnant and threatening Simin, saying, "I have nothing to lose. Tell your husband not to make me do something crazy." This incident terrifies Simin, as she is now even more afraid for Termeh's well-being, indeed her life, and strengthens her original aim to go abroad. The film portrays Simin's stress by showing her smoking at the flat, a controversial scene for Iranian films.[27] Another day Hojjat is waiting outside the school again when Nader goes to pick up Termeh, so he can also see the menace in the situation. Nonetheless, the magistrate is skeptical of his complaint about the harassment, telling him to bring in witnesses.

In an attempt to resolve the conflict between the couples, Simin goes to see Hojjat with his sister, Azam, at the cobbler's workshop. Through some negotiations and the assistance of Azam, who defends Nader and talks Hojjat into accepting the money, she gets him to reduce the blood money from 40 million rial to 15 million. These developments lead to a second argument, again in the kitchen. Nader still does not want to pay the blood money, as he thinks that paying would mean agreeing to extortion and admitting guilt, which he does not concede. However, Simin puts her point bluntly when she says, "I won't rest until my child's safety is guaranteed" and asks, "Is 15 million more important than your child's life?"[28] The increase in danger leads Simin to push harder for a compromise, as depicted when Simin and Razieh secretly meet at the school and Razieh states, "My husband will kill me if he finds out I told you this." She explains to Simin that she has doubts, that is, doubts about Nader's guilt, since as she says, "Even before [being fired] the child wasn't moving." She had felt pain the night before, as she was hit by a car while following the grandfather to the newsagent. Razieh tells Simin not to pay the money, as that would make her a sinner in the eyes of God for lying about the so-called murder. This scene is a crucial turning point, as here any question about whether Nader caused the abortion, intentionally or not, is answered.[29]

Finally, the film turns to a kind of climax, with the two families meeting to settle the situation. Farhadi cuts directly from the scene between

Simin and Razieh to a scene where Razieh, Hojjat, Azam, and Hojjat's creditors meet with Nader and Simin at Hojjat and Razieh's house to resolve issues through payment and acceptance of the blood money. The audience is not told why Nader changes his mind and accepts paying the blood money. It could be that he accepts Simin's argument that they need to do it for Termeh's safety. Nader was willing to lie so he would not go to prison and not be able to look after her, so it makes sense that he would agree to the exchange for her sake. He is principled, and hates lying, but puts Termeh first. For both parents, Termeh's welfare, and their promotion of it, is paramount, along with Nader's wish to care for his father, so their ethics and their resistance unite briefly at this point.

Nader asks for Razieh to be present to witness the deal: once Razieh and Hojjat give up their complaint, they will get the money. For a few moments it looks as if all will be smoothed over, but Nader unexpectedly asks Razieh, "a devout woman," to swear on the Koran that Nader caused the miscarriage. This suggests that he is still unwilling to accept guilt, even nominally.[30] In a sense, he is asserting his privilege as a man by risking the compromise Simin has negotiated. This request is too much for Razieh, who will not swear, since she fears the wrath of God for lying and taking the money falsely—her religious advisers have informed her that would be a sin. In an urgent consultation in the kitchen, Hojjat tries to placate Razieh by promising to take the sin on himself, but she will not accept that, and he hits himself in frustration.[31] Outside, the others are startled to hear an increasing level of shouts and banging, a cacophony that signals the breakdown of their peace deal. As Nader, Simin, and Termeh leave in their car, we see that rocks have been thrown through its windows (presumably by Hojjat), another sign that the conflict is now even further from resolution. Nader seemingly could not resist asserting his innocence at the last, instead of letting himself appear guilty, holding onto his personal ethical standards.

Two good, decent people have ended up making different ethical judgments that will split a family apart, separate them, and make them resist in different ways. One might argue that what they needed to do was hold the different ambiguities of human existence in tension (Beauvoir 1997, 133), but in the end, as she accepts, we must act "without knowing all the factors that are present" (1997, 123). Also, Nader and Simin weigh the factors differently, and here Simin is more concerned about the potential violence toward Termeh. As Beauvoir (1997, 148–49) contends, a free decision that is political is also ethical, and it "is a wager as well as a decision; one bets on the chances and risks of the measure under consideration; but whether chances and risks must be assumed or not in the given circumstances must be decided without help, and in doing so one sets up values."[32] Nader's and Simin's opposing forms of resistance mean that Termeh has to choose between her parents, a decision they leave to her (fig. 5.2).

FIG. 5.2. Termeh is asked which parent she chooses to stay with. Still from *A Separation*, directed by Asghar Farhadi (Asghar Farhadi Productions, Dreamlab Films, MPS APSA Academy Film Fund, and Memento Films, 2011).

CONCLUSION

A Separation is bookended by two courtroom scenes before a judge that stress ethical ambiguity, the first by leaving the situation unresolved, the second by concealing from the audience the final outcome, that is, Termeh's decision. The judge at the beginning of the film says, "Are you saying that there is no future for the children living in this country?" By the end of the film it is clear why Simin would think that Termeh would not have a future there, and why for her it is so essential to resist by leaving. The final scene shows Termeh, now alone before the judge, having to choose between her parents as their separation becomes indefinite. That is where the viewer is likely to experience "the feeling of loss" Williams (1998, 70) contends is central to melodrama. Filmed as if the audience is in the position of the judge, the shot is only of Termeh and her tears as she delays reporting which parent she has chosen to remain with. While Nader and Simin wait outside for the news of Termeh's decision, they remain on either side of an open glass door but do not really look at each other, although the camera shows them both look hopefully in the direction of the other, hoping to catch the other's eye. Nader and Simin's ethical judgments concerning the best way to resist cannot be reconciled, and the audience is left with that ambiguity and anguish of choice. They both try to follow Havel's prescription to live in the truth in different ways. Both are loving, good people, yet they cannot work out a compromise, although both conceded aspects of their ethical approach, Simin by being willing to pay the blood money, and Nader by lying about knowing that Razieh was pregnant and allowing Termeh to lie about it as well. Termeh's attempt to keep her mother in the country by staying with her father has failed, so she has to choose between them: this child has to make an adult's choice about resistance.

A Separation shows how both Nader and Simin recognize the ethical complexity and ambiguity of their situation, as Beauvoir argues is essential to a genuine ethics. For her, conditions of oppression make it impossible for all our freedoms to be recognized, and even in ordinary times individuals are sacrificed in conflicts (1997, 96). The film shows how the attempt to resist an authoritarian society can separate people, even a loving family. They pay a harsh penalty for their attempts to remain authentic and live in the truth. The arbitrary legal system, with its lack of representation, proper investigation, or reasonable penalties, leaves them to their own resources, leaves them struggling to maintain standards of honesty and integrity, though they are driven to abandon those standards for the protection of their loved ones. *A Separation* recognizes and highlights the ambiguity of situations Beauvoir identifies, in which both responses are understandable and justifiable in their own terms, so the audience is not drawn to take sides between Nader and Simin, even if it could be tempting to, perhaps through identifying or sympathizing more with the masculine or feminine perspectives. Nevertheless, the film presents the deep sense of loss that results from their opposing choices of resistance through Termeh's final dilemma. While *A Separation* presents a tragic choice, in the final chapter I consider a more hopeful possibility of resistance in terms of the amelioration of restrictions, through the eyes of a young girl in Saudi Arabia.

[CHAPTER SIX]

Wadjda

Realism and Resistance

In this final chapter, I consider how the realist film *Wadjda* depicts a resistance based on ameliorative changes to a political system. In philosophical and political terms, cinematic realism can be associated with ideological reinforcement of the status quo or propaganda for an oppressive regime.[1] I explore the contrary potential, also recognized, of realism in the cinema to philosophically articulate women and other oppressed groups' resistance to that oppression and restrictions on their lives.[2] While this phenomenon can be observed in a range of recent world cinema, such as Iranian and Romanian art films, *Wadjda* presents a special case in that it came from a country with almost no film industry, no film distribution system, and, at the time of release, no cinemas: Saudi Arabia.

Since its release, many more feature films have been made in Saudi Arabia, including Mahmoud Sabbagh's romantic comedy *Barakah yoqabil Barakah* (*Barakah Meets Barakah*, dir. Mahmoud Sabbagh, 2016), the satirical comedy *Amra and the Second Marriage* (dir. Mahmoud Sabbagh, 2018), Al Mansour's own *The Perfect Candidate* (2019), and Faris Godus's *Shams Alma'arif* (*The Book of Sun*, 2020). Cinemas to screen feature films opened in 2018 after more than thirty years of closure; the first Saudi Arabian international film festival, the Red Sea Film Festival, was held in Jeddah in 2021 (Ritman 2021); and there is an ambitious plan to greatly expand the industry (Goodfellow 2021). The director, Haifaa Al Mansour, has been praised by reviewers for making the film, the first feature made entirely in Saudi Arabia, there at all and being the first Saudi Arabian woman to make a film (Atakav 2020, 250). Furthermore, for some of the actors, it was their first time working with a female director (Lapin 2013).[3] *Wadjda* can be seen as an example of what is starting to be called "a new Arabic cinema" (El Rashidi 2019, 10).

Yet this exclusive focus on the director and location, while understandable, ignores the power of the film itself, which takes a slice of time, about six weeks, in the life of a ten-year-old Riyadh girl, Wadjda (Waad Mohammed), and focuses on the everyday desire of a child: to ride a bicycle. Wadjda's focus on this freedom of movement expresses her resistance, as does her engagement with her own form of Havelian "small-scale work." With reference to the neorealist fate of a certain bicycle in *Bicycle Thieves* (dir. Vittorio de Sica, 1948), the film is realist in describing the restrictive nature of life in Saudi Arabia; at the same time, it affirms hope in gradual change and resistance. *Wadjda* does this by exploring the natality, in Hannah Arendt's ([1958] 1998, 8–9) sense, of a young child who does not see life's restrictions as insurmountable obstacles. *Wadjda* is realist and tightly structured and planned, and it depicts a Riyadh just beyond reach. Set in the specific time and place of contemporary Riyadh, the realism of the film demonstrates the possibility of thinking otherwise and encourages viewers to consider the importance both of gradualism and nonviolent resistance in politics and of realistic filmmaking's capacities to anticipate and foster those advances.

Before making this film, Al Mansour had made three short films and one documentary called *Women without Shadows* (2005); since then, she has made *Mary Shelley* (2017), *Nappily Ever After* (2018), and *The Perfect Candidate*, all films centered on women who challenge society's expectations. She studied comparative literature at the American University in Cairo and film at the University of Sydney before starting to make feature films. Her determination to film on the specific location of Riyadh meant that her work was more challenging in various ways than if she had made it in a neighboring country, such as Jordan or Qatar. For instance, many of the scenes—those involving working with men, including her crew—had to be shot with Al Mansour in a van communicating with the actors via walkie-talkie or mobile phone (Atakav 2013). The crew were not allowed to shoot in a girl's school, so they had to shoot in a boy's school instead. They also often had to leave the scene quickly if the religious police were around (Bloom 2013). Al Mansour makes it clear that she followed all the censorship rules in making the film (Lapin 2013). Nevertheless, she was able to portray both men and women and how different their private and public lives are, in a society where women behave completely differently in their own homes than they do outside. Wadjda's mother (Reem Abdullah) is much more relaxed at home, casually dressed, moving quickly, singing and laughing. This sense of having a window onto a hidden world has marked many of the reviews of the film and leads directly to questions of realism and authenticity, so I examine André Bazin's and Rudolf Arnheim's discussions of realism and authenticity in film in relation to recent discussions of these issues by Daniel Morgan and Richard Rushton. Then I consider how *Wadjda*'s specific realism and location filming contributes to the way it presents women's nonconformity and resistance.

REALISM AND AUTHENTICITY

Bazin, in his classic treatment of realism as the ontology of cinema itself *and* an approach to filmmaking in his essay "The Ontology of the Photographic Image," speaks of only some films as achieving artistic realism, by distinguishing between true realism and pseudorealism. This account provides a context for understanding *Wadjda* as realist. True realism is "the need . . . to give significant expression to the world both concretely and [in] its essence," whereas pseudorealism is "a deception aimed at fooling the eye (or for that matter the mind); a pseudorealism content in other words with illusory appearances" (Bazin 1967a, 1:12). For Bazin, the realism of cinema comes from the mechanistic nature of the process: no matter how transformed the object, the audience believes that it really is the object rather than a representation of it. In his view, cinema takes this realism further than photography by providing us with a representation or image of change and the passing of time rather than a shot of an instant in time (1967a, 1:15). *Wadjda* is shot on digital film, so it is not mechanical in that sense, yet Al Mansour cites Italian neorealism as her main inspiration (O'Falt 2013). Bazin (1967a, 1:15) writes that "the cinema is objective in time. . . . The image of things is likewise the image of their duration, change mummified, as it were." Here Bazin refers to the idea that cinema's aim is to re-create the world without distorting it by the artist's interpretation or by the fact that time cannot be reversed, since it retains an image from the past.

In examining the cinema of the 1920s and 1930s, Bazin makes a distinction between those who trusted in the image and those who put their faith in reality. The legacy of the image involved reliance on sets, makeup, lighting, performance, shot framing, and montage, which made the language of cinema through the sequence of images in time, for example the work of D. W. Griffith, Sergei Eisenstein, Abel Gance, and Lev Kuleshov. In contrast to this approach to cinema, Bazin sets Robert Flaherty, F. W. Murnau, and Erich von Stroheim, who eschew these techniques and focus on images shown in real time, natural settings, and long takes, for instance.[4] In "The Evolution of the Language of Cinema," Bazin (1967a, 1:35–36) concludes that the structure of the filmic image is more realistic than reality itself, that the realistic style of filmmaking engages the viewer more, as they have to choose what they will attend to, and realist films allow ambiguity of meaning and expression to appear, while montage eliminates it.[5] His purpose is to link the ontology of cinema and a realistic approach to cinema with freedom of interpretation for the audience.

The paradoxical upshot of Bazin's (1967a, 1:40) discussion is that the realist film, "because it is founded on a much greater degree of realism," has access to "more means of manipulating reality and modifying it from within. The filmmaker is no longer the competitor of the painter and the playwright, he is, at last, the equal of the novelist."[6] In other words, the less an artist imposes a vision on the material, the more open are the possibilities for different perspectives on reality. Furthermore, Bazin claims that the aim of cinema is to express a mythic spirit and to create the myth of total cinema. This is an "integral realism," "a recreation of the world in its own image, an image unburdened by the freedom of interpretation of the artist or the irreversibility of time" (1967a, 1:21). While the logic of Bazin's argument is clear, it seems there is a flaw in the connection he makes between realism if thought of as specific filmmaking techniques and the potential for more varied interpretations. Does that mean, for example, that Richard Linklater's *Boyhood* (2014), because it was filmed over twelve years, is a better film than any film (at least fiction) than was made before, since it was filmed over a long time so that we could really see the process of aging and thus have more freedom of interpretation than in other films, where aging is depicted using makeup, wigs, and prostheses, or different actors, as in *Moonlight* (dir. Barry Jenkins, 2016)? *Boyhood* is a remarkable achievement and profound experience, yet what is more apposite is to consider that approach as simply different from other approaches and suitable for the particular film that was made.

While there can be a distinction between films that open up more interpretations and films that close interpretations off, it is not clear why that distinction would align with realism and other approaches, with long takes or montage, or even with filmmakers who would like to impose a narrow vision and those who would like to create the impression that the world is being revealed. For none of these things can be controlled; any creation of a new image is itself open to multiple interpretations, and any artistic decision always has unintended consequences. What is needed instead is an examination of films in their singularity, and if the aim is for the audience to be able to interpret a film in a variety of ways, then let us see and judge for ourselves whether that is the case. Daniel Morgan argues that Bazin is in fact more open about the kind of films that are realist than he appears to be in some essays, encompassing a variety of styles and forms of filmmaking, and that properly realist films are those in which what we learn can be transferred to our engagement with reality. They involve an engagement with things outside us that shows us something new about them (Morgan 2006, 481). For Morgan, such a realist engagement can occur with digital technologies as with traditional film and photography, so films like *Wadjda*, shot on digital film, can be considered realist.[7]

The making of *Wadjda* is inspired by Italian neorealist films in a number of ways. Al Mansour says she liked what she calls "their somewhat documentary style, mixed with the poetry of everyday life." For her, it was also critical to film outside, as those filmmakers did, so the constraints on Wadjda's life and movement could be seen. The content of the neorealist films matters to Al Mansour due to her desire to show the possibility of change in Saudi Arabia: "The films were always about people and kids, but also rebirth" (O'Falt 2013). This sense of rebirth and birth and the importance of childhood are themes I will return to in the final section of the chapter.

The film also attends to structure and enhancing effects, and I argue that the realist approach enables a specific form of resistance to be thought philosophically. A discussion of the relationship between realism and authenticity will enable my argument concerning this view of realism to become clearer. In a nuanced examination in "The Two Authenticities of the Photographic Media," Rudolf Arnheim (1993, 537) distinguishes between two senses of authenticity in art: "They are authentic to the extent that they do justice to the facts of reality, and they are authentic in quite another sense by expressing the quality of human experience by any means suitable to that purpose."[8] By doing justice to the facts of reality, Arnheim (1993, 537) explains, he means a representation that "offers recognizable images of creatures and objects." So in a reading of *Wadjda*, these two kinds of authenticity have to be examined to see how they work together and also to see how they might pull against each other. Arnheim's view is that the second, aesthetic sense of authenticity may actually be an obstacle to the first, more factual sense. By contrast, he sees Siegfried Kracauer's idea of film as the "redemption of physical reality" as taking the documenting aspect of film to further authenticity through film's ability to capture the fleeting and unclear moments of action in time. Kracauer (1960, 20) believes the photographic aspect of film is the most cinematic because it is the only feature of films that "afford[s] insight and enjoyment otherwise unattainable." In an attempt to break down the dichotomy between the two views of authenticity, Arnheim (1957) criticizes his own earlier work, *Film as Art*, for overemphasizing the aesthetic authenticity of film (1993, 538). Instead, what is needed is a "skilful union of the two authenticities" (1993, 538). Kracauer's (1960, 21) view is similar in that he argues for a "right" balance between what he calls the realistic and formative (formal) tendencies, with the proviso that the formative follows the realistic. So the singular film should be considered to see how it works on its own terms and to question its authenticity as a complete work rather than as an example of a style or set of techniques.

In his discussion of Bazin, Rushton (2010, 63) connects Bazin's conception of realism with authenticity, which he sees as filmic portrayals that are true to life. For him, it is not the distinction between analog and digital film that matters, but that between authentic and inauthentic works.[9] He suggests that the authenticity comes through in the way the characters are absorbed in their world (Rushton 2010, 73). But what does it mean for a film to be "true to life"? For Rushton it is not about copying reality or corresponding with it, but a commitment to a way of life. He says that realism in this sense concerns authenticity as "a matter of being in the presence of the authentic actions of persons absorbed in the world" (2010, 77). This authenticity is not based on style; what matters is the portrayal of a way of life. Thus I explore how *Wadjda* provides such a union or balance of reality, expressing human experience, and is true to life, how it relates to the cinematic realist tradition, and how that is significant to portraying everyday resistance.

THE REALISM OF *WADJDA*

One of the central points Al Mansour makes about *Wadjda* is that she insisted on shooting in Riyadh in order to make the film "authentic" (Brooks 2013; Lapin 2013). She resolved, for one thing, to have "this local voice. I wanted Saudis, when they see the film, to have this sense of ownership of that thing" (Al Mansour in Lapin 2013). Another reason is to have "new imagery coming from the kingdom" and the specific neighborhoods of Riyadh (Al Mansour in NPR Staff 2013). She also says that the film is "almost a documentary," so casting culturally appropriate actors, for example, was really imperative for her (Rosenberg 2013). German producers Gerhard Meixner and Roman Paul, with their production company, Razor film, which produced the Afghani film *The Patience Stone* (dir. Atiq Rahimi, 2012), supported the film financially, along with one of the Saudi princes, Alwaleed Bin Talal, through his production company, Rotana Video and Audio Visual, and other sources.[10] The script was chosen for the Sundance Screenwriters' lab in the Middle East, but it took over five years to set up, partly due to the difficulty of persuading investors it was possible to make a film in Saudi Arabia (Bloom 2013; Lucca 2013). Middle East investors would also have liked to have seen more melodrama, not "something that was more reflective of reality" (Al Mansour in Liston 2013).

What is it about *Wadjda* that makes it a realist film? *Wadjda* presents us with a recognizable world with recognizable objects, although perhaps of a surprising and unfamiliar place for some audiences, which does not generally draw attention to its own techniques, thus providing a sense of authenticity. However, *Wadjda* does obliquely refer to certain relevant films that have come before it, and uses cinematic techniques that enhance the scenes. For example, Wadjda's first sight of the green bicycle is presented as a vision, shot apparently moving through the air by itself, and then revealed to be on the back of a trailer, being taken to the local shop. The narrative unfolds in a linear fashion in that there are no flashbacks or flash-forwards, yet for all that there are unexpected depictions of human experiences along the way.[11] For those who are not familiar with Saudi Arabia, everyday incidents have fascinating and startling notes even though they are presented in a realistic style, such as the patterns of segregation of men and women and, to a lesser extent, boys and girls. The camera stays with Wadjda throughout, so the viewer sees the world that she sees, of home, streets, school, shopping center, and bathrooms, but not those places where men are, or when her father has his male friends over. Their own living room is off-limits for her and her mother while her father entertains, and they leave the food they have cooked at the door for the men to eat.

Furthermore, by insisting on filming in Riyadh, Al Mansour allows the audience to interpret the cityscape as they will, as Bazin suggests—for instance, to see the frequent building sites as a sign of progress or as a sign of alienation, and for audience members who know Riyadh to recognize and relate to the specific locations. *Wadjda* shows us the detail of life in Riyadh, expresses a vision that is both critical and sympathetic, and allows the spectator to reflect on whether the future for Wadjda is genuinely open, by contrasting her story with her mother's and other girls' and women's. While many of the scenes are of pale buildings and interiors, and dusty construction sites where the whiteness of the soil is exaggerated by the glare of the sun, bright colors appear as signs of hope and rebellion, in the green bike, the blue nail polish of two affectionate schoolgirls, the bracelets in soccer club colors, or the red dress Wadjda's mother hopes will keep her father faithful.

The realist aims and style of Al Mansour's film can be further understood by considering the broader filmic tradition that she both intentionally and unintentionally follows. While she grew up watching blockbusters and melodramas, she states that she is influenced in her filmmaking practice by a range of films, all realist: Jean-Pierre and Luc Dardenne's *Rosetta* (1999), *Bicycle Thieves*, and Jafar Panahi's *Offside* (2006) (Boo 2013; Rothe 2014).[12] Moreover, Wadjda's wild bike ride with her friend Abdullah (Abdullrahman Al Gohani) at the end of the movie is said by critics to echo the beach scene at the end of *The 400 Blows* (dir. François Truffaut, 1959) and to provide a "feminist renewal" of that scene (Luke Williams 2014; Lane 2013). The scenes are similar in their evocation of freedom and the visual representation of a border, in one case between the beach and the water, and the other that between a safe road and the highway (fig. 6.1). However, the final shots of their faces are very different, with Antoine looking apprehensive and defiant, and Wadjda expressing joyful expectation about what the future holds.

FIG. 6.1. Wadjda racing with Abdullah. Still from *Wadjda,* directed by Haifaa Al Mansour (Razor Film Produktion GmbH, Highlook Communications Group, and Rotana Film Production, 2012).

In developing her film practice in *Wadjda*, Al Mansour has traditions of French, Italian, and Iranian realist and neorealist films to draw inspiration from and refer to.[13] As Bazin (1967b, 2:50) notes of *Bicycle Thieves*, the plot of *Wadjda* would not deserve a line in a newspaper: a young girl would like a bicycle to ride, and after a number of unsuccessful attempts to get the bicycle, she gets it. Indeed, Al Mansour acknowledges that she was inspired by this film with a bike at its heart, as well as her own experiences during childhood, and one of her nieces who wanted to play soccer (Boo 2013; Barlow 2013; Moheb 2015). However, a lot happens along the way, as Wadjda studies the Koran and wins a competition based on her knowledge and harmonious recitation of a text concerning religious hypocrisy, planning to use the prize money to buy the bike. It is a hopeful ending, for her at least, in contrast to *Bicycle Thieves*' tragic one, as I discuss in more detail below. Both films use a child to highlight the difficulties of life in an unjust society. Furthermore, *Bicycle Thieves* also used nonprofessional actors, although they were carefully chosen. Al Mansour used some actors experienced with television, such as Reem Abdullah, who plays Wadjda's mother, and Ahd Kamel, also a film director, who plays Wadjda's school principal, Ms. Hussa. However, clearly she was looking for actors close to the characters, for instance in choosing a young girl who loved Western music and wore Converse sneakers, a symbol of nonconformity in the film, like Wadjda, for Wadjda and by choosing a non-Saudi actor (Mohammad Zahir) to play Iqbal, the non-Saudi driver (Rosenberg 2013). Moreover, Al Mansour was inspired by postwar Italian neorealism to film outside in the streets of Riyadh with its building sites (O'Falt 2013).

In addition to that acknowledged influence, Peter Debruge (2013) suggests that "Al Mansour modeled her simple story on Iranian films, which play like haikus in contrast with Hollywood's thundering Wagnerian operas." While studying for her cinema master's degree in Sydney, Al Mansour explored the work of Iranian filmmakers such as Abbas Kiarostami and Jafar Panahi, who directed *The White Balloon* (1995) and *Offside* (Moheb 2015). *Offside*, which is banned from screening in Iran, focuses on the issue of equality for girls and women to watch live soccer, in this case the World Cup qualifying match between Iran and Bahrain. Iranian women had been banned from stadiums since the 1979 revolution. Unlike *Wadjda*, *Offside* centers on a group of six girls disguised as boys, who are all caught and rounded up by young men on military service. It was filmed on location, including during the match depicted itself, and the use of handheld cameras gives it a documentary feel. The film's action takes place during the period of the match and ends in a joyful celebration of Iran's entry into the World Cup as the girls escape the bus taking them to "Vice HQ" when their guards are drawn into the cheering crowd to dance. It is difficult to say whether the film had an advocacy effect, although it further inspired protest groups, including the White Scarf Campaign. Iranian women were permitted to watch Iran play Spain in the 2018 World Cup, but it has not become generally permitted (Rannard 2018). *Offside*'s influences on the formal and realistic features of *Wadjda* are quite clear, in addition to the soccer references. Finally, Lee Marshall (2012) also comments that there is the "occasional hint of Egyptian melodrama" in *Wadjda*, and Al Mansour notes that Egyptian cinema is very dominant in Saudi Arabia and that she enjoyed these films as a child, including old films from the 1950s featuring a child star named Fairouz Arteen Kalevan (1943–2016) (Rosenberg 2013; Boo 2013; and Ahram Online 2016).

One way *Wadjda* contributes to a philosophical explication of resistance is by portraying in close detail and without didacticism the texture of daily life—the habits and routines, the everyday sights and sounds—in a conservative and constraining culture. Al Mansour shows the realities of life in a strongly patriarchal society, revealing the complexity and specificity of repression and oppression, their interlocking and conflicting aspects, especially showing how women are drawn into imposing restrictions on other women and the difficulties for immigrants in Saudi society. For instance, Wadjda's mother, who is sympathetic to Wadjda's dreams, is shocked when she sees a friend chatting to a male colleague in the hospital with her face uncovered. She is so scandalized that she feels she cannot work in such an environment and decides not to apply for a job there. Similarly, Wadjda's teachers (all women) are vigilant in ensuring that the schoolgirls abide by the country's strict law and customs, forbidding such behaviors as laughing, wearing toenail polish, and playing too close to the school wall; later in the film, after two girls are found together outside, the teachers also prohibit them from bringing flowers, exchanging affectionate letters, and holding hands. The school principal, Ms. Hussa, enforces society's strictures strongly on Wadjda, telling her she has to cover up her hair and stop wearing her sneakers, and takes her prize money from the Koran-reciting competition, which Wadjda wants to use to buy her beloved bike, to send to Palestine. To win the money, Wadjda hides her motivations, but once she wins, she is undone by her candor when she is asked how she will use it.

The film also shows the anomalous status of immigrant workers when it touches on the relationship between women and their drivers (women were not permitted to drive until 2018). They often conflict over who is in charge—the woman, who is the customer, or the man, who knows that the woman is dependent on him for transportation. Wadjda's mother's driver, Iqbal, constantly complains about her being late and then decides he will not drive her at all, leaving her unable to get to work. The power play between the two is resolved in a blunt way when Wadjda's friend Abdullah threatens to have his politician uncle investigate Iqbal's residence permit. In this situation, the children have more influence than the driver does. The film has numerous similar examples of what Rushton (2013, 21) notes is often considered necessary for "a film to be properly political": that is, contradiction. These can be contradictions between one group's freedoms and another's lack of those same freedoms, and the exploitation that makes that possible. Many such inconsistencies are portrayed in the film, as Omer M. Mozaffar describes in his review, including how "women enact the coercion, and suffer from it."[14] However, Rushton (2013, 23) adds that freedom "entails discovering *freedom with another*," and that can be seen in Wadjda learning to ride and riding her bike with her friend, her support for his uncle's political campaign, and the love and solidarity between mother and daughter.

Another complexity of the lived experience of repression is shown by the portrayal of Wadjda's father (Sultan Al Assaf) as kind and affectionate to both Wadjda and her mother, whom he fondly calls his "superstar." He is fun-loving and social, as he enjoys playing videogames in the lounge-room and spending time with Wadjda, her mother, and his friends, and is under a great deal of pressure from his own parents to father a son (fig. 6.2). His caring behavior seems more ambiguous at the end of the film, when the audience realizes that he has married again in order to have a wife who will produce a male heir. The everyday texture of lived experience and the complexity of cultural and political traditions is shown without comment so that viewers can interpret and respond on their own terms, as Bazin argues that film audiences should do. *Wadjda*'s realist approach involves a tight script, careful plotting, fine performances, and an aesthetic that stresses the beauty of the characters amid an environment that can appear harsh at times. The authenticity that Al Mansour strives for by filming in Riyadh is complemented by these other features of the film. Yet the realism of the film is not simply a pleasing depiction of reality; it has a political edge that communicates and suggests resistance to aspects of that reality. The realism of *Wadjda* points to the possibility of a slightly different world, a world that could come into being, and to some extent has since, as I will explain. That is what I mean by realism as resistance.

FIG. 6.2. Wadjda at home with her parents. Still from *Wadjda*, directed by Haifaa Al Mansour (Razor Film Produktion GmbH, Highlook Communications Group, and Rotana Film Production, 2012).

REALISM AND RESISTANCE

In certain ways, Al Mansour was not able to use all the precise locations required for the narrative, as the restrictions on women in Saudi Arabia she demonstrates in the film affected the making of the film itself. As I noted earlier, Al Mansour had to use a boys' school as the location for the girls' school in the film, as the partly male crew were not allowed to film in a girls' school. However, such small details do not alter her point in making the film in Saudi Arabia, since the location makes an impact on the reception of the film, especially for Saudi audiences, and even its visual texture, including the bright light, and the way that places like construction sites and highways play such a prominent role in the film. Key to the purposes of this chapter is how the realism of this specific film serves the goal of philosophizing resistance to a segregated and patriarchal state. Al Mansour herself sees the film as a celebration of resistance (Hoggard 2013). The resistance that can be thought through the film is a nonviolent and gradualist resistance. Todd May (2015, 163), in his account, describes this form of nonviolent resistance as one where "everyone—participants, adversaries, and bystanders—is considered to possess dignity, and because of this is to be approached in a dignified manner. . . . Moreover, and related, everyone is considered to be equally capable of conceiving and conducting a human life alongside others." In *Wadjda*, this form of nonviolence can be seen in how the protagonists act in their resistance, and in how each character is portrayed in the film.

The film has a simple plotline, although it is a bit more complicated than I suggested. The film contains two narratives: the story of Wadjda's quest for the green bicycle and that of her mother's loss of status since she has not borne a boy, which leads Wadjda's father to marry a second time. One story has a sweet, hopeful, ending and the other a quite bitter one, contributing to a sense that the film is not just there to gratify, and the idea that most hope must be found in the younger generation. The two narratives are tied together in that Wadjda's mother uses the money she was going to spend on a dress for herself on the bicycle, since her husband is remarrying, a decision that saddens her but that she accepts, saying, "We'll be fine." Her gift of the bike could be seen as her own gentle form of resistance and an acknowledgment of the greater possibilities for Wadjda's future. Furthermore, as Wadjda walks through the house, she glimpses a white lab coat on her mother's bed, at first out of focus and then in focus, suggesting that her mother has decided to take the better and closer job at the hospital after all.

Wadjda's resistance exemplifies the Arendtian sense of natality, a new birth, a different perspective on the world, and a lack of fear, in that her wish for the bicycle is untroubled by the thought that she might not be permitted to ride it. Wadjda's desire thrives even though she is told that girls do not ride bikes and that riding a bike will prevent her from having children, and being surrounded by classmates who are being "married off" and who seem relatively unfazed by that. For her, the only question is how to get enough money to pay for it. The bicycle is an object of desire that represents the freedom to move about the city and to engage in the pastimes that boys enjoy. Wadjda also "works" in the sense of selling the bracelets and delivering messages for the older girls. In that respect, Wadjda undertakes the small-scale work that resists the system she lives within, as Havel recommends.

In *The Human Condition* Hannah Arendt ([1958] 1998, 9) connects natality most closely to action, rather than work or labor, saying that "the new beginning inherent in birth can make itself felt in the world only because the newcomer possesses the capacity of beginning something anew, that is, of acting." Action for her goes beyond the repetitive subsistence and maintenance of labor and the means-end structure of making in work, to the free initiation of something new that is an end in itself. The different and new perspective Wadjda brings to her experience is why her life story seems to allow more possibilities than her mother's does, although that is not definitive. For instance, Ms. Hussa, the draconian school principal, suggests that Wadjda reminds her of herself at that age, a kind of foreboding of how young rebellion can be repressed in later life. Nevertheless, the concept of natality is one that is made concrete through the young girl's irrepressible spirit as the center of the film's narrative. Al Mansour (in Boo 2013) herself argues that she sees a generational shift in some girls the same age as Wadjda, who "were very feisty and they just didn't care. . . . They belonged to a different world." Such a shift in attitudes is one that sometimes only natality or the birth of a new generation can bring.

In some regards the film follows in a tradition of children's films, or films that have children as protagonists (rather than films made for children), especially those made in Iran, such as *The White Balloon*—partly in order to evade strict censorship, such as dress codes, and to present politically critical views by concentrating on the theme of childhood (ASL 19, in Decherney and Atwood 2014, 229–42). Fatemeh Hosseini-Shakib, in "The Image of Children," notes that the "children cinema" was made in Iran primarily in the late 1980s to 1990s (Jahed 2012, 227). She refers to Hamid-Reza Sadr's argument that in Iran after the revolution children were used as safe substitutes for things that adults were unable to represent—political and social criticism, and freedom in their dress and behavior. Moreover, children were cheap to hire as actors and unproblematic to work with (Sadr 2002, 228–31). This view might stand out as contradicting W. C. Field's famous quip "Never work with animals or children," but Sadr's point is that the dropping of prerevolutionary adult actors and the banning of sex along with singing and dancing were what made children less problematic subjects. Al Mansour has tapped into the tradition of children's films to make *Wadjda*, as protagonist and symbol, an expression of rebellion and change, exemplifying Arendt's concept of natality ([1958] 1998, 9, 177). Wadjda represents a more fearless generation, and her experience is contrasted to that of the adults around her.

Al Mansour's comments support Sadr's view, noting that issues about acting not being well-respected and the set as an inappropriate environment for a woman were easier to deal with in Waad Mohammad's case because "she is little and a kid" (Rosenberg 2013).[15] *Wadjda* follows in the tradition by suggesting that the lives of children offer possibilities for change and resistance that the lives of adults do not, but also by showing the pressure to conform in the tiniest details becoming stronger by the day. Part of the idea of hope comes from early resistance, the full experience of the new beginnings natality brings (Arendt [1958] 1998, 247).

Unlike Termeh and Somayeh in *A Separation*, Wadjda is the center of resistance and at the point of breaking free from authority. As Beauvoir (1997, 141) maintains in her discussion of childhood in *The Ethics of Ambiguity*, "even in this situation the child has a right to his freedom and must be respected as a human person." To some extent, this respect is accorded to Wadjda, by her mother, and the shopkeeper who has the bicycle, for example. The future for the child must be an open one, Beauvoir contends. By contrast, the school principal, Ms. Hussa, tries to limit and close Wadjda's future and decide for her what her future will be like. In beginning to question the adult world, Wadjda is leaving the world of the "serious," what Beauvoir (1997, 36) considers the world of ready-made values and the world that the child confronts and moving toward adolescence. For her, adolescence is a time of moral choice, where subjectivity must be assumed, where "freedom is then revealed and he must decide upon his attitude in the face of it" (1997, 40).[16] *Wadjda* shows Wadjda claiming her freedom against restrictions joyfully, and casting herself into the world, as Beauvoir would have it.

While her schooling aims at narrowing her horizons, the film suggests that at the very least, Wadjda's future will be more open than that of her mother and her mother's generation. In *The Second Sex*, Beauvoir paints a gloomier picture of the transition from childhood to adolescence, as she focuses on describing the process of a female child being inculcated into the role of "woman" in oppressive societies. While she believes that there are very few intellectual or physical differences between boys and girls, others begin to intervene from a girl's early years to prepare her to be a wife and mother (2010, 283). Beauvoir's descriptions of the dreams of "the girl" under these kinds of circumstances contrast with Wadjda's, showing how she is meant to be part of the feisty generation. Instead of dreaming of "everything" because she is responsible for "nothing," which Beauvoir sees as the compensatory wish of girls, Wadjda is like the person who has authentic projects and so "knows a finitude that is the gauge of one's concrete power" (2010, 371). To have and ride a bicycle and to be able to race on it is to retain confidence in one's body and independence. While to have expectations of marriage and motherhood can be burdensome and create what Beauvoir (2010, 372) sees as inauthentic flights, she notes that a young girl can also "have the courage to throw into question established optimism, preconceived values, and hypocritical and reassuring morality," an approach Wadjda exemplifies to the outrage of her teachers. Writing in 1949, Beauvoir (2010, 381) concludes, "Today, it is becoming possible for her [the girl] to take her future in her hands, instead of putting it in those of the man," a possibility that Al Mansour presents in *Wadjda*.

Wadjda's friendship with a boy her age, Abdullah, also evokes the possibilities of political change in natality and youth.[17] This relationship is one that shows the opportunities for those who have not been completely ground down by the restrictions of their society. It is an example of what Arendt ([1958] 1998, 177) means by the potential in natality: the coming into the world of new people always means that new ideas and crucial change are possible. Wadjda and Abdullah prefigure possible different relations between females and males in Saudi Arabia. While he says something to Wadjda about marrying her when they are older, she just smiles at the idea. Wadjda is not "waiting for Man," as Beauvoir (2010, 341) characterizes the girl captured by oppression. Their friendship suggests the possibility of genuine friendship between males and females. There are a number of simple and innocent relationships in the film, between children, and between children and adults. An example of the latter is Wadjda's relationship with the shop owner who has her bike, which is one of easy banter; she gives him a mixtape as a sign of friendship.

The resistance that is thought in the film is of a very particular sort, as it is nonviolent. Furthermore, it is a resistance that accepts gradualism while simultaneously believing in progress and human perfectibility. This approach to politics is called meliorism by Michèle Le Dœuff (2003, 44, 68) in *The Sex of Knowing*, and it can be considered insufficiently radical and ineffective compared to revolutionary political stances. She sees her own meliorism expressed in the thought that we can love the human condition and we "can also make [it] more loveable" (2003, 68). This gradual approach to change is evident in *Wadjda* in its gentle, respectful portraits of characters like Wadjda's father and its multifaceted, if slightly satirical depiction of Ms. Hussa and the other schoolteachers. Laws in Saudi Arabia are based on the conservative Wahhabi tradition of Islam, and Al Mansour aimed to stay respectful of the tradition while challenging some of its strictures. She says that "change is a painful process"; thus, she tries "to allow people to embrace change at their own pace," since "change has to come from the heart" (Al Mansour in Atakav 2013).

One review of the film by Saudi Tariq Al Haydar (2014) contends that *Wadjda* blames the society and culture at the expense of considering issues of politics and the state, and questions Al Mansour's motivation for making the film. However, culture and politics are not so easily separated, and meliorism should not necessarily be seen as a rival to or replacement of radical or revolutionary politics. Al Haydar's reaction to the film contrasts with the warm reviews previously cited, and Mozaffar (2014) testifies to these differences, even in a group where cultural mores are familiar: "This film is a masterful debut. It is indeed a great story. In a second viewing, I watched it with a number of students, male and female; almost all were Arab Muslims. Half the group was completely offended, while the other half could not stop laughing." Waleed F. Mahdi (2016, 101–2) provides a more mixed view, criticizing the film for not depicting "the complicity of government agencies in maintaining repressive status quo politics directed against both foreign laborers and women" and for focusing on a middle-class family, while praising the film for its insightful "critique of school and family as the perpetuators of social repression and discrimination." *Wadjda* allows for these differing interpretations that focus on both features and absences of the film, while giving insight into the intersection of restrictions and oppressions so that reflection on the film can suggest a need for change.

Radical politics can pave the way for gradualism, and gradualism can ultimately lead to radical changes. Changes can also occur on a number of levels: cultural, economic, legal, and political. Lulwa Shalhoub (2019), writing about recent changes in regulations, suggest that these support "gradual changes . . . at a societal level." The raft of progressive changes for women that have occurred in Saudi Arabia in the last few years, one of which is closely related to *Wadjda*, should be considered. Not long after the film was made, women were allowed to ride bicycles, albeit initially fully covered up, in parks and recreational areas, and with a male companion (Ramdani 2013). Likewise, women defied the ban on driving cars in concerted days of action in recent years and are now permitted to drive.[18] On the political front, women voted and stood as candidates in the elections in 2015, and 20 percent of the king's advisory council are now women. In relation to sports, two women competed in the Olympics for the first time in 2012; four women were also part of the team for Rio de Janeiro in 2016, and two for Tokyo in 2021. With regard to employment, women are now allowed to work in shops selling cosmetics, lingerie, and clothes to women, positions previously reserved for men (Zoepf 2013), and other positions in the public service and private enterprise are being opened up. Furthermore, the restrictions on dress and autonomous decision-making are being relaxed to some extent (Hvidt 2018), as is the need for permission from a male relative to travel (BBC News 2019). In the light of these changes, Al Mansour's most recent film, *The Perfect Candidate*, focuses on a female candidate in the municipal elections (AFP 2018), and she is one of three women on the new Saudi General Authority for Culture (Vadehra 2018). Progress continues: women are becoming taxi drivers, and increasingly employed (National Editorial 2022), including in the armed forces, as part of a wide program of economic and social reform called Saudi Vision 2030 (Issa 2021).

The film can be seen in the tradition of activist films, or social realist films, that effect change by highlighting and alerting people to injustice, such as Bertrand Tavernier's *It All Starts Today* (1999), which led to electricity not being turned off in France when people had not paid their bills; his film *The Other Side of the Tracks* (1997), after which the government allocated more funds for immigrants to the area (Montreuil) where he filmed; and the Dardenne brothers' *Rosetta* (1999), which was given as a name to the Rosetta law concerning fair wages for underage workers.[19] These may be small changes, but they are vital. Julia Hallam and Margaret Marshment (2000, 190) make a useful distinction between social realist films and social issue films, noting that social realist films focus on how problems are created by society, while social issue films look at an individual's problems as a problem for society. Through its conception of a small change and the meaning of freedom it could have for a young girl, the cinematic realism of a world a little different from this one, *Wadjda* is clearly the first, and shows the potential of social realist cinema to think otherwise, to portray resistance, and to light a path for viewers to change their thinking as well.

CONCLUSION

Realism in *Wadjda* is focused on authenticity in terms of its specific location and time in Riyadh, and in elucidating philosophical thinking about nonviolent, meliorist resistance by homing in on one form of freedom:

freedom of movement. The freedom of a girl to ride a bicycle can also be connected to the freedom of women to drive and so to work and to participate in political life. The film articulates a nonviolent and gradualist approach to changing oppressive or restrictive regimes, using a child to represent the innocence and hope of youth, the chance of new beginnings through natality, and emphasizing authenticity and realism to engage and to strengthen its philosophical and political plausibility. Realism here appears as a way of pointing to a possibility presently just beyond reach. Wadjda engages in her own forms of work, aiming at her chief goal, and lives in the truth on a small scale. My argument is aimed at demonstrating not that a cinematic articulation of resistance can only occur through realism, but that realism is well suited to representing a gradualist or meliorist resistance, and *Wadjda* is a particularly good example. Nevertheless, the film allows for spectators' differing interpretations, as Bazin thought was central to realism in cinema, by juxtaposing the two narratives of daughter and mother, the daughter who gains a key to freedom, and the mother whose husband has taken another wife. We must remember that she too was a young girl, not so long ago. While Wadjda's narrative of resistance is more hopeful than the others explored in this book, the possibilities for resistance in the future cannot be predicted.

Conclusion

Each of the films I reflect on in this book show through different styles and narratives the potential for resistance that is everyday, that challenges authoritarian regimes, that is not violent, and nor does it fall into the traditional category of dissent. One of the keys for thinking about this kind of resistance is Václav Havel's account of living within the truth, or resisting through political action, honest work, and authentic living, which may begin with small-scale work and develop into parallel structures. Films provide a powerful, textured, and moving representation of this resistance, and these films are inspiring depictions of its possibilities.

When *A Dry White Season* was first released, many critics and reviewers found the film limited in its understanding of the apartheid system in South Africa and of its true victims. Tracing responses to the film, analyzing and comparing it to the book on which it is based and considering director Euzhan Palcy's aims alongside Aimé Césaire's anticolonialism, I argue that bystanders can play a focal role in resistance through a search for truth. Of the six films I discuss, *A Dry White Season* is the most "Hollywood," with well-known stars working with South African actors to produce a film of high drama, harrowing scenes of torture, and detailed vignettes of racist attitudes and actions. The Afrikaner protagonist Benjamin Du Toit, while at first lacking in an authentic approach to his role, is transformed through his concern for Black South Africans into a secondary victim and witness. Then he begins to live in the truth, a process that the film shows has a high price not only for him but for those around him within such an extreme political system. I contend that the film pursues its activist stance through the fictional device of focusing on an initially privileged character in order to highlight the brutality of the regime and the risks of resistance for less privileged actors. *A Dry White Season* portrays resistance in a regime so brittle that even to ask questions and seek justice within its own legal system is life-threatening. It links the characters in a united resistance that involves sacrifice for the future.

By contrast, Joshua Oppenheimer's documentary *The Look of Silence* considers resistance through the lens of the revelation of truth and the attempt to seek atonement and reconciliation. Adi Rukun, whose brother was murdered in the 1965–66 genocide in Indonesia, interviews perpetrators about their deeds, sometimes using his profession as optometrist to engage with them. It is a much quieter film than its pair, *The Act of Killing*, using frequent close-ups of Adi Rukun's face to show his endurance as well as visuals of the surroundings that evoke a hidden menace. While the interviews are surprisingly effective in eliciting accounts of their actions from the killers, they rarely assume responsibility for what they have done or express remorse. Their function as a form of resistance is shown through the threats that emerge and the danger to Adi Rukun, Joshua Oppenheimer, and all those involved in making the film. There are moments of acknowledgment of the harm of the genocide, from the descendants of the perpetrators, but they are rare and ambivalently expressed. *The Look of Silence* depicts both the sadness engendered by and the determination to resist needed in an oppressive situation that is ongoing and unresolved.

A more positive kind of resistance, perhaps the closest to Havel's conception, appears in the film *Barbara*. Christian Petzold's *Barbara* is the most intertextual of the films analyzed here, with references to literature, painting, and music providing a layered commentary on the protagonist Barbara's moral dilemma concerning whether to stay in East Germany or escape to the West. The director created a portrait of East Germany that exposes both its cruelty and its beauty and coziness, as well as some of the drawbacks of life in the West. Barbara, the pediatric doctor faced with the dilemma, finds her focus in her work obligations as well as a growing attraction to another doctor. The film shows how resistance can occur within an authoritarian society as well as by leaving it. In the chapter, I suggest that Barbara's resistance is singular, exemplifying only one possibility of resistance. She lives in the truth by staying and caring for others, yet also enables a younger woman Stella to resist by exiting. The existential and moral features of resistance that Havel describes are highlighted in *Barbara*.

Pablo Larraín's film *No* demonstrates the possibility of resistance within an authoritarian legal system even when the odds are stacked against it in the 1988 Chilean plebiscite. Here it is the notion of happiness and its capacity to transform trauma that informs and supports the resistance. Like the films in the previous chapters, *No* centers on one protagonist, René Saavedra, to represent this kind of resistance and the creativity involved. Advertising director is an unlikely profession to embody living in the truth, yet *No* convincingly suggests that is possible, while still allowing that there are multiple dimensions to his occupation and the plebiscite campaign. Larraín used old cameras and film stock to re-create the year 1988, fit seamlessly with old footage used, and conjure an atmosphere of nostalgia for that earlier time. The continuous trauma is reworked into a new narrative, and the past and present are connected to a hopeful sense for the future. The very idea of simply saying no as a way of resisting implies that refusal itself takes courage and strength, like Wang Xiaobo's silent majority. However, *No* also shows in this case the importance of collective power in Hannah Arendt's sense to make a change on that political scale. The character René is shown to change from a traumatic lack of affect through his engagement with the campaign in its focus on happiness and working with others. This film allows a taste of the jubilance of victory, while still foreshadowing the difficulties ahead in the transition to democracy from this one act of collective resistance.

Asghar Farhadi's film *Nader and Simin: A Separation*, a mix of genres including melodrama, returns to the dilemma faced by Barbara, this time in contemporary Iran and embodied as an ongoing argument between a married couple about whether to exit Iran or stay and care for family. Many of these films focus on the importance of the next generation. *A Separation* does this too, through Nader and Simin's relationship with their daughter Termeh. Yet it also reminds us of duties to the previous generation who cared for the adults through Nader's concern for his father. Farhadi's film involves a complex plot and a tight script that articulates the views of the characters, as well as many scenes filmed through doors and windows and overheard conversations, conveying secrecy as well as boundedness and frustration. My view is that the film is even-handed between Nader's and Simin's approaches, with the ambiguity of their situation, heightened in Iran, exemplifying Simone de Beauvoir's idea of ethical ambiguity, although audience members may experience more empathy with one or other of the couple. Further, the film shows that sometimes, especially in authoritarian societies, antinomies of ethical action cannot be resolved, and that is how two such engaging and well-meaning characters can come to opposing conclusions. The arbitrariness and unreasonableness of the legal system leaves them to construct their own ethical responses and judgments. Their resistance is their way of authentically responding to the need to care for others. *A Separation* also does not shy away from showing the tragic consequence of even this everyday resistance in leading a child to choose between her parents, and the ethical remainder of sorrow and loss.

Wadjda is perhaps the most optimistic depiction of resistance. Haifaa Al Mansour's film shows further the resources of realist cinema to provide political critique. The director's insistence on filming on location in Riyadh, Saudi Arabia, despite the challenges that choice presented, adds to the specific texture through the recognizable neighborhoods and notable evidence of construction. *Wadjda* offers a very specific sense of resistance as nonviolent in that it is focused on gradual change. This time the central character is Wadjda, a ten-year-old girl who has her own ideas about how to live and would like to have a bicycle even though that is forbidden. While she does not have a profession yet, she uses her diligence as a school student and works selling bracelets as a way to start to create her own parallel structures. Her successful campaign for the bicycle has prefigured a raft of improvements in the life of Saudi Arabian women that have occurred since the film's release, and the film itself was the beginning of a sea change in the country's film industry, which has blossomed. *Wadjda* represents the possibility of hope in the future, new beginnings, in making a young girl the center of resistance. Realism works in this case to signify a possibility that is the next stage of improvement and the easing of restrictions and to make that seem possible and reasonable in the near future. Like the other films discussed in this book, however, *Wadjda* does not present a completely rosy picture, considering her father's remarriage; thus, it reminds us that resistance cannot address all forms of injustice and always carries risks.

Havel's approach to everyday resistance as "living within the truth" has great potential to be explored further in relation to film, as it opens up worlds that have previously been neglected in favor of protest and violence. I have been inspired by his philosophical ideas to consider profound and subtle details of each film I discuss and how they contribute to understanding resistance to authoritarian regimes and how they connect with the thought of other progressive philosophers. Havel enabled me to see how what is often "hidden" and prepolitical is or becomes authentic and political and to focus on understanding how this is portrayed in the language of cinema. Further study may explore how resistance appears in cinema since the flowering of the films discussed here and the recent rise of authoritarianism around the world. The role of work and professions, especially work in the creative arts, in enabling resistance is something that a Havelian approach highlights, so future studies could focus even more closely on this feature in both narrative and documentary films, or could take an authorial perspective by examining Havel's ideas' direct influence on filmmakers, as well as his own plays and involvement with film.[1] Havel's concept of resistance in a post-totalitarian polity has continuing relevance to cinema's power to represent everyday resistance.

Notes

INTRODUCTION

1. For instance, Walter Benjamin (1996, 239), in his well-known essay "Critique of Violence," acknowledges that while in one sense a strike is a nonaction, in another it is a use of threat and thus force.
2. Gandhi (2007, 120), for example, describes passive resistance as "love-force" and "soul-force."
3. See Brennan 2016, 91–109, for a discussion of living in the truth in relation to existentialism.
4. See Ashcroft 2021, 161–201, for a discussion of these conditions and Arendt's view of nonviolent politics.
5. Lash references approvingly Stanley Cavell's (1981, 10) view that "the way to overcome theory correctly, philosophically, is to let the object or the work of your interest teach you how to consider it."

CHAPTER ONE

1. Palcy was also the first Black director to have a film about apartheid released. In 1976, South African director and playwright Gibson Kente made *How Long?*, a film based on his play of the same name, but it was not released (Davis 1996, 109). Furthermore, Palcy was the only woman to direct Marlon Brando.
2. Lewis Gordon (2019, 682–83) describes this film "as a classic portrait of the struggle for dignity amid poverty in Martinique."
3. The main comparison films here are *Cry Freedom* (dir. Richard Attenborough, 1987) and *A World Apart* (dir. Chris Menges, 1987), although *Mapantsula* (dir. Oliver Schmitz, 1988) is also relevant and is considered "an exemplary anti-apartheid film of the period [the 1980s]" (Maingard 2007a, 513).
4. It took Palcy five years to arrange the financing for the film, and the well-known actors, like Marlon Brando, who came out of retirement and offered to work for free

(Gill 2000, 373) were all paid lower wages than usual (Collins 1989; S. G. Freedman 1989). Brando was nominated for an Academy Award for Best Supporting Actor.
5. See the actors' respective biographies at the Internet Movie Database: Zakes Mokae, https://www.imdb.com/name/nm0596310/bio?ref_=nm_ov_bio_sm; Thoko Ntshinga, https://www.imdb.com/name/nm0637680/bio?ref_=nm_ov_bio_sm; and Winston Ntshona, https://www.imdb.com/name/nm0637681/?ref_=fn_al_nm_1. Jacqueline Maingard (2019, 211–12) also comments on the music by Hugh Masekela, an exiled South African jazz musician, including the male choral group Ladysmith Black Mambazo, and sociologist Josef Gugler (2003, 85) notes that the cast of the musical *Sarafina!* provided additional vocals.
6. See Maingard 2007b for a discussion of South African cinema in the 1970s and 1980s.
7. Gugler (2003, 86) details many of these. Brink's novel was partly a response to the murder of prisoners, including Steve Biko, by the South African Special Branch, although Brink had begun writing the novel before Biko was killed (Brittan 2005, 58; Iannaccaro 2014, 71). Both the book and film were banned in South Africa, although Brink was able to circulate three thousand copies of the book. The ban on the book was lifted soon after publication (Iannaccaro 2014, 81–82), and the ban on the film was lifted after an appeal in September 1989 (Maingard 2019, 204).
8. Bickford-Smith (2003, 25) notes that the film was made during a period after the 1986 State of Emergency in which the government "prohibited both print and television journalists from reporting on unrest situations," so films in part took on the role that journalists could not.
9. See Alvis 2021 for an analysis of "victimhood culture," where people claim to be victims for the purpose of gaining power.
10. In the book, Gordon is a cleaner who works at Ben's school (Brink (1979) 1980, 37).
11. Brink was also harassed for opposing apartheid (Davis 1996, 110).
12. Ben provides information to journalist Melanie Bruwer, who reports on it for her paper. The book opens the narrative with Ben's death and then returns to the beginning of the narrative in time.
13. Nixon (1994, 88) reads Brink's novel as "scrambling a ride on the helter skelter of political change."
14. For a detailed analysis of the range of means used to overthrow apartheid in South Africa, see Zunes 2014.
15. The criticism also ignores the fact that a friendship between a Black man, Nelson Mandela, and a white man, F. W. De Clerk, played a central role in the overthrow of apartheid (Welsh and Spence 2011, 191). Bickford-Smith (2003, 31) details other examples of friendships between Black and white South Africans that were crucial to the transition to democracy.
16. However, Stanley is a powerful figure of resistance in the book as well.
17. Higgins (1992, 108–9) contends that the film's narrative aspects and identification with characters undermine its documentary realism.
18. Bickford-Smith's (2003, 33) interpretation of the film is that "the body of *Dry White Season*'s content, its argument to that moment, affirms Stanley's execution of the security policeman [Captain Stolz] at the end of the film."

19. See Enns (2012, 37–62) for a discussion of the issue of victims becoming killers.
20. This narrator does not feature in the film, so it makes sense that the romance is also less relevant. One can see this narrative as showing how someone even further removed from the realities of apartheid becomes drawn into concern about them.
21. Samuel G. Freedman (1989) links this scene to Brink's novel *Rumours of Rain* (1978).
22. Maynard, Kearney, and Guimond (2010, 137) detail how numerous government beer halls were destroyed in the Soweto uprising.
23. Soweto is an acronym for Southwestern Townships, where Blacks and Coloureds were relocated, away from what were considered by whites to be the more desirable, northern parts of Johannesburg (Ackerman and DuVall 2000, 336).
24. This approach contrasts with the villains in *Madiba* (dir. Kevin Hooks, 2017), who have cold empty eyes like Stolz's and no redeeming features.
25. Bickford-Smith (2003, 32) also notes that the African National Congress approved the making of the film.
26. Maynard, Kearney, and Guimond analyze the novel as presenting a counter to the secrecy of the apartheid government's state terrorism and an alternative to revenge or retribution (2010).
27. One scholar says that the people surrounding Ben are so "clearly evil" that the choices look easy (Herndon 1999, 238). However, that claim seems to overlook what the choices entail.
28. There is no sense that the film is trying to present an equivalence of white suffering, as has occurred in some milieus in South Africa (Conway 2017).
29. Readers should remember that Gandhi began his nonviolent resistance opposing discrimination against Indians in South Africa from 1907 (Ackerman and DuVall 2000, 339).
30. Nevertheless, Ben is being influenced in other ways as well. In short scenes Ben is shown reading a newspaper with the headline "What is happening to the children of Soweto?" and with Melanie's byline.
31. See Iannaccaro 2014, 75–76, for a discussion of this aspect of the novel.
32. Emily also takes the initiative by going to the school to ask for help finding out how Gordon was.
33. This is probably why the book presents an ironic reading of relationships due to the narrator and why Palcy in her film can remove those elements and allow this relationship between liberatory struggles emerge.
34. McKenzie's speeches also reflect in an obvious way on the perversion of the justice system under apartheid.

CHAPTER TWO

1. Other films made about the genocide include Robert Lemelson's documentary *40 Years of Silence: An Indonesian Tragedy* (2010), which explains the history and interviews four families affected by it; Chris Hilton's documentary *Shadow Play* (2003), which examines the West's involvement and the propaganda used to attempt to

justify the crimes; and Peter Weir's *The Year of Living Dangerously* (1982), which dramatizes events leading up to the failed coup attempt.

2. As Rafter (2015, 137) notes, it is incredible that Adi confronts them when they are still dominant.

3. The movement held its eighteenth summit in Baku, Azerbaijan, in 2019.

4. See Simpson 2012 for a discussion of international involvement in and responses to the genocide. PKI chairman Aidit was captured and killed, while Omar Dhani, air force commander, spent thirty years in jail (1965–95) and died in 2009.

5. Furthermore, Melvin (2018, chap. 7) describes how from "April 1966 ethnic Chinese in Aceh were targeted as a group." Melvin and Pohlman (2018, 38; 39) note the IPT65's findings that motivations against ethnic Chinese played a role in Medan, Makasar, and Lombok, and other reports that Chinese were targeted in Central Java, Sumbawa, and South and West Kalimantan.

6. See Margaret Scott 2018 for a clear summary of the events; see Harff 2003 for a discussion of politicide. Melvin and Pohlman (2018) argue that the killings should be understood as genocide, with ideological, ethnic, and religious elements.

7. He says the United States may have been behind the killings of the military that were used to excuse or justify the genocide (Goodman 2015). Following the New Order Regime, the Reformation Era began (1999–).

8. Oppenheimer (*Look of Silence*, DVD notes) notes that the NBC news report shown in *The Look of Silence* celebrates the genocide. *Time* magazine and the *New York Times* both praised the killings (Campbell 2015).

9. Johannes Lang (2018) argues that, similarly, many of the perpetrators of the Holocaust, particularly members of the SS, were proud of their actions and boasted about them.

10. This film's executive producers are Werner Herzog and Errol Morris, who were also producers for *The Act of Killing*, along with Joram Ten Brink and André Singer.

11. Oppenheimer is now working on a musical about the apocalypse (Nussbaum 2020).

12. Adi Rukun intended to start an optometry shop, using funds from the True/False Film Festival (Buckley 2016).

13. See "Indonesian Roundtable" 2014 for discussions of this film.

14. I discuss Radzik's view of atonement in more detail in La Caze 2018, 130–38, where I argue that atonement should be understood as moral transformation and as related to but not constituted by reconciliation, as she contends.

15. Kara Barnette (2017, 68–72) considers atonement in relation to memory.

16. He was the forty-first perpetrator Oppenheimer (2014) filmed.

17. Julian Stallabrass (2013, 12) observes that the twenty-first century's first decade saw a return to documentary.

18. By contrast, Buruma (2015, 61–62) states that "Oppenheimer's second film, *The Look of Silence*, is a quieter, less flamboyant work and all the stronger for it."

19. Grierson (2015) calls *The Act of Killing* a "vérité-hybrid classic."

20. Oppenheimer (in O'Falt 2016) says his influences include Werner Herzog's *Even Dwarves Started Small* (1970) and *Stroszek* (1977), Tsai Min-Liang's *The Hole* (1998), and Robert Bresson's *Diary of a Country Priest* (1951).

21. Abbott (2017, 408) notes that Inong and the others have a kind of "epistemic impunity" or culpable unclarity of vision.
22. *The Look of Silence* was originally called *Snake River*, and that is how it is referred to by Anderson (2012, 269) and Brink and Oppenheimer (2012, 9).
23. Adi's two older brothers and Ramli's wife moved, so he has at least three other siblings. Sinnerbrink (2017, 37) suggests that the focus on Adi provides "a source of narrational authority."
24. There is also a ban on grandchildren of communists from getting government jobs (Goodman 2015), and in 2018 an environmental activist was jailed for supposedly "spreading communist ideology" (Reuters Staff 2018). The army lifted the ban on children and grandchildren of Communist Party members in 2022 (Hariyadi 2022).
25. The eye tests were Oppenheimer's idea, as a way to build "an instant intimacy and rapport, to show the perpetrators that Adi sees them, no matter what, as a human being, as any doctor will with their patients" (Blyth 2016). Adi gives an eye test to Inong Syah and also to his uncle.
26. For instance, he is threatened by M. Y. Basrun, speaker in the regional parliament (Schenkel 2015, 100).
27. The massacre was denied until 1990, when Mikhail Gorbachev acknowledged the crime, although the Soviet government refused to categorize it as a war crime, an act of genocide, or Stalinist repression and thus claimed no further accountability was needed. Putin has commemorated Katyn, and expressed regret and contrition, but did not apologize or offer compensation or full disclosure (Bidder 2010). There has been no progress since then (Scollon 2020).
28. However, the Indonesian government did not take part. The fifty-year anniversary in 2015 also drew more international attention to the atrocities.
29. Both films were also shown widely in the Netherlands, where survivors and children of survivors have been led to reflect on and discuss the events (Dragojlovic 2018).
30. However, Pohlman (2015, 133) argues that neither film is a story of "redemption, or reconciliation, or hope."

CHAPTER THREE

1. The film was shot in chronological order in single takes by director Christian Petzold, except for the scene at André's house when Barbara kisses André (Wood 2014, 107; Pinfold 2014, 283).
2. The town is not named, but the region is thought by German audiences to be Mecklenburg-Vorpommern (Gerhardt 2016, 555). Petzold did film in Ahrenshoop in that region for the Baltic coast (Prager 2017) and in a village called Kirchmöser, in Brandenburg, to the South (Cook 2017).
3. Buhanan (2016, 492) refers to Jörg as her "husband," but this is probably an assumption he makes. Abel (2013, 72) argues that all of Petzold's films revolve around a search for a home in some way.

4. The film won a Silver Bear for Best Director at the Berlin Film Festival and was nominated for Best Foreign Film at the 2013 Oscars.
5. He also plays opposite her in *Phoenix*.
6. Petzold (in Wood 2014, 105) says that he was most influenced by Herman Broch's novel *Barbara*, although, as Prager (2017) observes, the adaptation is very loose. Another book he mentions as background is *Rummelplatz* (Bräunig 2016; Oselund 2012). A closer connection is with Roland Gräf's film *The Flight* (1977), which concerns a doctor specializing in the care of infants considering whether to defect to the West. Pinfold (2014, 288) notes the connection with Wolf's novel.
7. Gerhardt (2016, 555, 563) suggests that this character's name could be a reference to *Stella Dallas* (dir. King Vidor, 1937) due to the related theme of maternal sacrifice.
8. Barbara was also in prison before being sent to the small town. Fulbrook (2008, 284) notes that applicants for an exit visa were sometimes imprisoned for two years before being allowed to leave.
9. Buhanan (2016, 491) notes the importance of images in representing Barbara's choice of "how to live in an unjust society."
10. Cook (2017) and Prager (2017) suggest that these scenes evoke Caspar David Friedrich's painting *Cross on the Baltic Sea*.
11. See Roland Bleiker (1993, 6, 10–13) and Andrew I. Port (2007, 112–39) for discussions of what is called "exit" as a form of popular protest, although Port (2007, 137) suggests that the departure of those who opposed the regime could also be seen as a "safety valve." Around 4 million East Germans from a population of 18 million are estimated to have left; most before the wall was erected in 1961 (3.5 million), and almost 80 were killed trying to leave. About 300,000 people went from West to East. In Škvorecký et.al, 1989, Werner Krätschell explains some of the reasons people stayed.
12. Nina Hoss is playing the piano herself in these scenes—for instance, Frédéric Chopin's Nocturne in G Minor, op. 15, no. 3.
13. István Szabó's film *Taking Sides* (2001) dramatizes the postwar denazification investigation.
14. Lyrics are by Matthias Claudius and music by Johann Abraham Peter Schulz. Stella only sings the first verse, so the rest of the song would need to be known for its significance to be recognized.
15. It was written by band members Nile Rodgers and Bernard Edwards.
16. Pinfold (2014, 290) observes that the song is "bitterly ironic" if one knows the words. Similarly, at the end of *Transit*, the Talking Heads' "Road to Nowhere" is played, signifying Georg's impossible situation of fleeing the Nazis. *Phoenix* is different in using the song "Speak Low" (1943) by Kurt Weill throughout.
17. Gerhardt (2016, 553) notes that Jörg lives in Düsseldorf.
18. There is a philosophical debate concerning whether Huck's decision to save Jim is a case of sympathy or an expression of his true morality. See Clarke 2020, 503–6 for the argument that the novel shows the dangers of Huck Finn's failure to reflect on his morality. Pinfold (2014, 296–97) sees Barbara as Huck and the use of novel as pointing to the range of possible interpretations of the film. The novel's presentation of Huck's vacillation can be compared with Barbara's deep reflection on her decision.

19. By contrast, Thomas Elsaesser (2019, 267) finds that the reading of the (first) passage where "Finn fakes his own murder" should be linked to André's discussion of the painting and the thought of Barbara being dissected like a corpse.
20. *Barbara* is often compared to Florian Henckel von Donnersmarck's *The Lives of Others* (2007) because of its GDR setting, although critics (Gerhardt 2016, 556) have noted the absence of GDR kitsch in *Barbara*, despite its attention to period detail, and Petzold insists that the setting is not just a backdrop (Cook 2017; Berghahn 2016, 325). Elsaesser (2019, 256) rebuts the idea that the portrayal is "particularly realistic" by saying it is "extremely stylized" and is a thought experiment about what the GDR might have felt like from the inside.
21. Barbara is body-searched after her train trip to get the money, and after the visit to the Interhotel. Hackeling (2003) notes that moving elsewhere within East Germany was one way that citizens could defy the authorities.
22. See Leask's (2013) article on humiliation, which discusses the humiliation of party members.
23. The film was shot on Kodak 35 mm film so that the color would suit the era (Prager 2017).
24. Reds and blues are particularly noticeable (Oselund 2012). For example, the light is pink or rose when Barbara is in Stella's room, and blue at the beach. Barbara often wears blue when she is not in her doctors' jacket. A more recent film, *Balloon* (dir. Michael Herbig, 2018), also uses bright colors.
25. Beauvoir's work is a rich source for thinking about film and is discussed again in chapters 5 and 6. See Lucy Fischer's (1990) reading of Max Ophül's *Letter from an Unknown Woman* (1948); Gwendolyn Doske's (2012) analysis of Marc Abraham's *Flash of Genius* (2008); Jean-Pierre Boulé and Ursula Tidd's (2012) edited collection; Jean-Pierre Boulé's (2013–14) reading of Claire Denis's *Chocolat* (1988); Daniel Shaw's (2017) discussion of Sam Mendes's *Revolutionary Road* (2008); chapters in Lori Jo Marso's (2017) book on films by Chantal Akerman, Lars von Trier, and Margarethe von Trotta; Lauren Du Graf's (2018) essay on the importance of cinema for Beauvoir and Kelli Fuery's (2022) book on Beauvoir and cinema.
26. See my chapter "The Time of Possible and Impossible Reciprocity: Love and Hate in Beauvoir" (2015) for a discussion of reciprocity in love.
27. Buhanan (2016, 493) claims that if Barbara stays out of love for André "then the film's ethical dilemma dissolves into superficial romanticism," which he contrasts negatively with ethical commitment to the state. Castro (2017) criticizes Buhanan for not recognizing how Barbara, like many other women, was otherwise forced to choose between love and her profession. Elsaesser (2019, 261) makes the point that "respect and self-respect through work" is central to Barbara's relationship with André. His conclusion notes, moreover, how Barbara makes an ethical choice and how that choice "challenges the regime, by not giving into the system's own cynicism and taking literally the values it only pretends to defend" (Elsaesser 2019, 273).
28. A high proportion of the population, about one in every hundred or 189,000 people, were recruited as informers (DW 2008).
29. Buhanan (2016, 492), Elsaesser (2019, 268), and Pinfold (2014, 292) point out that this discussion is taken from Sebald, *The Rings of Saturn* (1998, 12–13). Furthermore, Prager (2017) questions André's interpretation as "at least two of the surgeons

are . . . staring outward from Rembrandt's painting, looking neither at the corpse nor at the anatomical textbook." Krakenberg (2017) makes a similar point, as does Pinfold (2014, 292). Petzold says the painting is a symbol for the lack of empathy in the socialist society (Saito 2012).

30. Krakenberg (2017) suggests that André is urging Barbara to see the human beings beyond the system in the GDR.

31. This is an odd reference, because New Zealand switched to Celsius in 1969.

32. Paul Freedman (2013, 191) describes the way "endless conversations took place accompanied by low-quality but comforting coffee" in the GDR. Slavoj Žižek (1994, 64). observes that while the private sphere could be a place of escape into pleasures, there was also "an extraordinary flourishing of authentic friendship, of paying visits, of shared dinners, of passionate intellectual conversations in closed societies."

33. Because Mario attempted to kill himself, the assistant doctor, Schulze, says they must report him.

34. Earlier André had told Barbara, "You're always abrupt."

35. See Velleman 1999, 338–74, for a detailed argument showing that love is a moral emotion from a Kantian perspective.

36. She shows and cultivates sympathy for her patients, and gratitude can be seen both from Stella to Barbara, for example, and in Barbara's response to André's support for her work as a doctor. See my chapter on love and respect in *Wonder and Generosity* (2013, 35–58).

37. The parachutists fly over Stella while she is working clearing a river, and she uses that moment to escape.

38. Wolle (2019, 15) refers to the "cosy atmosphere' of the GDR, and Cook (2017) notes how "the warmth and appeal of everyday life" portrayed in the film is stressed in scholarship on *Barbara*. James F. Pontuso (2014) argues that *The Lives of Others* and *Good Bye Lenin!* (dir. Wolfgang Becker, 2003) show the power of everydayness to inspire individuals to question the regime.

39. The Ivan Turgenev story "The District Doctor" in *Sketches from a Hunter's Album* (1852) is the one André describes. It is a story of how a district doctor fell in love with a dying girl, and she imagines the ugly doctor is her lover. André is yet again putting his case to Barbara. It should be noted that Turgenev's portraits of the cruelty of the ruling class and the suffering of the peasants led to his arrest and confinement to his estate. Pinfold (2014, 293) points out that in this scene André addresses Barbara using the informal *du* rather than *Sie* for the first time. Wim Staat (2016, 195) notes that Barbara does likewise.

40. Fisher (2013, 141) calls this the "watershed moment."

41. At one point she asks about the plan, "Will it involve water?," which combined with her claim that she hates the sea, suggests another, albeit less serious, reason that she does not want to carry out the plan. She also says wonderingly "Denmark?" Perhaps she does not want to go through that experience.

42. She disappoints Steffi by letting her know that even if Gerhard marries Steffi, she will not be able to leave the GDR. Wolle (2019, 339) observes that "prostitution only existed in hard-currency hotels."

43. The catalog they browse through is a *Quelle* from 1980 (Gerhardt 2016, 558).

44. Prager (2017) analyzes the scene as like the doctors in the Rembrandt painting that stare out at the viewer, and Krakenberg (2017) makes a very similar point about the shots of Barbara and André being like the painting, although her look is hard to interpret.

CHAPTER FOUR

1. *No* was nominated for the Best Foreign Language Film of the Year Oscar in 2013; it won the Art Cinema Award at the 2012 Cannes Film Festival and many other awards.
2. Radstone (2007, 26) suggests that advocates of trauma theory need to be wary of promoting a Manichean view of the world where all negative ideas and actions come from without.
3. Dzero (2015, 120) cites 3,000 people killed and more than 80,000 tortured. Chile had a commission into human rights abuses resulting in death or disappearance, which delivered the National Commission for Truth and Reconciliation (Rettig) Report in 1991 and the National Commission on Political Imprisonment and Torture (Valech) Report in 2004. Thakkar (2017b, 248) gives figures from the Valech Report as 3,225 murdered or disappeared and 37,055 tortured, out of approximately 10 million people.
4. Feierstein explains how during the Argentinian military dictatorship (1976–83) almost any actual or potential criticism or rebellion against the regime was characterized as criminal subversion (2014, 161–66) and how such subversion was treated as defining of the group subjected to genocide (2014, 29).
5. For example, Chile has a Museum of Memory and Human Rights in Santiago to commemorate the victims of the civic-military regime.
6. See Di Stefano 2018 for a comparison of *No* and *Neruda*.
7. See Toledo 2013; Jung 2015; and Thakkar 2017a, 2017b for analyses of *Tony Manero* and *Post Mortem*.
8. However, as Kaplan (2005, 39) contends, viewers of films about trauma may also experience vicarious or secondary trauma.
9. Wells (2017, 514) acknowledges that "Larraín could never tell the entire story," Cilento (2015) also argues that the film "catalyzes a larger historical discussion," and Cronovich (2016, 166) defends the value of the film as an "introduction to the plebiscite." See Hirmas 1993, 82, for an analysis of the role of television in the campaign in reminding viewers of social, economic, and political conditions.
10. See Ackerman and DuVall 2000, 296–97, for a discussion of opinion polls and the background to the plebiscite. There was a long registration drive from 1980 to ensure that people were enrolled to vote, and 92 percent of the electorate was registered (Khazan 2013).
11. Khazan's (2013) article details how the positive theme had also been based on work with focus groups. Hirmas (1993, 87) states that the profile of undecided voters were women and young people, as represented in the film. By contrast, Cronovich (2016, 167) says they were women, poor people, and rural voters.

12. It also pointed to a conciliatory mood in another slogan, "Without hatred, without fear, and without violence, vote 'No.'"

13. Hirmas (1993, 85) notes that another slogan was "YES. You decide. We continue moving ahead or we return to the UP." Unidad Popular, or Popular Unity, is the coalition of left-wing parties that supported Allende.

14. Jung (2015, 127–28) is an exception in acknowledging the importance of happiness as a substantial political concept and the creativity of the campaign.

15. Zucconi (2016, 142–43) suggests that having a copywriter at the center of the political transition both allows recognition of the importance of mass media and encourages critical reflection on that history.

16. Cilento (2015) also sees René as going through an "anguishing dilemma" in both his professional and private life.

17. Wells (2017, 504) similarly argues that there is no possibility of redemption in Larraín's films. Simón (2018, 54) concurs that it is not clear that anything has changed between René and his boss after the campaign.

18. Harvey (2018, 56) suggests that René's ambivalence is paired with an ambivalence between realism and self-reflexivity in alluding to Larraín's presence.

19. Qandt's (2016) and Caldwell's (2013) humorless readings focus on René's first mentioning the possible damage to his car.

20. René also protects a crucial tape by taking it to the censor, while the others leave with empty video boxes. This tape is the one censored. Simón (2018, 110–11) notes that the only censorship of the campaign occurred on day 8, when the "No" program included testimony from a judge concerning fifty cases of torture. After a national and international outcry, the *Sí* campaign self-censored its own program the following day.

21. James Cisneros (2018, 53–54) observes that Larraín exaggerates the quality of the video by allowing rather than controlling blurring and overexposure.

22. Jung (2015, 120) notes that "video—U-matic, VHS-C, Hi-8, Super VHS and Betacam—was central for the development of an alternative 'imaginary' of Chilean society and, later, as part of the audio-visual battle of the 1980s, as well as the NO campaign." See Chanan 2013 for an account of the importance of video to resistance in Chile and other Latin American countries and the U-matic Project website (http://www.prypecyoidis.org/umatic) for documentaries and other films made on video during the dictatorship.

23. It is also referred to in another slogan, "We are more" (Hirmas 1993, 91), which can be seen as a response to the "Yes" campaign's "We are millions."

24. Applebaum (2013) notes these aspects of the film, and Wells (2017, 517, 504) recognizes that Larraín's films may help viewers to work through the trauma by helping them to see themselves as implicated subjects, as well as acting it out. See Traverso 2011 for a discussion of how Chilean documentaries since the regime have involved representations that work through the traumatic memories rather than acting them out.

CHAPTER FIVE

1. *A Separation* was highly honored at the state-endorsed Fajr Film Festival and was a box office success in Iran (Cheshire 2012, 78). In addition, it won the Golden Bear at the 2011 Berlinale and the 2012 Academy Award for Best Foreign Language Film, suggesting that it appeals to both local and international audience.
2. Ramin Jahanbegloo and Nojang Khatami (2013, 331–36) explain why Iran should be seen as an authoritarian and antidemocratic state, but not a totalitarian one.
3. Lisa Tessman (2000, 190) develops further the idea of moral residue or remainder from Bernard Williams (1973), where following a choice that is the best under the circumstances, we are still left with concerns about the unmet competing moral obligations.
4. See Tapper 2002 and Gow 2011 for discussions of new Iranian cinema.
5. One of Farhadi's students claims that he took the idea for the film from her (Byrnes 2022; Roxborough 2022).
6. As A. O. Scott (2011) notes, *A Separation* is both "family melodrama and legal thriller."
7. Lane (2012) comments that while you feel for the characters, "you don't quite know what to think."
8. Julia Hallam and Margaret Marshment (2000, 190) describe this distinction as that between social issue films and social realist films.
9. See Hengehold 2017 for a discussion of how separation and connection are focal concepts for Beauvoir.
10. Sattar Oraki, an Iranian composer, created the music used for the end title and trailer.
11. Linnell Secomb (in Boulé and Tidd 2012, 81–96) argues that Beauvoir's work enables us to interpret the issues of melodrama in "a richer and more nuanced way," using the films *Far from Heaven* (dir. Todd Haynes, 2002) and *All That Heaven Allows* (dir. Douglas Sirk, 1955).
12. Iran has a rapidly aging population, very few nursing homes, and a strong expectation that families will care for parents. It is also difficult to find private nurses other than uneducated people from rural areas (Peyrovi, Mortazavi, and Joolaee 2010). Thus, the family's situation is quite a typical one.
13. The children are of consequence for Farhadi, as they are judging what is going on. As he expresses it, the grandfather is at the end of life and does not remember his past, whereas the children have not had much experience, and both are controlled by others (Special Features: *A Separation*, 2011).
14. This has not happened before, and the audience can surmise that it is partly due to his reliance on Simin.
15. An article on dementia as cultural metaphor notes that "throughout the film, Nader's father is mute, but his emotional life is evident" (Zeilig 2013, 263).
16. Azam phoned Simin to tell her what had happened.
17. When Simin tries to stop Hojjat hitting Nader, Hojjat punches her, inflicting a black eye.
18. In his review, Romig (2012) explains that it is criminal abortion that carries the penalty of blood money and possibly one to three years in prison in Iranian law. The

fetus was nineteen weeks, yet to some extent it is treated as if it had been a living person. Simin's mother (Shirin Yazdanbakhsh) remarks ironically that they say "my child" as if it was an eighteen-year-old.

19. In addition, Nader files a complaint about Razieh's treatment of his father.

20. Iranian law is a blend of sharia law (Twelver Shia version) and French-influenced civil law (Romig 2012; Maranlou 2015, 50–87).

21. Razieh shows the judge that Hojjat needs to take antidepressants since he lost his job.

22. Ms. Ghahraii (Merila Zarei), Termeh's tutor, testifies for Nader, saying that he could not have heard their discussion about Razieh's pregnancy and that her pregnant state was not yet visible. But Farhadi discloses that she gave Razieh the number for the gynecologist and that Nader had heard everything—that is the only way he could have known about the number to ask her for it. And after Nader rings Ms. Ghahraii for the number, she revokes her testimony to the magistrate.

23. Nader also insists that Termeh asks for the money for a tip back from a service station attendant, as she was the one who had filled the tank.

24. Somayeh is also brought into the dispute when she is questioned by Ms. Ghahraii.

25. Christine Daigle (2014, 202) notes that social conceptions do generate ambiguity for women, "but it is an inauthentic ambiguity."

26. The situation of women in Iran is difficult, as they face legal and practical discrimination in relation to divorce, employment, inheritance, and political office and in family and criminal law (Amnesty International 2018).

27. See Burke 2011 for a useful discussion of censorship in Iranian films.

28. Simin had been planning to come back to the family as Termeh points out she had all her things in the car, but when Nader still refuses to pay the blood money, she changes her mind. Robert Sinnerbrink (2016, 95–102) has a detailed discussion of the shifts of empathy and sympathy for the different characters in this scene.

29. Another scene the viewer might remember is when Nader tells Termeh not to sit down on the wet stairs, so it is most likely that Razieh slipped on them rather than that she was pushed by Nader.

30. Clearly Hojjat's sister, Azam, also knows the truth, from her expression and comments. Razieh appears to assume that Simin has told Nader what really happened, although the viewer is not shown that. If she had, that would be another reason he agrees to the deal: because his innocence has been acknowledged, at least in private.

31. Razieh says, "Don't beat yourself," implying that he must beat himself often. In fact, he is shown in an earlier scene hitting himself against the door in the investigator's office, and she has said that he is depressed.

32. In her account of Beauvoir's view of political judgment, Sonia Kruks (2012, 124–50) stresses the features of the wager and of the less rational aspects of the self.

CHAPTER SIX

1. This critique could condemn social realism for glorifying socialist regimes, for example. Similarly, feminist theorists have criticized realist film for reinforcing patriarchal and bourgeois stereotypes (Kaplan 1996, 125–41). By contrast, Theodor Adorno (2003, 178–86) faulted Hollywood films for reinforcing prejudices and stereotypes, arguing that only avant-garde art can be socially critical. However, Michael Ryan and Douglas Kellner (1988, 269) argue that some uses of some *forms* are ideological, such as "camera techniques that suggest natural hierarchies, spectacles that idealize violence as a solution to social problems, voyeuristic objectifications that debase others."

2. For example, Ryan and Kellner (1988, 268) suggest that realist narratives can provide challenges to domination through "different character representations, different plot strategies, different moral configurations, different tropes of action." E. Ann Kaplan (1996, 132–35) also contends that there is nothing in realist cinema per se that means it cannot be critical of prevailing ideologies.

3. *Wadjda* was submitted for the Best Foreign Language Film Oscar in 2013 but was not nominated. Al Mansour has also written a children's book based on the film, *The Green Bicycle* (2015). Prior to *Wadjda*, a documentary called *Arabia 3D* (2011) was made by Greg MacGillivray.

4. Techniques to promote realism, such as long takes, or methods, such as following the sequence of events, can be called naturalistic. Non-naturalistic techniques include those like the montage Bazin eschews, slow motion, and freeze frames. While this distinction between naturalism and critical realism has featured in discussions of literature (Lukács 1972, 85–96), Hallam and Marshment (2000, 5–6) maintain that they cannot be distinguished formally and that the distinction tends to rest on either a value judgment or assumptions about the intentions of authors. Cavell (1971, 73, 133–46) is open-minded about the techniques or methods filmmakers use, depending on their significance and effectiveness, and the integrity, in the particular film.

5. As Tom Gunning (2007, 46) observes, films do not have to be realistic "to have a 'realistic' effect, that is, to invite the empathic participation, both imaginative and physiological, of viewers."

6. Smith (2006, 131) stresses that for Bazin, emotions and our reflection on them are also enhanced in film by narrative and drama.

7. This view contrasts with the view that Bazin's concerns with cinema of a certain period "can be seen to have been eroded, epistemologically, by the advent of postmodernism, and, technologically, by the movement from analogue to digital modes of image capture and construction" (Grist 2009, 28), although Grist believes that Bazin's work is of continuing interest.

8. Robert Sinnerbrink (2012, 98), in his discussion of Bazin, suggests that genuine realism tries to express a meaningful world "with as much authenticity as possible, combining concrete detail, unity of composition, with openness to interpretation."

9. Richard Rushton criticizes Stephen Prince's (2004, 27) view that the use of digital film makes an ontological change to film itself. In his more recent work, Prince (2019, 72) says that the filmmakers' objectives and the contexts films are made in are more significant than whether they are made digitally.

10. Alwaleed Bin Talal also supported the first Saudi woman pilot, Hanadi Al-Hindi, to fly planes in Saudi Arabia (BBC 2014). IMDb lists seventeen production companies for the film.

11. Tom Gunning (1990, 61) argues that the "attractions" or spectacle of early cinema can be reconciled with later narrative cinema.

12. *Bicycle Thieves* is also known as *The Bicycle Thief.*

13. Bazin (1967b, 2:60) refers to *Bicycle Thieves* as "pure cinema," where there are "no more actors, no more story, no more sets, which is to say that in the perfect aesthetic illusion of reality there is no more cinema." Lane also notes this connection, and the one with Jacques Tati's *Jour de fête* (1949), François Truffaut's *Les mistons* (*The Mischief Makers*, 1957), and the Dardenne brothers' *The Kid with a Bike* (2013). Shiel (2006, 1) sees neorealism as "a historically and culturally-specific manifestation of the general aesthetic quality known as 'realism' which is characterized by a disposition to the ontological truth of the physical, visible world." For Deleuze (1986, 141, 3), realism is "milieux and modes of behavior, milieux which actualize and modes of behavior which embody," while neorealism in cinema "is the purely optical and sound situation which takes the place of the faltering sensory-motor situations."

14. Omer M. Mozaffar (2014) notes that the film "zeroes in on many inconsistencies" and how "women enact the coercion, and suffer from it."

15. However, Fatemeh Hosseini-Shakib questions this analysis by suggesting that it neglects the important absences in the kinds of films made, such as fantasy films created for child audiences, or representations of ordinary children (Jahed 2012, 231). Deleuze (1989, 3) suggests that children are limited in their movement, but this allows them to see and hear more. This comment about children taking the role of observers is relevant to *A Separation*, but is not a compelling description of *Wadjda*, as they are absorbed in their own lives.

16. Kelli Fuery (2022, 61–90) considers Beauvoir's idea of adolescence in relation to ambiguity to interpret Debra Granik's *Leave No Trace* (2018).

17. Lane (2013) sees this friendship "as the weak spot in the tale. No boy, whatever his background, will risk the jibes of his pals to go and hang out with a girl. Compared with the rooted figures who surround him, he seems a bit of a dream." However, this claim seems to miss the film's point concerning the possibility for positive change in the future. Armes (2015, 304) also addresses this aspect of the film.

18. Al Mansour herself responded to the restrictions on driving by going to her wedding in a golf cart (Hoggard 2013). This decision is a way of simultaneously acknowledging the existence of the limitations on driving and overcoming those limitations.

19. Ryan and Kellner (1988, 266–95) discuss activist Hollywood and independent films. A different approach is taken in *Lemon Tree* (dir. Eran Riklis, 2008), which was based on an incident that had already occurred and a court case that was not successful.

CONCLUSION

1. For example, César Ballester (2016) has written on Havel and other Central European dissidents' influence on Krzysztof Kieślowski's films; Yana Meerzon (2011, 479–50) considers Havel's plays in relation to memory; Timothy Barney (2015) analyzes the documentary about Havel's presidential terms directed by Pavel Koutecký and Miroslav Janek, *Citizen Havel* (2008); and Jesse Bryant Wilder (1991) reviews another film about Havel, Wojtech Jasný's *Why Havel?* (1991).

Works Cited

Abbott, Mathew. 2017. "*The Look of Silence* and the Problem of Monstrosity." *Film-Philosophy* 21, no. 3: 392–409.

ABC News. 2023. "Indonesia President Joko Widodo Acknowledges His Country's Past 'Gross Human Rights Violations.'" January 11. https://www.abc.net.au/news/2023-01-11/indonesia-president-joko-widodo-acknowledges-rights-violations/101845560.

Abel, Marco. 2008. "The Cinema of Identification Gets on My Nerves: An Interview with Christian Petzold." *Cineaste*, December 2. https://www.cineaste.com/summer2008/the-cinema-of-identification-gets-on-my-nerves.

———. 2010. "Imaging Germany: The (Political) Cinema of Christian Petzold." In *The Collapse of the Conventional: German Film and Its Politics at the Turn of the Twenty-First Century*, edited by Jaimey Fisher and Brad Prager, 258–84. Detroit: Wayne State University Press.

———. 2013. *The Counter-cinema of the Berlin School*. Suffolk: Boydell & Brewer.

Ackerman, Peter, and Jack DuVall. 2000. *A Force More Powerful: A Century of Nonviolent Conflict*. New York: St. Martin's.

Adorno, Theodor. 2003. *The Culture Industry: Selected Essays on Mass Culture*. Edited by J. M. Bernstein. London: Routledge.

AFP. 2018. "Al Mansour Is Returning to Film in Saudi Arabia." *The National*, August 6. www.thenational.ae/arts-culture/film/haifaa-al-mansour-is-returning-to-film-in-saudi-arabia-1.757336.

Ahmed, Sara. 2010. *The Promise of Happiness*. Durham, NC: Duke University Press.

Ahram Online. 2016. "Famous Egyptian Actress Fayrouz Dies at 73." January 30. www.english.ahram.org.eg/NewsContent/5/32/186277/Arts—Culture/Film/Famous-Egyptian-actress-Fayrouz-dies-at-.aspx.

Al Haydar, Tariq. 2014. "Haifaa Al Mansour's *Wadjda*: Revolutionary Art or Pro-State Propaganda?" *Jadaliyya*, January 13. www.jadaliyya.com/Details/30078.

Al Mansour, Haifaa. 2015. *The Green Bicycle*. London: Puffin.

Alvis, Jason W. 2021. "Christianity and the Culture (Wars) of Victimhood: Persecution, Purity, Patience." *Philosophy Today* 65, no. 4: 881–98.

Amnesty International. 2018. "Iran 2017/18." https://www.amnesty.org/en/countries/middle-east-and-north-africa/iran/report-iran/.

Anderson, Benedict. 2012. "Impunity." In *Killer Images: Documentary Film, Memory and the Performance of Violence*, edited by Joram Ten Brink and Joshua Oppenheimer, 268–86. New York: Columbia University Press.

Apor, Péter. 2022. *Socialism Goes Global: The Soviet Union and Eastern Europe in the Age of Decolonisation.* Edited by James Mark and Paul Betts, 115–47. Oxford: Oxford University Press.

Applebaum, Stephen. 2013. "Mad Men vs. Augusto Pinochet: Pablo Larraín's New Film *No*." *The Scotsman*, February 4.

Arendt, Hannah. (1958) 1998. *The Human Condition*. 2nd ed. Chicago: University of Chicago Press.

———. (1961) 1993. *Between Past and Future: Eight Exercises in Political Thought*. 2nd ed. London: Penguin.

———. 1968. *Between Past and Future: Eight Exercises in Political Thought*. London: Penguin.

———. 1970. *On Violence*. San Diego: Harcourt Brace.

———. 1972. *Crises of the Republic*. New York: Harcourt Brace Jovanovich.

———. 1976. *The Origins of Totalitarianism*. 2nd ed. San Diego: Harcourt Brace.

———. 1992. *Eichmann in Jerusalem: A Report on the Banality of Evil*. London: Penguin.

———. 2003. *Responsibility and Judgment*. New York: Schocken.

Aristotle. 1984 (350 BCE). *Nicomachean Ethics*. In *The Complete Works of Aristotle*, vol. 2, edited by Jonathan Barnes. Princeton, NJ: Bollingen.

Armes, Roy. 2015. *New Voices in Arab Cinema*. Bloomington: Indiana University Press.

Arnheim, Rudolf. 1957. *Film as Art*. Berkeley: University of California Press.

———. 1993. "The Two Authenticities of the Photographic Media." *Journal of Aesthetics and Art Criticism* 51, no. 4: 537–40.

Ashcroft, Caroline. 2021. *Violence and Power in the Thought of Hannah Arendt*. Philadelphia: University of Pennsylvania Press.

Associated Press. 2016. "Memorial Monument Shines Light on 1965 Indonesia Massacre." *Indian Express*, October 5. https://indianexpress.com/article/world/world-news/memorial-monument-shines-light-on-1965-indonesian-massacre-3066332/.

Atakav, Eylam. 2013. "Wadjda: A Girl Who Changes the World on Her Bicycle." *Huffington Post*, August 23. www.huffingtonpost.com/dr-eylem-atakav/wadjda-movie-review_b_3763952.html.

———. 2020. "Women, Islam, and Cinema: Gender Politics and Representation in Middle Eastern Films and Beyond." In *The Routledge Companion to Cinema and Gender*, edited by Kristin Lené Hole, Dijana Jelača, E. Ann Kaplan, and Patrice Petro, 244–53. London: Routledge.

Ballester, César. 2016. "From *Personnel* to *Dekalog*: Michnik, Havel, Konrad, Camus, and the Search for the Individual in the Cinema of Krzysztof Kieślowski." *Central Europe* 14, no. 2: 106–24.

Barlow, Helen. 2013. "*Wadjda*: Haifaa Al Mansour Interview." *SBS*, June 4. http://www.sbs.com.au/movies/article/2013/06/04/wadjda-haifaa-al-mansour-interview.

Barnette, Kara. 2017. "Haunting Guilt, Communities of Memory, and the Process of Atonement." *The Pluralist* 12, no. 1: 60–73.

Barney, Timothy. 2015. "*Citizen Havel* and the Construction of Czech Presidentiality." *Quarterly Journal of Speech* 101, no. 4: 585–611.

Bazin, André. 1967a. *What Is Cinema? Essays*. Vol. 1. Translated by Hugh Gray. Berkeley: University of California Press.

———. 1967b. *What Is Cinema? Essays*. Vol. 2. Translated by Hugh Gray. Berkeley: University of California Press.

BBC News. 2014. "Saudi Arabia: First Woman to Get Pilot License." *BBC News*, April 23. http://www.bbc.com/news/blogs-news-from-elsewhere-27125689.

———. 2019. "Saudi Arabia Allows Women to Travel Independently." *BBC News*, August 2. http://www.bbc.com/news/world-middle-east-49201101.

Beauvoir, Simone de. 1997. *The Ethics of Ambiguity*. Translated by Bernard Frechtman. Secaucus: Citadel. [*Pour une morale de l'ambiguïté*. Paris: Gallimard, 1947.]

———. 2010. *The Second Sex*. Translated by Constance Borde and Sheila Malovany-Chevallier. New York: Knopf. [*Le deuxième sexe*, Paris: Gallimard, 1949.]

———. 2018. "Brigitte Bardot and the Lolita Syndrome." In *The Continental Philosophy of Film Reader*, edited by Joseph Westfall, 380–87. London: Bloomsbury.

Beckett, Lois. 2022. "'With My Camera I Don't Shoot, I Heal': Director Euzhan Palcy Receives Honorary Award." *The Guardian*, November 20.

Behlil, Melis. 2015. "*The Look of Silence*: An Interview with Joshua Oppenheimer and Adi Rukun." *Cineaste*, 26–31.

Benjamin, Walter. 1996. *Walter Benjamin: Selected Writings*. Vol. 1, *1913–1926*. Edited by Marcus Bullock and Michael W. Jennings. Cambridge, MA: Belknap Press.

Benson, Sheila. 1989. "The Art of Politics and Passion." *Los Angeles Times*, October 15.

Benson-Allott, Caetlin. 2013. "An Illusion Appropriate to the Conditions: *No* (Pablo Larraín, 2012)." *Film Quarterly* 66, no. 3: 61–63.

Berghahn, Daniela. 2016. "DEFA's Afterimages: Looking Back at the East from the West in *Das Leben der Anderen* (*The Lives of Others*, 2006) and *Barbara* (2012)." *Re-imagining DEFA: East German Cinema in Its National and Transnational Contexts*, edited by Seán Allan and Sebastian Heiduschke, 312–34. New York: Berghahn Books.

Bickford-Smith, Vivian. 2003. "Reviewing Hollywood's Apartheid: *Cry Freedom* (1987) and *A Dry White Season* (1989)." *South African Historical Journal* 48, no. 1: 23–34.

Bidder, Benjamin. 2010. "Remembering the Katyn Massacre: Putin Gesture Heralds New Era in Russian-Polish Relations." *Spiegel Online*, April 8. https://www.spiegel.de/international/europe/remembering-the-katyn-massacre-putin-gesture-heralds-new-era-in-russian-polish-relations-a-687819.html.

Blanchot, Maurice. 2010. "Refusal." In *Political Writings, 1953–1993*, translated by Zakir Paul, 7. New York: Fordham University Press.

Bleiker, Roland. 1993. *Nonviolent Struggle and the Revolution in East Germany*. Cambridge: Albert Einstein Institution.

Bloom, Julie. 2013. "Where a Bicycle Is Sweetly Subversive." *New York Times*, September 15. http://www.nytimes.com/2013/09/15/movies/wadjda-by-haifaa-al-mansour-made-in-saudi-arabia.html.

Blustein, Jeffrey. 2018. "Traumatic Emotions." In *Emotions and Mass Atrocity: Philosophical and Theoretical Explorations*, edited by Thomas Brudholm and Johannes Lang, 234–61. Cambridge: Cambridge University Press.

Blyth, Antonia. 2016. "*The Look of Silence's* Joshua Oppenheimer: 'We Had a Getaway Car and Bags Packed, Ready to Evacuate'—Awardsline." *Deadline*, February 4.

Bobo, Jacqueline. 2016. "Black Women Filmmakers: A Brief History." In *The Routledge Companion to Cinema and Gender*, edited by Kristin Lené Hole, Dijana Jelača, E. Ann Kaplan, and Patrice Petro, 265–74. London: Routledge.

Boo, Bernard. 2013. "Interview: Haifaa Al Mansour of *Wadjda." Way Too Indie*, September 18. http://waytooindie.com/interview/interview-haifaa-al-mansour-wadjda/.

Boulé, Jean-Pierre. 2013–14. "A Reading of Claire Denis's *Chocolat* in the Light of Simone de Beauvoir's *The Second Sex*." *Simone de Beauvoir Studies* 29: 56–65.

Boulé, Jean-Pierre, and Ursula Tidd, eds. 2012. *Existentialism and Contemporary Cinema: A Beauvoirian Perspective*. Oxford: Berghahn Books.

Bräunig, Werner. 2016. *Rummelplatz*. Translated by Samuel P. Willocks. London: Seagull Books.

Brennan, Daniel. 2016. *The Political Thought of Václav Havel: Philosophical Influences and Contemporary Applications*. Leiden: Brill.

Brink, André. 1978. *Rumours of Rain*. London: W. H. Allen.

———. 1980. *A Dry White Season*. New York: Morrow.

Brink, Joram Ten, and Joshua Oppenheimer, eds. 2012. *Killer Images: Documentary Film, Memory and the Performance of Violence*. London: Wallflower Press.

Brison, Susan. 2003. *Aftermath: Violence and the Remaking of the Self*. Princeton, NJ: Princeton University Press.

Brittan, Alice. 2005. "Reading Sex and Violence in André Brink's *Rumours of Rain* and *A Dry White Season*." *Tydskrif vir Letterkunde* 42, no. 1: 55–77.

Broch, Herman. 1936 [1994]. *Barbara. Novelle*. Frankfurt: Suhrkamp.

Brooks, Xan. 2013. "Interview with Haifaa Al Mansour." *The Guardian*, July 16. http://www.theguardian.com/film/video/2013/jul/16/wadjda-saudi-arabia-female-director-video.

Brudholm, Thomas. 2008. *Resentment's Virtue: Jean Améry and the Refusal to Forgive*. Philadelphia: Temple University Press.

Buckley, Cara. 2016. "Adi Rukun, Neither Silent nor Intimidated." *New York Times*, February 12.

Buhanan, Kurt. 2016. "What's Wrong with This Picture? Image-Ethics in Christian Petzold's Films." *German Quarterly* 89, no. 4: 480–95.

Burke, Joseph. 2011. "Rediscovering Morality through Asghar Farhadi's *A Separation*." *Senses of Cinema*, no. 61. http://sensesofcinema.com/2011/feature-articles/rediscovering-morality-through-ashgar-farhadi%E2%80%99s-a-separation/.

Buruma, Ian. 2015. "The Violent Mysteries of Indonesia." *New York Review of Books*, October 22, 60–62.

Butler, Judith. 2020. *The Force of Nonviolence: An Ethico-Political Bind*. London: Verso.

Byrnes, Paul. 2022. "Two-Time Oscar Winner's Superb New Drama Is Not without Controversy." *Sydney Morning Herald*, June 9.

Caldwell, Thomas. 2013. "Film Review—*No* (2012)." *Cinema Autopsy*. https://blog.cinemaautopsy.com/2013/04/18/film-review-no-2012/.

Campbell, Meagan. 2015. "A Few Questions for His Brother's Killers." *Maclean's*, July 27.

Carchidi, Victoria K. 1994. "South Africa from Text to Film: *Cry Freedom* and *A Dry White Season*." *Departmental Papers (Landscape Architecture)* 7, University of Pennsylvania, 47–61.

Caruth, Cathy. 1996. *Unclaimed Experience: Trauma, Narrative, and History*. Baltimore: Johns Hopkins University Press.

Castro, Joy. 2017. "'A Place without Parents': Queer and Maternal Desire in the Films of Christian Petzold." In *Senses of Cinema* 2017.

Cavell, Stanley. 1971. *The World Viewed: Reflections on the Ontology of Film*. New York: Viking.

———. 1981. *Pursuits of Happiness: The Hollywood Comedy of Remarriage*. Cambridge, MA: Harvard University Press.

Césaire, Aimé. (1950) 2000. *Discourse on Colonialism*. Translated by Joan Pinkham. New York: Monthly Review Press.

———. 2020. *Resolutely Black: Conversations with Françoise Vergès*. Translated by Matthew B. Smith. Cambridge: Polity.

Chanan, Michael. 2013. "Video Speech in Latin America." In *The Oxford Handbook of New Audiovisual Aesthetics*, edited by John Richardson, Claudia Gorbman, and Carol Vernallis, 194–212. Oxford: Oxford University Press.

Chenoweth, Erica, and Maria J. Stephan. 2011. *Why Civil Resistance Works: The Strategic Logic of Nonviolent Conflict*. New York: Columbia University Press.

Cheshire, Godfrey. 2012. "Iran's Cinematic Spring." *Dissent* 59, no. 2: 76–80.

Chirot, Daniel. 2020. *You Say You Want a Revolution? Radical Idealism and Its Tragic Consequences*. Princeton, NJ: Princeton University Press.

Cilento, Fabrizio. 2015. "Pablo Larraín's *No* and the Aesthetics of Television." *Seismopolite*, April 30. https://www.seismopolite.com/pablo-Larraín-no-and-the-aesthetics-of-television.

Cisneros, James. 2018. "Precarious Images: Media and Historicity in Pablo Larraín's *No*." In *The Precarious in the Cinemas of the Americas*, edited by Constanza Burucúa and Carolina Sitnisky, 41–59. London: Palgrave Macmillan.

Clarke, Steve. 2020. "Huckleberry Finn's Conscience: Reckoning with the Evasion." *The Journal of Ethics* 24, no. 4: 485–08.

Claudius, Matthias. 1916. "Evening Song." In *A Harvest of German Verse*, translated by Margarete Münsterberg. Whitefish: Kessinger. https://www.bartleby.com/177/27.html. Accessed March 11, 2022.

Collins, Glenn. 1989. "A Black Director Views Apartheid." *New York Times*, September 25.

Conway, Daniel. 2017. "Shades of White Complicity: The End Conscription Campaign and the Politics of White Liberal Ignorance in South Africa." In *Exploring Complicity: Concept, Cases and Critique*, edited by Afxentis Afxentiou, Robin Dunford, and Michael Neu, 119–41. London: Rowman and Littlefield.

Cook, Roger. 2017. "The Texture of History: Petzold's *Barbara* and *The Lives of Others*." In *Senses of Cinema* 2017.

Cox, Damian. 2015. "Overcoming Victimhood: Stoicism, Anti-Stoicism and *Le Fils*." In *Victim Victorious; From Fire to Phoenix*, edited by Marie-Claire Patron and Stephen Holden, 1–15. Hauppauge: Nova.

Cronovich, Paula T. 2016. "'No' and *No*: The Campaign of 1988 and Pablo Larraín's Film." *Radical History Review*, no. 124: 165–76.

Dadar, Taraneh. 2014. "Framing a Hybrid Tradition: Realism and Melodrama in *About Elly*." In *Melodrama in Contemporary Film and Television*, edited by Michael Stewart, 223–38. London: Palgrave Macmillan.

Daigle, Christine. 2014. "*The Second Sex* as Appeal: The Ethical Dimension of Ambiguity." *philoSOPHIA* 4, no. 2: 197–220.

Daigle, Christine, and Louise Renée. 2015. "Performing Philosophy: Beauvoir's Methodology and Its Ethical and Political Implications." *Janus Head* 14, no. 2: 71–86.

Dargis, Manohla. 2013. "Try Freedom: Less Filling! Tastes Great! *No* with Gael García Bernal." *New York Times*, February 14.

Davis, Peter. 1996. *In Darkest Hollywood: Exploring the Jungles of Cinema's South Africa*. Athens: Ohio University Press.

Debruge, Peter. 2013. "Why *Wadjda* Matters: Tiny Saudi Movie Makes Waves." *Variety*, September 26. www.variety.com/2013/film/columns/rearview-why-wadjda-matters-saudi-arabia-oscar-1200662946/.

Decherney, Peter, and Blake Atwood, eds. 2014. *Iranian Cinema in a Global Context: Policy, Politics, and Form*. London: Routledge.

Deleuze, Gilles. 1986. *Cinema I: The Movement-Image*. Translated by Hugh Tomlinson and Barbara Habberjam. Minneapolis: University of Minnesota Press.

———. 1989. *Cinema II: The Time-Image*. Translated by Hugh Tomlinson and Robert Galeta. Minneapolis: University of Minnesota Press.

Di Stefano, Eugenio. 2018. "Forms of Freedom in Pablo Larraín's *No* and *Neruda*." *Open Library of Humanities* 4, no. 2: 1–28. https://olh.openlibhums.org/articles/10.16995/olh.361/.

Dolske, Gwendolyn. 2012. "More than a Windshield Wiper: A Beauvoirian Analysis of Project and Other in *Flash of Genius*." *Film and Philosophy Journal* 16: 1–14.

Dos Passos, John. 1939. *Adventures of a Young Man*. Boston: Houghton Mifflin.

Dragojlovic, Ana. 2018. "Violent Histories and Embodied Memories: Affectivity of 'The Act of Killing' and 'The Look of Silence.'" In *The Indonesian Genocide of 1965: Causes, Dynamic and Legacies*, edited by Katharine McGregor, Jess Melvin, and Annie Pohlman, 269–85. London: Palgrave.

Du Bois, W. E. B. (1903) 1996. *The Souls of Black Folk*. London: Penguin.

Du Graf, Lauren. 2018. "Cinema in the Eyes of Simone de Beauvoir." *Screen* 59, no. 3: 381–90.

DW. 2008. "East German Stasi Had 189,000 Informers, Study Says." March 11. https://www.dw.com/en/east-german-stasi-had-189000-informers-study-says/a-3184486-1.

Dzero, Irina. 2015. "Larraín's Film *No* and Its Inspiration, *El plebiscito*: Chile's Transition to Democracy as a Simulacrum." *Confluencia: Revista Hispánica de Cultura y Literatura* 31, no. 1: 120–32.

Ebert, Roger. 1989. "*A Dry White Season*." RogerEbert.com, September 22. https://www.rogerebert.com/reviews/a-dry-white-season-1989.

Edelstein, David. 2012. "Iranian Devolution." *New York Magazine*, January 6. https://nymag.com/movies/reviews/a-separation-edelstein-2012-1/.

Eichendorff, Joseph Von. https://freies-deutsches-hochstift.de/en/mediaguide/romantik-ausstellung/3-obergeschoss/suche-nach-dem-zauberwort/. Accessed November 21, 2022.

El Rashidi, Yasmine. 2019. "Growing Up in Hell: *Capernaum*, a Film Directed by Nadine Labaki." *New York Review of Books* 66, no. 10, June 6–26: 8–10.

Elsaesser, Thomas. 2019. "Anatomy Lesson of a Vanished Country: Christian Petzold's *Barbara*." In *European Cinema and Continental Philosophy: Film as Thought Experiment*, 253–73. New York: Bloomsbury.

Enns, Diane. 2012. *The Violence of Victimhood*. University Park: Pennsylvania State University Press.

Enzenberger, Hans Magnus. 1997. *Zigzag: The Politics of Culture and Vice Versa*. New York: New Press.

Feierstein, Daniel. 2014. *Genocide as Social Practice: Reorganizing Society under the Nazis and Argentina's Military Junta*. New Brunswick, NJ: Rutgers University Press.

Felperin, Leslie. 2012. "*No*." *Variety* 427, no. 3: 16.

Fiala, Andrew. 2018. *Transformative Pacificism: Critical Theory and Practice*. London: Bloomsbury.

Fischer, Lucy. 1990. "Seduced and Abandoned: Recollection and Romance in *Letter from an Unknown Woman*." In *Issues in Feminist Film Criticism*, edited by Patricia Erens, 163–82. Bloomington: Indiana University Press.

Fisher, Jaimey. 2013. *Christian Petzold*. Champaign: University of Illinois Press.

———. 2017. "Petzold's *Phoenix*, Fassbinder's *Maria Braun*, and the Melodramatic Archaeology of the Rubble Past." In *Senses of Cinema* 2017.

Fjellström, Roger F. 2002. "On Victimhood." *SATS: Nordic Journal of Philosophy* 3, no. 1: 102–17.

Free, Erin. 2022. "Unsung Auteurs: Euzhan Palcy." *FilmInk*, March 31. https://www.filmink.com.au/unsung-auteurs-euzhan-palcy/.

Freedman, Paul. 2013. "Luxury Dining in the Later Years of the German Democratic Republic." In *Becoming East German: Socialist Structures and Sensibilities after Hitler*, edited by Mary Fulbrook and Andrew I. Port, 179–97. New York: Berghahn Books.

Freedman, Samuel G. 1989. "Black Agony Pierces the Heart of an Afrikaner." *New York Times*, September 17.

Fuery, Kelli. 2022. *Ambiguous Cinema: From Simone de Beauvoir to Feminist Film-Phenomenology*. Edinburgh: Edinburgh University Press.

Fulbrook, Mary. 2008. *The People's State: East Germany from Hitler to Honecker*. New Haven, CT: Yale University Press.

Gandhi, Mohandas K. 2007. "Hind Swaraj, or Indian Home Rule." In *On Violence: A Reader*, edited by Bruce B. Lawrence and Aisha Karim, 110–26. Durham, NC: Duke University Press.

Gerhardt, Christina. 2016. "Looking East: Christian Petzold's *Barbara* (2012)." *Quarterly Review of Film and Video* 33, no. 6: 550–66.

Gill, June M. 2000. "The Films of Euzhan Palcy: A Voice for Black History." *Quarterly Review of Film and Video* 17, no. 4: 371–81.

Gledhill, Christine. 1987. "The Melodramatic Field: An Investigation." In *Home Is Where the Heart Is: Studies in Melodrama and the Women's Film*, edited by Christine Gledhill, 5–39. London: BFI.

Glicksman, Marlaine. 1989. "Tempest: Euzhan Palcy's *Dry White Season*." *Film Comment* 25, no. 5: 64–69.

Goodfellow, Melanie. 2021. "Saudi Arabia Sets Sights on 100 Feature Films by 2030." *Screen Daily*, December 10. https://www.screendaily.com/news/saudi-arabia-sets-sights-on-100-feature-films-by-2030/5165902.article.

Goodman, Amy. 2015. "*The Look of Silence*: Will New Film Force U.S to Acknowledge Role in 1965 Indonesian Genocide?" *Democracy Now*, August 3. https://www.democracynow.org/2015/8/3/the_look_of_silence_will_new.

Gordon, Lewis R. 2019. "Race in Film." In *The Palgrave Handbook of the Philosophy of Film*, edited by Noël Carroll and Laura T. di Summa, 677–97. London: Palgrave Macmillan.

Gorsevski, Ellen W. 2004. *Peaceful Persuasion: The Geopolitics of Nonviolent Rhetoric*. Albany: State University of New York Press.

Gottlieb, Akiva. 2019. "30 Years after Making History with *A Dry White Season*, Director Euzhan Palcy Looks Back." *Los Angeles Times*, February 1. https://www.latimes.com/entertainment/movies/la-ca-mn-euzhan-palcy-dry-white-season-20190201-story.html.

Gow, Christopher, 2011. *From Iran to Hollywood and Some Places In-Between: Reframing Post-revolutionary Iranian Cinema*. London: I. B. Tauris.

Grierson, Tim. 2015. "*The Look of Silence*: How a New Doc Revisits Indonesia's Genocide." *Rolling Stone*, July 17. https://www.rollingstone.com/tv-movies/tv-movie-news/the-look-of-silence-how-a-new-doc-revisits-indonesias-genocide-113990/.

Grist, Leighton. 2009. "Whither Realism? Bazin Reconsidered." In *Realism and the Audiovisual Media*, edited by Lúcia Nagib and Cecilia Mello, 20–30. London: Palgrave Macmillan.

Gugler, Josef. 2003. *African Film: Reimagining a Continent*. Bloomington: Indiana University Press.

Gunning, Tom. 1990. "The Cinema of Attractions: Early Film, Its Spectator and the Avant-Garde." In *Early Cinema: Space, Frame, Narrative*, edited by Thomas Elsaesser and Adam Barker, 56–62. London: British Film Institute.

———. 2007. "Moving Away from the Index: Cinema and the Impression of Reality." *Differences: A Journal of Feminist Cultural Studies* 18, no. 1: 29–52.

Gutmann, Peter. 1999. "Wilhelm Furtwängler: Genius Forged in the Cauldron of War." *Classical Notes*. http://www.classicalnotes.net/features/furtwangler.html. Accessed February 28, 2022.

Hackeling, Joan. 2003. "Remembering Ordinary Agency under East German State Socialism: Revelations of the Rostock District Record, 1978–89." In *Political Transition: Politics and Cultures*, edited by Paul Gready, 183–95. London: Pluto Press.

Hallam, Julia, and Margaret Marshment. 2000. *Realism and Popular Cinema*. Manchester: Manchester University Press.

Hansberry, Lorraine. 1969. *To Be Young, Gifted and Black: Lorraine Hansberry in Her Own Words*. Englewood Cliffs, NJ: Prentice Hall.

Harff, Barbara. 2003. "No Lessons Learned from the Holocaust? Assessing Risks of Genocide and Political Mass Murder since 1955." *American Political Science Review* 97, no. 1: 57–73.

Hariyadi, Mathias. 2022. "Indonesian Military Lifts Ban on Communist Descendants." *AsiaNews*, May 4. https://www.asianews.it/news-en/Indonesian-military-lifts-ban-on-communist-descendants-55519.html.

Harvey, James. 2018. "Larraín's Ambivalence." In *Jacques Rancière and the Politics of Art Cinema*, 42–60. Edinburgh: Edinburgh University Press.

Havel, Václav. (1978) 1987. "The Power of the Powerless." In *Václav Havel; or, Living in Truth: Twenty-Two Essays Published on the Award of the Erasmus Prize to Václav Havel*, edited by Jan Vladislav, 36–122. London: Faber & Faber.

Hemphill, Jim. 2019. "'Pushing for Black Actors to Tell Black Stories': Euzhan Palcy on *A Dry White Season*." *Filmmaker*, February 5. https://filmmakermagazine.com/107007-pushing-for-black-actors-to-tell-black-stories-euzhan-palcy-on-a-dry-white-season/.

Hengehold, Laura. 2017. "Separation and Queer Connection in *The Ethics of Ambiguity*." In *A Companion to Simone de Beauvoir*, edited by Laura Hengehold and Nancy Bauer, 286–98. Hoboken: John Wiley & Sons.

Herman, Judith Lewis. 1992. *Trauma and Recovery*. New York: Basic Books.

Herndon, Gerise. 1999. "From *Rue Cases-Nègres* to *A Dry White Season*: The Evolution of Resistance in Euzhan Palcy's Films." In *Beyond Survival: African Literature and the Search for New Life*, vol. 5, edited by Kofi Anyidoho, Abena P. A. Busia, and Anne V. Adams, 233–41. Trenton, NJ: 1st Africa World Press.

Higgins, John. 1992. "Documentary Realism and Film Pleasure: Two Moments from Euzhan Palcy's *A Dry White Season*." *Literator* 13, no. 3: 101–9.

Hill, Thomas E., Jr. 2010. "Moral Responsibilities of Bystanders." *Journal of Social Philosophy* 41, no. 1: 28–39.

Hirmas, María Eugenia. 1993. "The Chilean Case: Television in the 1988 Plebiscite." In *Television, Politics, and the Transition to Democracy in Latin America*, edited by Thomas E. Skidmore, 82–96. Washington, DC: Woodrow Wilson Center Press.

Hirsch, Joshua. 2004. *Afterimage: Film, Trauma, and the Holocaust*. Philadelphia: Temple University Press.

Hoffman, Karen D. 2017. "Deceiving into the Truth: The Indirect Cinema of *Stories We Tell* and *The Act of Killing*." In *The Philosophy of Documentary Film: Image, Sound, Fiction, Truth*, edited by David LaRocca and Timothy Corrigan, 517–36. Lanham, MD: Lexington Books.

Hoggard, Liz. 2013. "Interview with Haifaa Al Mansour." *The Guardian*, July 14. www.theguardian.com/theobserver/2013/jul/14/haifaa-mansour-wadjda-saudi-arabia.

hooks, bell. 2015. *Yearning: Race, Gender, and Cultural Politics*. New York: Routledge.

Howe, Alexis. 2015. "Yes, No, or Maybe? Transitions in Chilean Society in Pablo Larraín's *No*." *Hispania* 98, no. 3: 421–30.

Hunt, Aaron E. 2020. "Misfortunes That Have No Mouth: A Conversation with Euzhan Palcy." *MUBI*, July 2020. https://mubi.com/notebook/posts/misfortunes-that-have-no-mouth-a-conversation-with-euzhan-palcy.

Hvidt, Martin. 2018. "The New Role of Women in the New Saudi Arabian Economy." Center for Mellemøststudier. Odense: Syddansk Universitet. http://www.sdu.dk/-/media/files/om_sdu/centre/c_mellemoest/videncenter/artikler/2018. Accessed March 4, 2022.

Iannaccaro, Giuliana. 2014. "Apartheid Spies: The Character, the Reader, and the Censor in André Brink's *A Dry White Season*." *Altre modernità*, no. 11: 69–84.

"Indonesian Roundtable: *The Act of Killing*." 2014. *Critical Asian Studies* 46, no. 1: 145–207.

International Commission of the Latin American Studies Association to Observe the Chilean Plebiscite. 1989. *The Chilean Plebiscite: A First Step towards Redemocratization*. Pittsburgh: Latin American Studies Association.

Issa, Tala Michel. 2021. "Everything You Need to Know about Saudi's Vision 2030 Five-Year Progress: Report." *Al Arabiya English*, May 6. https://english.alarabiya.net/features/2021/05/06/Everything-you-need-to-know-about-Saudi-s-Vision-2030-five-year-progress-Report.

Jahanbegloo, Ramin, and Nojang Khatami. 2013. "Acting under Tyranny: Hannah Arendt and the Foundations of Democracy in Iran." *Constellations* 20, no. 2: 328–46.

Jahed, Parviz, ed. 2012. *Directory of World Cinema: Iran*. Bristol: Intellect.

Joseph-Vilain, Mélanie. 2009. "'First Hand Becomes Second Hand': André Brink's *A Dry White Season*." *Commonwealth Essays and Studies* 32, no. 1: 98–109.

Jung, Nike. 2015. "History, Fiction and the Politics of Corporeality in Pablo Larraín's Dictatorship Trilogy." In *Film, History and Memory*, edited by Jennie M. Carlsten and Fearghal McGarry, 118–33. London: Palgrave Macmillan.

Kamenka, Eugene. 1995. "Totalitarianism." In *A Companion to Contemporary Political Philosophy*, edited by Robert E. Goodin and Philip Petit, 629–37. Oxford: Blackwell.

Kant, Immanuel. 1996. *Metaphysics of Morals*. In *Practical Philosophy*, translated and edited by Mary J. Gregor. Cambridge: Cambridge University Press.

Kaplan, E. Ann. 1996. *Women and Film: Both Sides of the Camera*. London: Routledge.

———. 2005. *Trauma Culture: The Politics of Terror and Loss in Media and Literature*. New Brunswick, NJ: Rutgers University Press.

Kashdan, Todd B., Jon D. Elhai, and B. Christopher Frueh. 2007. "Anhedonia, Emotional Numbing, and Symptom Overreporting in Male Veterans with PTSD." *Personality and Individual Differences* 43, no. 4: 725–35.

Kasman, Daniel, and David Phelps. 2012. "Spatial Suspense: A Conversation with Christian Petzold." MUBI. https://mubi.com/notebook/posts/spatial-suspense-a-conversation-with-christian-petzold. Accessed February 28, 2022.

Khazan, Olga. 2013. "4 Things the Movie *No* Left Out about Real-Life Chile." *The Atlantic*, March 29.

Kierkegaard, Søren. 1992. *Concluding Unscientific Postscript to Philosophical Fragments*. Edited and translated by Howard V. Hong and Edna H. Hong. Princeton, NJ: Princeton University Press.

Kirkland, Paul E. 2015. "Sorrow Songs and Self-Knowledge: The Politics of Recognition and Tragedy in W. E. B. Du Bois's *Souls of Black Folk*." *American Political Thought: A Journal of Ideas, Institutions, and Culture* 4, no. 3: 412–37.

Kracauer, Siegfried. 1960. *Theory of Film: The Redemption of Physical Reality*. Oxford: Oxford University Press.

Krakenberg, Jasmin. 2017. "Moving Portraits: Christian Petzold and the Art of Portraiture." In *Senses of Cinema* 2017.

Kraus, Michael. 2007. "Did the Charter 77 Movement Bring an End to Communism?" *New England Review* 28, no. 2: 134–46.

Kruks, Sonia. 2012. *Simone de Beauvoir and the Politics of Ambiguity*. Oxford: Oxford University Press.

Kurlansky, Mark. 2006. *Non-violence: The History of a Dangerous Idea*. New York: Modern Library.

Kwok, Yenni. 2016. "*The Look of Silence* and Indonesia's Quest for Truth and Reconciliation." *Time*, June 27. https://time.com/4383283/the-look-of-silence-indonesia-1965-1966-killings-massacre-pki/.

La Caze, Marguerite. 2013. *Wonder and Generosity: Their Role in Ethics and Politics*. Ithaca, NY: SUNY Press.

———. 2015. "The Time of Possible and Impossible Reciprocity: Love and Hate in Beauvoir." In *Thinking about Love: Essays in Contemporary Continental Philosophy*, edited by Antonio Calcagno and Diane Enns, 186–200. University Park: Penn State University Press, 2015.

———. 2018. *Ethical Restoration after Communal Violence: The Grieving and the Unrepentant*. Lanham, MD: Lexington Books.

Lane, Anthony. 2012. "Tehran Tales: *A Separation* and *The Hunter*." *New Yorker*, January 9, 87(43): 78.

———. 2013. "How They Roll." *New Yorker*, September 16, 89(28): 72.

Lang, Johannes. 2018. "The Proud Executioner: Pride and the Psychology of Genocide." In *Emotions and Mass Atrocity: Philosophical and Theoretical Explorations*, edited by Thomas Brudholm and Johannes Lang, 64–80. Cambridge: Cambridge University Press.

Lapin, Andrew. 2013. "Interview: *Wadjda* Director Haifaa Al Mansour." *The Dissolve*, September 19. https://thedissolve.com/features/interview/168-wadjda-director-haifaa-al-mansour/. Accessed August 8, 2019.

Laplanche, Jean, and Jean-Bertrand Pontalis. 1973. *The Language of Psychoanalysis*. Translated by Donald Nicholson-Smith. New York: Norton.

Larraín, Pablo. 2012. "The Problems of Fiction." Interview with José Miguel Palacios. *Brooklyn Rail: Critical Perspectives on Arts, Politics, and Culture*, November 6. https://brooklynrail.org/2012/11/film/the-problems-of-fictionpablo-larran-with-jos-miguel-palacios.

Lash, Dominic. 2020. *The Cinema of Disorientation: Inviting Confusions*. Edinburgh: Edinburgh University Press.

Leask, Phil. 2013. "Humiliation as a Weapon within the Party: Fictional and Personal Accounts." In *Becoming East German: Socialist Structures and Sensibilities after Hitler*, edited by Mary Fulbrook and Andrew I. Port, 237–56. New York: Berghan Books.

Le Dœuff, Michèle. 2003. *The Sex of Knowing*. Translated by Kathryn Hamer and Lorraine Code. Routledge [*Le sexe du savoir*, Paris: Aubier, 1998].

Liston, Enjoli. 2013. "Haifaa Al Mansour Interview: Saudi Arabia's First Female Film Director Talks about New Release *Wadjda*." *Independent*, July 18. www.independent.co.uk/arts-entertainment/films/features/haifaa-al-mansour-interview-saudi-arabias-first-female-film-director-talks-about-new-release-wadjda-8717438.html.

Lodge, Tom. 2009. "The Interplay of Non-violent and Violent Action in the Movement against Apartheid in South Africa." In *Civil Resistance and Power Politics: The Experience of Non-violent Action from Gandhi to the Present*, edited by Adam Roberts and Timothy Garton-Ash, 213–30. Oxford: Oxford University Press.

Lucca, Violet. 2013. "Review: *Wadjda*." *Film Comment*, August 16. www.filmcomment.com/blog/review-wadjda-haifa-al-mansour/.

Lukács, Georg. 1972. *Studies in European Realism*. Translated by Edith Bone. London: Merlin Press.

Lyttelton, Oliver. 2013. "Interview: Director Pablo Larraín on the Unique Aesthetic of *No* and Working with Star Gael García Bernal." *Indiewire*, February 12. https://www.indiewire.com/2013/02/interview-director-pablo-Larraín-on-the-unique-aesthetic-of-no-working-with-star-gael-garcia-bernal-101511/.

Mahdi, Waleed F. 2016. "Review of *Wadjda* by Haifaa Al Mansour, Gerhard Meixner, Roman Paul." *Journal of Islamic and Muslim Studies* 1, no. 1: 100–102.

Mahmoudi, Hassan. 2021. "Iran Loses Highly Educated and Skilled Citizens during Long-Running 'Brain Drain.'" *Migration Policy Institute*, April 2022. https://www.migrationpolicy.org/article/iran-brain-drain-emigration.

Maingard, Jacqueline. 2007a. "South African Cinema: Histories and Futures." *Screen* 48, no. 4: 511–15.

———. 2007b. *South African National Cinema*. London: Taylor & Francis.

———. 2019. "A Pan-African Perspective on Apartheid, Torture, and Resistance in Euzhan Palcy's *A Dry White Season*." *Black Camera* 11, no. 1: 201–13.

Maranlou, Sahar. 2015. *Access to Justice in Iran: Women, Perceptions, and Reality*. Cambridge: Cambridge University Press.

Marshall, Lee. 2012. "*Wadjda*." *Screen Daily*, September 1.

Marso, Lori Jo. 2017. *Politics with Beauvoir: Freedom in the Encounter*. Durham, NC: Duke University Press.

Maslin, Janet. 1989. "Sutherland Catches On to Apartheid Slowly." *New York Times*, September 20.

Matheou, Demetrios. 2013. "*No*." *Sight and Sound* 23, no. 3: 101–2.

May, Todd. 2015. *Nonviolent Resistance: A Philosophical Introduction*. Oxford: Polity.

Maynard, Katherine, Jarod Kearney, and James Guimond. 2010. "State Terrorism and Revenge in André Brink's *A Dry White Season*." In *Revenge versus Legality: Wild Justice from Balzac to Clint Eastwood to Abu Ghraib*, 133–53. London: Routledge.

McCartney, Kristin. 2009. "W. E. B. Du Bois and the Sorrow Songs: Unburying Resistance in the Roots of Trauma." *Radical Philosophy Review* 12, nos. 1–2: 79–86.

McGregor, Katharine, Jess Melvin, and Annie Pohlman, eds. 2018. *The Indonesian Genocide of 1965: Causes, Dynamics and Legacies*. London: Palgrave Macmillan.

McKenna, Kristine. 1989. "Tough, Passionate, Persuasive." *American Film* 14, no. 10: 32–37.

Meerzon, Yana. 2011. "Dancing on the X-Rays: On the Theatre of Memory, Counter-Memory, and Postmemory in the Post-1989 East-European Context." *Modern Drama* 54, no. 4: 479–510.

Melvin, Jess. 2018. *The Army and the Indonesian Genocide*. London: Routledge.

Melvin, Jess, and Annie Pohlman. 2018. "A Case for Genocide: Indonesia, 1965–1966." In *The Indonesian Genocide of 1965: Causes, Dynamics and Legacies*, edited by Katharine McGregor, Jess Melvin, and Annie Pohlman, 27–47. London: Palgrave Macmillan.

Milani, Farzaneh. 2015. "The Haunting Obituary of a Dying Patriarch: *A Separation*." In *Iranian Cinema in a Global Context: Policy, Politics, and Form*, edited by Peter Decherney and Blake Atwood, 208–12. London: Routledge.

Moheb, Yasser. 2015. "Interview: Haifaa Al Mansour, Female Saudi Filmmaker, Talks about Her Aspirations." *Ahram Online*, August 10. https://english.ahram.org.eg/News/137441.aspx.

Morgan, Daniel. 2006. "Rethinking Bazin: Ontology and Realist Aesthetics." *Critical Inquiry* 32, no. 3: 443–81.

Mozaffar, Omer M. 2013. "Pinochet: The Choice of a New Generation." RogerEbert.com, March 6. https://www.rogerebert.com/reviews/no-2013.

———. 2014. "Western Wrestling with *Wadjda*." RogerEbert.com, February 27. www.rogerebert.com/far-flung-correspondents/western-wrestling-with-wadjda.

Mrovlje, Maša. 2019. *Rethinking Political Judgement: Arendt and Existentialism*. Edinburgh: Edinburgh University Press.

Mueller, Gabriele. 2013. "Re-imaging the Niche: Visual Reconstructions of Private Spaces in the GDR." In *Remembering and Rethinking the GDR*, edited by Anna Saunders and Debbie Pinfold, 197–213. London: Palgrave Macmillan.

Murphy, Ann. 2012. *Violence and the Philosophical Imaginary*. Albany: State University of New York Press.

National Editorial. 2022. "Where Progress on Saudi Women's Rights Is Heading in 2022." *The National*, January 13. https://www.thenationalnews.com/opinion/editorial/2022/01/13/where-progress-on-saudi-womens-rights-is-heading-in-2022/.

Nixon, Rob. 1994. *Homelands, Harlem and Hollywood: South African Culture and the World Beyond*. New York: Routledge.

NPR Staff. 2013. "Interview: *Wadjda* Director: 'It Is Time to Open Up.'" NPR.org, September 22. http://www.npr.org/2013/09/22/224437165/wadjda-director-haifaa-al-mansour-it-is-time-to-open-up.

Nussbaum, Karen. 2020. "'Impunity Is the Story of Our Times': An Interview with Filmmaker Joshua Oppenheimer." *American Prospect*, July 10. https://prospect.org/culture/impunity-is-the-story-of-our-times-interview-joshua-oppenheimer/.

O'Falt, Chris. 2013. "Influences: The Movies That Inspired *Wadjda* Director Haifaa Al Mansour to Make History." *Hollywood Reporter*, December 18. http://www.hollywoodreporter.com/news/influences-movies-inspired-wadjda-director-665035.

———. 2016. "How the Oscar-Nominated *The Look of Silence* Uses Art to Spread Activism." *Indiewire*, February 26. https://www.indiewire.com/features/craft/how-the-oscar-nominated-the-look-of-silence-uses-art-to-spread-activism-63862/.

Oppenheimer, Joshua. 2014. "The Act of Killing Has Helped Indonesia Reassesses Its Past and Present." *The Guardian*, February 26.

———. 2015. "Director's Notes." http://thelookofsilence.com/.

Oppenheimer, Joshua, and Michael Uwemedimo. 2012. "Show of Force: A Cinema-Séance of Power and Violence in Sumatra's Plantation Belt." In *Killer Images; Documentary Film, Memory and the Performance of Violence*, edited by Joram Ten Brink and Joshua Oppenheimer, 287–310. London: Wallflower Press.

Oselund, Kurt R. 2012. "Christian Petzold on *Barbara*." *Filmmaker Magazine*, December 21. https://filmmakermagazine.com/61159-christian-petzold-on-barbara/.

Palcy, Euzhan. 1990. "Putting Apartheid on Screen: Talking with Euzhan Palcy." *Spareribr*, February, no. 209: 12–15.

Peirano, María Paz. 2018. "Larraín's *No*: A Tale of Neoliberalism." In *Contemporary Latin American Cinema: Resisting Neoliberalism*, edited by Claudia Sandberg and Carolina Rocha, 135–52. Basingstoke, UK: Palgrave Macmillan.

Peyrovi, Hamid, Hamed Mortazavi, and Soodabeh Joolaee. 2012. "Challenges of Iranian Family Members in Decision-Making to Put Elderly People with Chronic Diseases in Nursing Homes: A Qualitative Study." *Archives des Sciences* 65, no. 10: 178–88.

Pinfold, Debbie. 2014. "The End of the Fairy Tale? Christian Petzold's *Barbara* and the Difficulties of Interpretation." *German Life and Letters* 67, no. 2: 279–300.

Plato. 1989. *The Collected Dialogues of Plato*. Edited by Edith Hamilton and Huntington Cairns. Princeton, NJ: Princeton University Press.

———. 2006. *Plato on Love*. Edited by C. D. C. Reeve. Indianapolis: Hackett.

Pohlman, Annie. 2015. "Film Review: *The Act of Killing*." *Genocide Studies and Prevention: An International Journal* 9, no. 2: 131–34.

———. 2016. "A Year of Truth and the Possibilities for Reconciliation in Indonesia." *Genocide Studies and Prevention: An International Journal* 10, no. 1: 60–78.

Pontuso, James F. 2014. "*The Lives of Others, Good Bye Lenin!* and the Power of Everydayness." In *Totalitarianism on Screen: The Art and Politics of "The Lives of Others,"* edited by Carl Eric Scott and F. Flagg Taylor IV, 137–53. Lexington: University Press of Kentucky.

Popper, Karl. 2020. *The Open Society and Its Enemies*. Princeton, NJ: Princeton University Press.

Port, Andrew I. 2007. *Conflict and Stability in the German Democratic Republic*. Cambridge: Cambridge University Press.

Prager, Brad. 2017. "No Time like the Present: The Edges of the World in Christian Petzold's *Barbara*." In *Senses of Cinema* 2017.

Pribram, E. Deidre. 2018. "Melodrama and the Aesthetics of Emotion." In *Melodrama Unbound: Across History, Media, and National Cultures*, edited by Christine Gledhill and Linda Williams, 238–51. New York: Columbia University Press.

Prince, Stephen. 2004. "The Emergence of Filmic Artifacts: Cinema and Cinematography in the Digital Era." *Film Quarterly* 57, no. 3: 24–33.

———. 2019. *Digital Cinema*. New Brunswick, NJ: Rutgers University Press.

Qandt, James. 2016. "Post Mortem: Pablo Larraín's Chile Trilogy: A Look Back at Larraín's Trio of Films about the Pinochet Regime." *Toronto International Film Festival*, December 13.

Rabaka, Reiland. 2016. *The Negritude Movement: W. E. B. Du Bois, Leon Damas, Aimé Césaire, Leopold Senghor, Frantz Fanon, and the Evolution of an Insurgent Idea*. Lanham, MD: Lexington Books.

Radstone, Susannah. 2007. "Trauma Theory: Contexts, Politics, Ethics." *Paragraph* 30, no. 1: 9–29.

Radzik, Linda. 2009. *Making Amends: Atonement in Morality, Law, and Politics*. Oxford: Oxford University Press.

Rafter, Nicole. 2015. "Film Review: The Look of Silence." *Genocide Studies and Prevention: An International Journal* 9, no. 2: 135–37.

Ramdani, Nabila. 2013. "Saudi Women Are Allowed to Ride Bikes—But Only in Circles." *The Guardian*, April 4. www.theguardian.com/lifeandstyle/the-womens-blog-with-jane-martinson/2013/apr/03/saudi-women-allowed-to-cycle.

Rannard, Georgina. 2018. "World Cup 2018: Women Finally Allowed in Iranian Football Stadium." *BBC News*, June 21. www.bbc.com/news/blogs-trending-44561909.

Reichle, Niklaus. 2014. "Melodrama and Censorship in Iranian Cinema." *Film International* 12, no. 3: 64–76.

Repucci, Sarah, and Amy Slipowitz. 2021. "Freedom in the World 2021: Democracy under Siege." *Freedom House*. https://freedomhouse.org/report/freedom-world/2021/democracy-under-siege. Accessed February 8, 2022.

Reuters Staff. 2018. "Indonesia Jails Activist under Controversial Anti-communist Law." Reuters, January 24. https://www.reuters.com/article/uk-indonesia-communism-idUKKBN1FD18H.

Ritman, Alex. 2021. "Saudi Arabia's Red Sea Festival Wraps Star-Studded First Edition." *Hollywood Reporter*, December 15. https://www.hollywoodreporter.com/movies/movie-news/saudi-arabia-red-sea-film-festival-omicron-1235063061/.

Rohter, Larry. 2013. "One Prism on the Undoing of Pinochet: Oscar-Nominated *No* Stirring Debate in Chile." *New York Times*, February 8.

Romig, Rollo. 2012. "Blood Money: Crime and Punishment in *A Separation*." *New Yorker*, February 24. https://www.newyorker.com/culture/culture-desk/blood-money-crime-and-punishment-in-a-separation.

Rosenberg, Alyssa. 2013. "*Wadjda* Director Haifaa Al Mansour on Saudi Women, What Sexism Denies Men, and Digital Filmmaking." *Thinkprogress*, September 20. http://www.thinkprogress.org/alyssa/2013/09/20/2658481/wadjda-haifaa-mansour/.

Rothe, E. Nina. 2014. "'The Shawati' Interviews: *Wadjda* Filmmaker Haifaa Al Mansour." *HuffPost*, August 1. www.huffpost.com/entry/the-ishawatii-interviews_b_4561223.

Roxborough, Scott. 2022. "Did Oscar Winner Asghar Farhadi Steal the Idea for *A Hero*?" *Hollywood Reporter*, March 23. https://www.hollywoodreporter.com/movies/movie-features/asghar-farhadi-a-hero-legal-battle-1235116214/.

Rushton, Richard. 2010. *The Reality of Film: Theories of Filmic Reality*. Manchester: Manchester University Press.

———. 2013. *The Politics of Hollywood Cinema: Popular Film and Contemporary Political Theory*. London: Palgrave Macmillan.

Ryan, Michael, and Douglas Kellner. 1988. *Camera Politica: The Politics and Ideology of Hollywood Film*. Bloomington: Indiana University Press.

Sadr, Hamid-Reza. 2002. "Children in Contemporary Iranian Cinema: When We Were Children." In *The New Iranian Cinema: Politics, Representation and Identity*, edited by Richard Tapper, 227–37. London: I. B. Tauris.

Saito, Stephen. 2012. "Interview: Christian Petzold on the Skilful Seduction of Barbara." *Moveable Feast*, December 20. https://moveablefeast.com/christian-petzold-barbara-interview/.

Santoso, Aboeprijadi, and Gerry van Klinken. 2017. "Genocide Finally Enters Public Discourse: The International People's Tribunal 1965." *Journal of Genocide Research* 19, no. 4: 594–608.

Schenkel, Hanna. 2015. "Clarifying the Past: Joshua Oppenheimer's *The Look of Silence*." *Metro Magazine* 186: 96–101.

Scollon, Michael. 2020. "After 80 Years, the 'Katyn Lie' Lives On in Russia." *RadioFreeEuropeRadioLiberty*, March 5. https://www.rferl.org/a/after-80-years-the-katyn-lie-lives-on-in-russia/30470317.html.

Scott, A. O. 2011. "A House Divided by Exasperation: *A Separation*." *New York Times*, December 30.

Scott, Carl Eric, and F. Flagg Taylor IV, eds. 2014. *Totalitarianism on Screen: The Art and Politics of "The Lives of Others."* Lexington: University Press of Kentucky.

Scott, Margaret. 2018. "The Truth about the Killing Fields." *New York Review of Books*, June 28, 33–35.

Sebald, W. G. 1998. *The Rings of Saturn*. Translated by Michael Hulse. New York: New Directions.

Senses of Cinema. 2017. "Christian Petzold: A Dossier." No. 84 (September). http://sensesofcinema.com/?s=christian+petzold.

Serote, Mongane. 1974. *Tsetlo*. Johannesburg: Ad Donker.

Shalhoub, Lulwa. 2019. "How Saudi's 'New Direction' Is Changing Life for Women like Me." *BBC News*, August 4. www.bbc.com/news/world-middle-east-49208737.

Shaw, Daniel. 2017. *Movies with Meaning: Existentialism through Film*. London: Bloomsbury.

Shiel, Mark. 2006. *Italian Neorealism: Rebuilding the Cinematic City*. New York: Wallflower.

Simón Salazar, Harry L. 2018. *Television, Democracy and the Mediatization of Chilean Politics*. Lanham, MD: Lexington Books.

Simpson, Bradley. 2012. "International Dimensions of the 1965–68 Violence in Indonesia." In *The Contours of Mass Violence in Indonesia*, edited by Douglas Kammen and Katharine McGregor, 50–74. Singapore: NUS Press.

Sinnerbrink, Robert. 2012. "Cinematic Belief: Bazinian Cinephilia and Malick's *The Tree of Life*." *Angelaki: Journal of the Theoretical Humanities* 17, no. 4: 95–117.

———. 2016. *Cinematic Ethics: Exploring Ethical Experience through Film*. New York: Routledge.

———. 2017. "The Act of Witnessing: Cinematic Ethics in *The Look of Silence*." *Post Script* 36, nos. 2–3: 31–45.

Skármeta, Antonio. n.d. *El plebiscito*. Unpublished play.

Škvorecký, Josef, et al. 1989. "The State of Europe: Christmas Eve 1989." *Granta Magazine*. https://granta.com/the-state-of-europe-christmas-eve-1989/. Accessed November 18, 2022.

Smith, Greg M. 2006. "Reflecting on the Image: Sartrean Emotions in the Writings of André Bazin." *Film and Philosophy*, no. 10: 117–33.

Staat, Wim. 2016. "Christian Petzold's Melodramas: From Unknown Woman to Reciprocal Unknownness in *Phoenix*, *Wolfsburg*, and *Barbara*." *Studies in European Cinema* 12, no. 3: 185–99.

Stallabrass, Julian, ed. 2013. *Documentary: Documents of Contemporary Art*. Cambridge, MA: MIT Press.

Steinbeck, John. 1963. *In Dubious Battle*. New York: Viking.

Stern, Steve J. 2004. *Remembering Pinochet's Chile*. Durham, NC: Duke University Press.

Stevens, Dana. 2015. "*The Look of Silence*: The Follow-Up to Joshua Oppenheimer's *Act of Killing* Is Just as Beautiful—and Just as Disturbing." *Slate*, July 17.

Strangio, Sebastian. 2021. "Declassified Files Illuminate UK Role in Indonesian Anti-Communist Purges." *The Diplomat*, October 18. https://thediplomat.com/2021/10/declassified-files-illuminate-uk-role-in-indonesian-anti-communist-purges/.

Suleiman, Susan Rubin. 2008. "Judith Herman and Contemporary Trauma Theory." *Women's Studies Quarterly* 36, nos. 1–2: 276–81.

Sutopo, Oki Rahadianto. 2020. "Using Bourdieu to Understand Perpetrators in *The Act of Killing* and *The Look of Silence*." *Continuum: Journal of Media and Cultural Studies* 34, no. 2: 286–98.

Tapper, Richard, ed. 2002. *The New Iranian Cinema: Politics, Representation, and Identity*. London: I. B. Tauris.

Tessman, Lisa. 2005. *Burdened Virtues: Virtue Ethics for Liberatory Struggles*. Oxford: Oxford University Press.

Thakkar, Amit. 2017a. "The Perpetrating Victim: An Allegorical Reading of Pablo Larraín's *Tony Manero* (2008)." *Journal of Latin American Cultural Studies* 26, no. 4: 523–37.

———. 2017b. "Unclaimed Experience and the Implicated Subject in Pablo Larraín's *Post Mortem*." In *Scars and Wounds: Film and Legacies of Trauma*, edited by Nick Hodgin and Amit Thakkar, 243–66. London: Palgrave Macmillan.

Toledo, Vania Barraza. 2013. "Reviewing the Present in Pablo Larraín's Historical Films." *Iberoamericana* 13, no. 51: 159–72.

Torchin, Leshu. 2012. *Creating the Witness*. Minneapolis: University of Minnesota Press.

———. 2015. "Chronicle of a Quest: Silence after Killing." *Film Quarterly* 69, no. 2: 25–35.

Traverso, Antonio. 2011. "Dictatorship Memories: Working through Trauma in Chilean Post-dictatorship Documentary." In *Interrogating Trauma: Collective Suffering in Global Arts and Media*, edited by Mick Broderick and Antonio Traverso, 179–91. London: Routledge.

Turgenev, Ivan. (1852) 1990. *Sketches from a Hunter's Album*. London: Penguin.

Twain, Mark. (1884) 1942. *The Adventures of Huckleberry Finn*. Santa Cruz, CA: Sandstone.

Vadehra, Pranav. 2018. "Three Women Appointed to Saudi Culture Authority Board." Digitalstudiome.com, April 11. http://www.digitalstudiome.com/production/29613-three-women-appointed-to-saudi-culture-authority-board.

Varagur, Krithika. 2017. "How the US Came to Declassify 30,000 Pages of American Embassy in Indonesia Files." *Voanews*, October 18. https://www.voanews.com/a/us-declassified-indonesian-embassy-files/4075504.html.

Vasanthakumar, Ashwini. 2018. "Epistemic Privilege and Victims' Duties to Resist Their Oppression." *Journal of Applied Philosophy* 35, no. 3: 465–80.

Velleman, David. 1999. "Love as a Moral Emotion." *Ethics* 109, no. 2: 338–74.

Vieira, Mónica Brito. "The Great Wall of Silence: Voice-silence Dynamics in Authoritarian Regimes." *Critical Review of International Social and Political Philosophy* 24, no. 3: 368–91.

Vivarelli, Nick. 2019. "First Saudi Film Fest Hires Former Sundance Programmer, Sets Dates." *Variety*, June 27. http://www.variety.com/2019/film/news/red-sea-film-festival-saudi-arabia-2020-1203254537/.

Vogler, Christopher. 2007. *The Writer's Journey: Mythic Structure for Writers*. 3rd ed. Studio City, CA: Michael Wiese Productions.

Wadi, Romana. 2022. "Uncovering Dictatorship Violence in Chile." *Inkstick*. https://inkstickmedia.com/uncovering-dictatorship-violence-in-chile/. Accessed December 6, 2022.

Walker, Margaret Urban. 2006. *Moral Repair: Reconstructing Moral Relations after Wrongdoing*. Cambridge: Cambridge University Press.

Walters, Margaret. 1990. "Acts of Faith." *The Listener* 123, no. 3149, January 25: 40.

Wang Xiaobo. 1996. "The Silent Majority." Translated by Eric Abrahamsen. *Asia Literary Review*. https://media.paper-republic.org/files/09/04/The_Silent_Majority_Wang_Xiaobo.pdf. Accessed February 1, 2022.

Wartenberg, Thomas. 2007. *Thinking on Screen: Film as Philosophy*. London: Routledge.

Wartenberg, Thomas E., and Angela Curran, eds. 2005. *The Philosophy of Film: Introductory Text and Readings*. Oxford: Blackwell.

Watson, Ruby S. 1994. *Memory, History and Opposition under State Socialism*. Santa Fe: School of American Research Press.

Wells, Robert. 2017. "Trauma, Male Fantasies, and Cultural Capital in the Films of Pablo Larraín." *Journal of Latin American Cultural Studies* 26, no. 4: 503–22.

Welsh, David, and J. E. Spence. 2011. *Ending Apartheid*. Harlow: Pearson Education.

Westfall, Joseph, ed. 2018. *The Continental Philosophy of Film Reader*. London: Bloomsbury.

Wilder, Jess Bryant. 1991. "Intimate Lighting." *Film Comment* 27, no. 4: 4–6.

Williams, Bernard. 1973. "Ethical Consistency." In *Problems of the Self: Philosophical Papers 1956–1972*, 166–86. Cambridge: Cambridge University Press.

Williams, Linda. 1998. "Melodrama Revised." In *Refiguring American Film Genres: History and Theory*, edited by Nick Browne, 42–88. Berkeley: University of California Press.

Williams, Luke. 2014. "Movie Review: *Wadjda*." MovieClub.net, May 13. www.themovieclub.net/review-wadjda.

Wilson, Jake. 2015. "*The Look of Silence* Review: Joshua Oppenheimer's *The Act of Killing* Follow-Up Powerful but Too Polished." *Sydney Morning Herald*, November 25.

Wolf, Christa. 1963. *Der geteilte Himmel, Erzählung* [Divided heaven, narrative]. Halle (Saale): Mitteldeutscher Verlag.

——. 1997. *Parting from Phantoms: Selected Writings, 1990–1994*. Translated by Jan van Heurck. Chicago: University of Chicago Press.

Wolle, Stefan. 2019. *The Ideal World of Dictatorship: Daily Life and Party Rule in the GDR 1971–1989*. Translated by David Burnett. Berlin: Ch. Links Verlag.

Wood, Jason. 2014. *Last Words: Considering Contemporary Cinema*. London: Wallflower Press.

Zeilig, Hannah. 2013. "Dementia as a Cultural Metaphor." *The Gerontologist* 54, no. 2: 258–67.

Žižek, Slavoj. 1994. *The Metastases of Enjoyment: Six Essays on Woman and Causality*. London: Verso.

Zoepf, Katherine. 2013. "Shopgirls." *New Yorker*, December 23, 89(42). www.newyorker.com/magazine/2013/12/23/shopgirls.

Zucconi, Francesco. 2016. "When the Copywriter Is the Protagonist: History and Intermediality in Pablo Larraín's *No* (2012)." *Acta Universitatis Sapientiae, Film and Media Studies* 12, no. 1: 129–47.

Zunes, Stephen. 2014. "South Africa: The Townships Rise Up." In *Civil Resistance and Conflict Transformation: Transitions from Armed to Nonviolent Struggle*, edited by Véronique Dudouet, 100–125. London: Routledge.

Filmography

About Elly [Darbareye Elly]. Directed by Asghar Farhadi. Iran/France: Dreamlab, 2010.

The Act of Killing. DVD. Directed by Joshua Oppenheimer. UK/Denmark/Norway: Final Cut for Real / Piraya Film A/S / Novaya Zemlya / Novaya Zemlya / Spring Films, 2012.

Aimé Césaire, a Voice for History [Une voix pour l'histoire]. Television documentary. Directed by Euzhan Palcy. France/Senegal: Saligna and So On / France 3 / L'Institut National de l'Audiovisuel Radio France Outremer and Radio-Télévision Sénégalaise, 1994.

All That Heaven Allows. Directed by Douglas Sirk. United States: Universal International Pictures, 1955.

Amra and the Second Marriage. Directed by Mahmoud Sabbagh. Saudi Arabia: El Housh Productions, 2018.

Arabia 3D. Directed by Greg MacGillivray. United States: MacGillivray Freeman Films, 2011.

Balloon [Ballon]. Directed by Michael Herbig. Germany: herbX Film / Studio Canal / SevenPictures Film / ARP Sélection / Amazon Prime Video, 2018.

Barakah Meets Barakah [Barakah yoqabil Barakah]. Directed by Mahmoud Sabbagh. Saudi Arabia: El Housh Productions, 2016.

Barbara. Directed by Christian Petzold. Germany: Schramm Film Koerner & Weber / ZDF / ARTE, 2012.

Bicycle Thieves [Ladri di biciclette]. Directed by Vittorio de Sica. Italy: Produzioni de Sica, 1948.

The Book of Sun [Shams Al-Ma'arif]. Directed by Faris Godus. Saudi Arabia: Tape Productions, 2020.

Born in '45 [Jahrgang 45]. Directed by Jürgen Bötttcher. East Germany: Deutsche Film, 1966.

Boyhood. Directed by Richard Linklater. United States: IFC Productions / Detour Filmproduction, 2014.

The Boy in the Striped Pajamas. Directed by Mark Herman. United Kingdom / United States: BBC Films / Heyday Films, 2008.

Chariots of Fire. Directed by Hugh Hudson. United Kingdom: Film. Enigma Productions / Allied Stars Limited, 1981.

Citizen Havel [Občan Havel]. Directed by Miroslav Janek and Pavel Koutecký. Czech Republic: Nadace Film a Sociologie / Negativ / Krátký Film Praha, 2008.

Cry Freedom. Directed by Richard Attenborough. United Kingdom: Universal Pictures / Marble Arch Productions, 1987.

Dancing in the Dust. Directed by Asghar Farhadi. Iran: Neshane, 2003.

Deutschland 89. Television series. Directed by Anna Winger and Jörg Winger. Germany: UFA Fiction / Big Window Productions, 2020.

Diary of a Country Priest. Directed by Robert Bresson. France: Union Générale Cinématographique, 1951.

Divided Heaven [Der geteilte Himmel]. Directed by Konrad Wolf. East Germany: Deutsche Film, 1964.

A Dry White Season. Directed by Euzhan Palcy. United States: Davros Films / Star Partners II Ltd. / Sundance Productions, 1989.

Ema. Directed by Pablo Larraín. Chile: La Fábula, 2019.

Even Dwarves Started Small. Directed by Werner Herzog. West Germany: Werner Herzog Filmproduktion, 1970.

Everybody Knows. Directed by Asghar Farhadi. Spain/France/Italy/Argentina/Germany: Memento Films Production / Morena Films / Lucky Red, 2018.

Far from Heaven. Directed by Todd Haynes. United States / France: Focus Features / Vulcan Productions / Killer Films / John Wells Productions / Section Eight / Clear Blue Sky Productions / TFI International / USA Films, 2002.

Fireworks Wednesday. Directed by Asghar Farhadi. Iran: Boshra Film, 2006.

Flash of Genius. Directed by Marc Abraham. Canada / United States: Universal Pictures / Spyglass Entertainment / Strike Entertainment / Intermittent Productions, 2008.

The Flight [Die Flucht]. Directed by Roland Gräf. East Germany: VEB DEFA-Studio für Spielfilme / Künstrlische Arbeitsgruppe "Roter Kreis," 1977.

40 Years of Silence: An Indonesian Tragedy. Directed by Robert Lemelson. Indonesia / United States: Elemental Productions, 2010.

The 400 Blows [Les quatre cents coups]. Directed by François Truffaut. France: Les Films du Carrosse / Sédif Productions, 1959.

Fuga. Directed by Pablo Larraín. Argentina/Chile: La Fábula, 2006.

Goodbye Lenin! Directed by Wolfgang Becker. Germany: X-Filme Creative Pool / Westdeutscher Rundfunk / ARTE, 2003.

A Hero. Directed by Asghar Farhadi. Iran/France: Arte France Cinéma / Aghar Farhadi Productions / CNC, 2021.

The Hole. Directed by Tsai Min-Liang. Taiwan/France: Arc Light Films / Central Motion Pictures / China Television / Haut et Court / La Septe-Arte, 1998.

It All Starts Today [Ça commence aujourd'hui]. Directed by Bertrand Tavernier. France: Canal+ / Le Films Alain Sarde / Little Bear / TF1 Films Production, 1999.

Jackie. DVD. Directed by Pablo Larraín. United States: Fox Searchlight, 2016.

Jour de fête. Directed by Jacques Tati. France: Cady Films / Panoramic Films, 1949.

The Kid with a Bike [Le gamin au vélo]. Directed by Jean-Pierre Dardenne and Luc Dardenne. Belgium/France/Italy: Les Films du Fleuve / Archipel 35 / Lucky Red, 2012.

The Killing Yard. Directed by Euzhan Palcy. United States / Canada: Harris & Company / Paramount Television, 2001.

Leave No Trace. Directed by Debra Granik. United States / Canada: BRON Studios / Topic Studios / Harrison Productions / Reisman Productions / Still Rolling Productions, 2018.

Lemon Tree [Etz limon]. Directed by Eran Riklis. Germany/France: Heimatfilm / MACT Productions / Eran Riklis Productions, 2008.

Letter from an Unknown Woman. Directed by Max Ophüls. United States: William Dozier Productions / Rampart Productions, 1948.

The Lives of Others. Directed by Florian Henckel von Donnersmarck. Germany: Wiedemann and Berg Filmproduktion / Bayerisher Rundfunk / ARTE / Creado Film, 2006.

The Look of Silence. DVD. Directed by Joshua Oppenheimer. Denmark / Indonesia / Finland / Norway / United Kingdom / Israel / France / United States / Germany / Netherlands: Anonymous / Britdoc Foundation / Final Cut for Real /Making Movies Oy / Participant Media / Piraya Film A/S / Spring Films, 2014.

Madiba. Television miniseries. Directed by Kevin Hooks. South Africa: Showtime Networks / Blue Ice Pictures, 2017.

Mapantsula. Directed by Oliver Schmitz. South Africa: Haverbeam / One Look Productions / David Hannay Productions, 1988.

Mary Shelley. Directed by Haifaa Al Mansour. United Kingdom / Luxembourg / United States / Ireland / Australia: BFI Film Fund / Film Fund Luxembourg / Gidden Media, 2017.

The Mischief Makers [Les mistons]. Directed by François Truffaut. France: Les Films du Carrosse, 1957.

Moonlight. Directed by Barry Jenkins. United States: A24 / PASTEL / Plan B Entertainment, 2016.

Nader and Simin, A Separation [Jodaeiye Nader az Simin]. Directed by Asghar Farhadi. Iran/France/Australia: Asghar Farhadi Productions / Dreamlab Films / MPS APSA Academy Film Fund / Memento Films, 2011.

Nappily Ever After. Directed by Haifaa Al Mansour. United States: Netflix / Marc Platt Productions / Badabing Pictures, 2018.

Neruda. Directed by Pablo Larraín. United States: Sony Pictures, 2016.

Night and Fog. Directed by Alain Resnais. France: Argos Films, 1956.

No. Directed by Pablo Larraín. Chile / France / Mexico / United States: Participants / Funny Balloons / La Fábula / Canana, 2012.

Offside. Directed by Jafar Panahi. Iran: Jafar Panahi Film Productions, 2006.

The Other Side of the Tracks [De l'autre côté du périph]. Directed by Bertrand Tavernier. France: Little Bear, 1997.

The Past. Directed by Asghar Farhadi. France/Italy/Belgium: Memento Films Production / France 3 Cinéma / BIM Distribuzione / BIM Production, 2013.

The Patience Stone. Directed by Atiq Rahimi. France/Afghanistan: Film/Razor Film, 2012.

The Perfect Candidate. Directed by Haifaa Al Mansour. Saudi Arabia / Germany: Al Mansour Est. for Audiovisual Media / Razor Film Produktion GmbH / NDR, 2019.

Phoenix. Directed by Christian Petzold. Germany: Schramm Film Koerner & Weber, 2014.

Post Mortem. Directed by Pablo Larraín. Chile: La Fábula, 2010.

Revolutionary Road. Directed by Sam Mendes. United States / United Kingdom: Dreamworks Pictures / BBC Films / Evamere Entertainment / Neal Street Productions / Goldcrest Pictures / Scott Rudin Productions, 2008.

Rosetta. Directed by Jean-Pierre Dardenne and Luc Dardenne. France/Belgium: ARP Sélection / Canal+ / CNC, 1999.

Ruby Bridges. Directed by Euzhan Palcy. United States: Marian Rees Associates / Walt Disney Television, 1998.

The Salesman. Directed by Asghar Farhadi. Iran/France: ARTE / Arte France Cinéma / Doha Film Institute, 2016.

Saturday Night Fever. Directed by John Badham. United States: Paramount, 1977.

Scenes from a Marriage. Directed by Ingmar Bergman. Sweden: Cinematograph AB, 1973.

Schindler's List. Directed by Steven Spielberg. United States: Universal Pictures / Amblin Entertainment, 1993.

Shadow Play: Indonesia's Year of Living Dangerously. Directed by Chris Hilton. Australia: Hilton Cordell Productions, 2003.

Shoah. Directed by Claude Lanzmann. France / United Kingdom: British Broadcasting Corporation / Historia / Les Films Aleph / Ministère de la Culture de la Republique Française, 1985.

Siméon. Directed by Euzhan Palcy. France/Guadeloupe/Martinique: Saligna Production / France 2 Cinéma / Club d'investissement Média, 1992.

Spencer. Directed by Pablo Larraín. United Kingdom / Germany / United States / Chile: Shoebox Films / Komplizen Film / FilmNation Entertainment / Topic Studios / La Fábula, 2021.

The Spitfire Grill. Directed by Lee David Zlotoff. United States: Castle Rock Entertainment, 1996.

The State I Am In [Die innere Sicherheit]. Directed by Christian Petzold. Germany: Schramm Film, 2001.

Stella Dallas. Directed by King Vidor. United States: Samuel Goldwyn Company, 1937.

Stroszek. Directed by Werner Herzog. West Germany: Werner Herzog Filmproduktion / Zweites Deutsches Fernsehen, 1977.

Sugar Cane Alley [La rue cases-nègres]. Directed by Euzhan Palcy. France/Martinique: NEF Diffusion / Orca Productions / SU.MA.FA., 1983.

Taking Sides. Directed by István Szabó. Germany/France: Paladin Production S.A. / Maecenas Film-und Fernseh GmbH / Studio Babelsberg / Little Big Bear Filmproduktion GmbH / Canal + / Enterprise Films / France 2 Cinéma / Jeremy Isaacs Productions Ltd. / MBP / Satel Film / Spice Factory / TwanPix Ltd., 2001.

Tony Manero. DVD. Directed by Pablo Larraín. Chile/Brazil: La Fábula / Prodigital, 2008.

Transit. Directed by Christian Petzold. Germany: Schramm Film, 2018.

12 Years a Slave. Directed by Steve McQueen. United States / United Kingdom: New Regency Productions / River Road Entertainment / Plan B Entertainment, 2013.

Wadjda. Directed by Haifaa Al Mansour. Saudi Arabia / Netherlands / Germany / Jordan / UAE / United States: Razor Film Produktion GmbH / Highlook Communications Group / Rotana Film Production, 2012.

Way Down East. Directed by D. W. Griffith. United States: D. W. Griffith Productions, 1920.

The White Balloon [Badkonake sefid]. Directed by Jafar Panahi. Iran: Farabi Cinema Foundation / Ferdos Films / I.R.I.B. Channel 2, 1995.

Why Havel? Directed by Wojtech Jasný. Czechoslovakia/Canada: Rock Demers, 1991.

Women without Shadows. Directed by Haifaa Al Mansour. Saudi Arabia: Pretty Pictures, 2005.

A World Apart. Directed by Chris Menges. United Kingdom / Zimbabwe: Atlantic Entertainment Group / British Screen Productions / Channel Four Films, 1987.

The Year of Living Dangerously. Directed by Peter Weir. Australia / United States: McElroy & McElroy / Metro-Goldwyn-Meyer, 1982.

Index

Page numbers in italics indicate illustrations.